MUTABARUKA
THE VERBAL SWORDSMAN

MUTABARUKA
THE VERBAL SWORDSMAN

Perspectives from the
Cutting Edge and *Steppin Razor*

MUTABARUKA
SEBASTIAN SCHWAGER
WERNER ZIPS

Published with the support of the
Department of Social and Cultural Anthropology,
University of Vienna.

IAN RANDLE PUBLISHERS
Kingston • Miami
www.ianrandlepublishers.com

First published in Jamaica, 2023 by
Ian Randle Publishers
16 Herb McKenley Drive
Box 686
Kingston 6
www.ianrandlepublishers.com

National Library of Jamaica Cataloguing-In-Publication Data
Names: Mutabaruka, author. | Schwager, Sebastian, author. |
    Zips, Werner, author.
Title: Mutabaruka : the verbal swordsman : perspectives from
    the Cutting Edge and Steppin Razor / Mutabaruka, Sebastian
    Schwager, Werner Zips.
Description: Kingston, Jamaica : Ian Randle Publishers, 2023. |
    Published with the support of the Department of Social and
    Cultural Anthropology, University of Vienna.
Identifiers: ISBN 9789768286826 (pbk).
Subjects: LCSH: Mutabaruka, 1952- – Criticism and interpretation.
    | Black nationalism. | Pan-Africanism. | Black people – Race
    identity. | Radio journalists – Jamaica. | Poets, Black – Jamaica. |
    Rastafari movement.
Classification: DDC 305.8969729 -- dc23.

Cover and Book Design by Ian Randle Publishers
Printed and Bound in the United States of America

Cover Photo by Werner Zips:
Muta with Katana sword, Vienna, Austria 2011

IN MEMORY OF

Sylvia Chambers
Sybil Spence
Raymond Spence

Sevana Leona Schwager

Emsley 'Ras T' Smith

i am de man
you love to hate
sitting in the slums of
ghost town
trench town
back o' wall
no clothes
to hide my nakedness
filth and mosquitoes smelling
biting 400 years of black flesh
scarred by whips and sticks
i am de man
locks entangled in
your nightmares of
medusas and gorgons
unkept religious beliefs
that pierce the side of
your jesus in the sky
your vinegar has turned to blood
your water to mud
crucifix
choking on your life
of neo-colonialistic attitudes
yes I am de man

Mutabaruka,
I Am De Man (2005, 34)

CONTENTS

FOREWORD

'Word-Sound-Power':
Mutabaruka on the Airwaves

Carolyn Cooper

Werner Zips and Sebastian Schwager offer a compelling rationale for their long-sustained engagement with Mutabaruka that has resulted in this powerful book:

> As born Austrians, we may appear as fairly strange fruits of Muta's inspirational influence. But if you consider the global dimension of justice, relentlessly rallied for by Haile Selassie I. in his struggle for international morality and collective security, it becomes much less inexplicable, why Romans join into Muta's cry for 'fire 'pon Rome,' Germans edit his poetry books, and people around the world flock to his concerts (he still tours) or tune into his radio shows, blogs, and other media of expression nowadays.

Deploying the trope of the verbal swordsman, Zips and Schwager conceive Mutabaruka as 'The Hattori Hanzō Sword of Rasta':

> Like the famous Samurai of the sixteenth century who has appeared in manga, video games, novels, and feature films, Muta brings with him the real component of a historical actor/activist fighting for a cause – the cause of Black Liberation. On the symbolic level, the legendary sharpness of the sword refers to his fearlessness in confrontation with the powerful. His reputed invincibility in disputations justifies the reference to the Japanese warrior and leader of a Ninja clan.

Zips and Schwager's perception of Mutabaruka as the Hattori Hanzō Sword of Rasta also evokes the ritual cutting and clearing practised by Revivalists in Jamaica around the seal, the sacred ground on which ancestral spirits are summoned. On his radio programmes,

Mutabaruka effaces the conventional distinction between sacred and secular discourse. He becomes both priest and poet. Drawing on ancestral wisdom, Mutabaruka is the *griot*, the oral historian who poetically documents the collective narrative of survival of Africans in the diaspora. Mutabaruka speaks into conscious memory the history of his community.

One of Mutabaruka's most powerful poems is 'Killin' on his *Melanin Man* album, released in 1994. In an informal interview with me, Mutabaruka disclosed that the poem was inspired by a visit to the Holocaust Memorial Museum in Washington, DC. He frames the poem with a brief meditation on the role of museums, libraries, and public monuments as sites of communal memory and formal education:

> Everyone remembers their past
>
> Buildin monuments museums
>
> Writin books
>
> So that their children children will never forget
>
> We must all learn from the past
>
> So as not to repeat those things
>
> That have kept us back for over five hundred years.

Mutabaruka acknowledges the need to dredge up the past, bringing to the surface histories that have been deliberately submerged. He establishes the human need to memorialize the past – especially to document those historical facts that can be so systematically erased from collective memory by the perpetrators of horrific crimes. The poet repeatedly invites us to talk. This talk is not idle chatter. It is an incantation, a mystical vibration, an intellectual engagement, a reasoning that dispels lies and reclaims truth:

> Mek wi talk
>
> Mek wi talk
>
> Mek wi talk, mek wi talk, mek wi talk
>
> Mek wi talk bout de killin
>
> De killin dat dem neva mention
>
> Killin was their intention

. . .

Suh mek wi talk bout de bottom a de sea

Escaping from slavery

Millions tryin to be free

Preferrin death

Yet

Not to mention the plantation

Fighting for liberation

No mention

Cause killin was their intention

Suh mek wi talk

. . .

Dyin at their will

In the name of Jesus they killed

Still, wi deh yah

Mutabaruka's imperative talk illustrates a foundational element of Rastafari philosophy and *livity*: acknowledgement of the potent vibrations of speech and music that shape consciousness and define community. This 'overstanding' – to use a Rastafari coinage – is eloquently articulated in the formulaic compound, 'word-sound-power.' Its genesis is multivalent. Rastafari discourse and biblical epistemology are, undeniably, imbricated. Identifying with the Children of Israel who endured slavery, Rastafari have appropriated the poetic language of the Old and New Testaments to speak their own truth of survival: 'In the beginning was the Word, and the Word was with God, and the Word was God.'[1] Divine power and authority are manifested in the spoken word.

The signifier 'word-sound-power' also evokes ancestral memories of African origins. All across the African continent, the verbal arts flourish: proverbs, riddles, stories, songs, incantations, acts of divination – a whole gamut of orality. For instance, the Dogon people of Mali conceive *Nommo* as the articulation of the power of the spoken word. It is the spirit force that engenders and sustains life. Just as the Old Testament Jehovah 'spake' and the world came into being, even so the Dogon people claim the productive and predictive authority of the spoken word.

Jahlani Niaah, Rastafari Studies academic and cultural activist, confirms the centrality of 'word-sound-power' in the rituals of Rastafari that substantiate divine creativity:

> Glory to word
>
> Glory to sound
>
> Glory to power
>
> This is an often-used opening remark, especially within the Nyahbinghi congregation of Rastafari. This affirmation is in keeping with the moral compass that holds word-sounds as the root of all creation.[2]

Niaah elucidates the ideological grounding of the resonant term:

> In this space, there is, as is reasoned generally within Rastafari, a responsibility to speak the impeccable word-sounds for there is power in word. Word-sound is thus a reference to conversations, messages, gossip, and other aspects of family communication used almost as a substitute for elaboration of an idea or a statement. It is especially in the Nyahbinghi context (including ritualistic performances) that 'word-sound-power' becomes a refrain consistently echoed to affirm ideas as well as to issue a proverbial caution about the weight of words and the consequent need to weigh one's words.[3]

It is precisely this philosophy of 'word-sound-power' that informs Mutabaruka's practice as a radio talk show host. His philosophical and political engagements with his local and international audience are a mediated extension of the 'reasoning' that is a traditional element of Rastafari praxis. Regular listeners of Mutabaruka's show become part of a community akin to a congregation of believers. But Mutabaruka does not claim divine infallibility. He admits his own doubt on certain matters. And he does not valorize uncritical acceptance of received wisdom. As he perceptively puts it: 'I think for myself! Critical thinking is the business of understanding something that you doubted. When you want to understand something that you doubt, you start to examine it more. Because doubt is the first step towards knowing. Through doubt you are going to examine the thing.'

Zips and Schwager give a trenchant account of Mutabaruka's incisive words on his radio programmes *Cutting Edge* and *Steppin Razor*:

> His approach to communicative rationality – enshrined in the Rastafari notion of 'reasoning' or higher dialogues ('Iyahlogue') – opened doors to like-minded people globally. After all, justice is indivisible. It stands or falls universally. There is no justice for some, without regard to all. This is where his international followers – not to say fans – come into the play, not least ourselves, as the co-authors of this book.

Zips and Schwager also allow Mutabaruka to speak for himself. The centrepiece of the book is Mutabaruka's reflection on his own life. His words also envision the future. One of the most moving passages in this section is Mutabaruka's celebration of the transformative language of Rastafari, which empowers the downtrodden:

> 'Inna the dung, the filth, inna the shit they would put we into,' we come with that. 'The dutty locks and the ganja smoking, who can't get no work,' being despised and all these things. And you tell a man: 'Love?' You live in the shit and a man passes you and you tell him: 'Love?' You call a woman, who has never seen a palace yet, a queen and empress. The man who lives in the shit, lives in the piss, and who can't get any work, and people despise him, looks at his woman and says: 'She is a queen!' You can't get better than that. I do not care what a man says; you can't get better than that because Rasta is the only set of people who bring that to the table.

For countless years, I have been encouraging Mutabaruka to collect his wide-ranging ideas for publication as a book. The working title of the volume I envisaged was, *Philosophy and Opinions of Mutabaruka*, in tribute to Marcus Garvey, his ideological ancestor. The title also signified the weight of Mutabaruka's own world view. I anticipated that his words would be presented on their own, unmediated by others. I must concede that Werner Zips's and Sebastian Schwager's authoritative account of the breadth and depth of Mutabaruka's long-lasting radio programmes is absolutely valuable, especially since Mutabaruka's voice reverberates throughout the book. They have expertly amplified the word-sound-power of an extraordinary public intellectual.

NOTES

1. John 1:1, King James Version.
2. In personal correspondence with me.
3. Ibid.

PREFACE

Mutabaruka:
The Hattori Hanzō Sword of Rasta

Werner Zips and Sebastian Schwager

No name, no name
I knew no name
I, the forgotten soul
Whipped to live
Whipped because I lived
Whipped to death
Today I sing songs
Redemption songs
Free mother, free father
I sing songs to be free
Free, I the slave
I, the slave.
   – Mutabaruka, Cape Coast/Ghana (1996)

'Free, I the Slave'

Mutabaruka was born in 1952 and grew up with his mother in Rae Town, a ghetto district of Kingston that is also home to the *General Penitentiary*. Influenced by the philosophy of Black Nationalism, the young *Muta*, as many people call him, poured his social criticism into biting poems while still at school.[1] Rastafari philosophy gave him a spiritual depth, which he used to enrich a Reggae subgenre often coined *Dub Poetry*.[2] In Jamaica, he was attacked by the elite, whose members he targeted in many of his poems, radio broadcasts, and other public appearances. But the young poet continued undeterred on his way to a world career as a Reggae *artiste* and as a social commentator on Jamaican radio and television – true to his life motto: 'If you don't have self-confidence, you will lose the race of your life in two ways.

With confidence, you've won before you've even started running. I repeat this philosophy all the time because it encourages me to achieve what I set out to do.'[3]

This preface has three intentions: 1. To provide an anecdotical preliminary rapprochement to a highly complex personality that resists any quick categorization; 2. To give an idea, how the three voices of the authors relate to each other and converge in this book; 3. To explain, why two Austrian anthropologists joined with Mutabaruka to explore some important aspects of his worldviews, based on his public speech acts on Jamaican radio.

The two Austrians belong to different generations and therefore met Mutabaruka at different times in his career: Sebastian Schwager encountered Mutabaruka by chance for the first time in 2008 at the legendary *Rae Town Old Hits* sound system session in Jamaica, then in 2011 at the University of Vienna, and in 2018 (again in Jamaica) to interview him on a selection of his radio shows he analysed for his master's thesis in 2019, supervised by Werner Zips, professor of social and cultural anthropology at the University of Vienna.[4] The latter had his first encounter while still a student himself, in 1989 to interview Mutabaruka after a performance at the legendary Austrian festival arena of Wiesen for his own PhD thesis. In some ways, both (Austrian) authors are therefore scholarly engaged with the work and thoughts of Mutabaruka, though at times wide apart. They have their own personal history with Mutabaruka, which gave Sebastian Schwager the privilege to appear at Mutabaruka's famous radio show *Steppin Razor* and Werner Zips the once-in-a-lifetime chance to experience and record the historic performance of Mutabaruka in the Cape Coast Castle of Ghana during Panafest 1997 on film for posterity.

This preface attempts to give a personal account of the person Mutabaruka to allow some first glimpses behind the icon of Black resistance and insubordination. It has in mind a smiling Mutabaruka saying about himself: 'I was always a rebel, born a rebel, and I am still a rebel.' It further recalls moments that we consider characteristic for a man that is above else very human in the most positive sense of the word. These first-hand impressions are picked from a period of time spanning more than three decades. Since the bigger part of this book is based on his public speeches on radio in his own shows *Cutting Edge* and *Steppin Razor,* the few snapshots we wish to provide here should enhance an understanding where he is coming from in both meanings, as a person with a life experience and a folk philosopher or 'public intellectual' as he might be called by some.

We are very much aware that Mutabaruka afforded us the privilege of openness and friendship across a divide that in many ways defines present-day global relations: the colour line. It was accordingly self-evident that this book can only be a joint effort. Huge parts of the text were either spoken by Mutabaruka himself – either in his biographical sketches taken from an interview/reasoning or in his speeches on radio – or analysed in the broader contexts and social meanings of his 'words, sounds, and power,' to quote the Rasta wording for a righteous and mighty speech act. However, the responsibility for misinterpretations and any other mistakes lies with Sebastian Schwager and Werner Zips, transferring Mutabaruka's oratory into written text, thereby adding their own interpretations. This book intends a preliminary synopsis of the contributions Mutabaruka and his cultural politics broadcasts have had in Jamaica and beyond, being fully aware that we can only offer a relatively small compendium of his entire accomplishments. However, we believe and indeed suggest that a more comprehensive inventory of a 'Philosophy and Opinions of Mutabaruka' may be a rewarding task for future researchers, particularly at Jamaican academic institutions perfectly equipped with access to the necessary sources. Three decades of reasoning from the *Cutting Edge* and one decade from the *Steppin Razor* have piled up to historical reflections, critical social analyses, and debates with eminent personalities representing Black consciousness from diverse angles.

Beyond doubt, transcultural encounters with Mutabaruka are not without tension. It should suffice to take the above-mentioned slave castle performance in Ghana following a joint visit to the dungeons as a graphic illustration, pars pro toto. Yet, this tension does not only animate the sweat glands of the Austrian interviewee on a *Steppin Razor* show or the Austrian filmmaker during a performance of the poem

Free, I the Slave (quoted above) at the very location where transatlantic slavery robbed millions of Africans of their freedom, identity, and dignity. It may also prove fertile for a process of healing that Haile Selassie I. had in mind with his famous UN speech of 1963, which is quoted further below. The idea, inherent criticism, and utopian moment of reconciliation mark the motivation behind this book, although Mutabaruka in our (virtual) joint meeting smilingly warned the two Austrian authors against any premature gesture of harmony:

> I can accept a white man. I accept you both. I don't see you as a problem to me. Because we are fighting against a system. It is a system, you know. But guess what? The system is mostly controlled by white people. ... Look what the British, French, and Portuguese did to the Africans during slavery. And they haven't apologized! They say that they didn't do it. You didn't do it? But you are benefitting from it! Most of the banks in England benefit from slavery. William Beckford, who used to have a slave plantation in Jamaica, became one of the richest men in the world because of sugar cane and slavery in Jamaica itself. And we still have to fight for that! I can't stop the fight. Haile Selassie said that we Africans fight when it is necessary because we are confident in the victory of good over evil. We cannot paint a utopian scenario right now because too many things are going on. We can't live with it! When I come to Europe to your (Werner Zips's) house, I don't feel no way. When white people come to my house, we don't feel no way. It is not that I put this thing upon my head.[5]

A Universal Struggle

Mutabaruka's frequent performances to sold out enthusiastic venues in Austria show that his radical Rastafari Black Power messages fell on fertile grounds in unforeseen cultural habitats. Having travelled to literally 'all four corners of the earth,' he finds it no longer surprising that people in Rome may cheerfully embrace an imperative such as 'fire 'pon Rome.' As he reflects in his own chapter to this book (see chapter 1), the invitation of Reggae to radically change a system of white supremacy, responsible for transatlantic slavery, colonialism, neocolonialism, racial discrimination, exploitation, and various forms of inequality is not limited to people of African origin. It has universal appeal, perhaps only for a minority so far, but a minority many millions strong. And indeed, a minority visibly getting stronger every day, if we interpret the anti-racist, decolonization, and anti-discrimination youth movements correctly.

Since freedom is as much indivisible as justice, no human can truly feel free without universal freedom, in a global environment of social justice. Mutabaruka's agreement to have two Austrians working with him on this book must be seen in this context. Although he thoroughly researched the aims behind this effort, as Sebastian Schwager experienced on the *Steppin Razor* show while interviewed on air and asked by Mutabaruka why he wants to write a thesis on one of the most radical voices of Black Liberation, himself being an Austrian with no historical experience of systematic racism? His skilful live interrogation in the *Steppin Razor* broadcast tested inter alia for self-serving interests of self-righteousness, a potentially hypocritical ingratiation or cultural appropriation of the Black struggle, or quasi-religious motives of salvation from historical guilt.[6]

In the case of the other author, Werner Zips, Mutabaruka had the personal experiences of professional cooperation that dates to the aforementioned Panafest of 1997 in Ghana and led to several joint efforts from books to films, articles, conferences, concerts, and performances that built not only trust but friendship. These remarks may be important for the reader, who should not expect an academic critique of a social activist, but rather a respectful appreciation of his public appearances, particularly in his two radio shows. Although belonging to different age groups, Sebastian Schwager and Werner Zips both see themselves as students of Mutabaruka, spanning a time frame of almost four decades, when the latter was first introduced to Mutabaruka's work by Emsley 'Ras T' Smith, a Reggae record shop owner and Rastafari of Jamaican origin living in Vienna in 1983, namely to Mutabaruka's first album *Check It!* (1983a).

This now classic Reggae (or 'Dub Poetry') album kicked off a lifelong interest and, in fact, fascination with an artiste/activist/philosopher that is never predictable in his readings of 'the world' and its global structures of injustice. When the student turned professor over time, sharing his admiration for Muta with his students in turn, it perhaps captured Sebastian Schwager to choose Mutabaruka's *Steppin Razor* shows as the topic of his master's thesis. His decision finally came through, when Mutabaruka lectured at the University of Vienna in various courses of Werner Zips on Reggae, Rastafari, and the Caribbean. These special appearances in lecture halls filled to capacity triggered as a rule standing ovations by an audience composed in its majority by – what Muta would refer to as – 'white people from Austria.' Narrating these events to our Jamaican and African friends often led to great surprise, challenging beliefs that Muta only appeals to Black people. In contrast to this view, we have witnessed on any number of occasions, how he easily transcends barriers of all kinds, be it language, culture, experience, colour, gender, age, and so forth. His peculiar art of communication expresses itself in the book title *The Verbal Swordsman*, who can equally strike in any circumstances.

The sharp social commentaries and ever-ready challenges to the status quo he is universally known for, made us choose the heading for this preface: 'Mutabaruka: The Hattori Hanzō Sword of Rasta.'[7] Like the famous Samurai of the sixteenth century who has appeared in manga, video games, novels, and feature films, Muta brings with him the real component of a historical actor/activist fighting for a cause – the cause of Black Liberation. On the symbolic level, the legendary sharpness of the sword refers to his fearlessness in confrontation with the powerful. His reputed invincibility in disputations justifies the reference to the Japanese warrior and leader of a Ninja clan. The Hattori Hanzō sword from *Kill Bill* by Quentin Tarantino makes a direct reference to the historic figure. It is said to be forged by a successor of the famous Ninja, counting among the best Samurai swords ever made. Since the beginning of his career, Muta has cultivated a similar nimbus of sharpness as his own manager and promoter, advertising his talk master skills as the *art of war* and claiming not to avoid verbal combat. Mutabaruka's radio show titles *Cutting Edge* and *Steppin Razor* suggest the allegory. But what we consider much more important, not least for the choice of this heading, is his readiness to walk the walk, beyond merely talking the talk. The following sequence gives but one example, how the African-Jamaican blade interferes in real life. It may only be a small incident but says a lot on his personality.

On the *Cutting Edge*

A Sunday morning, after an amazing night-long Rebel Salute festival, Mutabaruka drives his Mitsubishi jeep out of the parking lot.[8] He does not seem tired at all, although he worked on stage as one of the MCs for the show. The venue, Port Kaiser Sports Club, fits perfectly with the 'strictly ital livity' of Tony Rebel's annual birthday (*earth strong*) party.[9] Here on Jamaica's (almost) untouched south coast, everyday Caribbean life still matches its (foreign) image: *island in the sun*. Fishermen in their elaborately painted boats from nearby Alligator Pond control the nets in front of slopes of hills gliding gently into the sea.[10] Their fishing grounds extend to the dramatic Lover's Leap, the steep cliff from which two enslaved lovers are said to have thrown themselves to their deaths during slavery. With their suicide, they prevented their separation, permanently freed themselves from slavery and, at least in legend, remained united forever.

Passing through this rural landscape, everyone recognizes Muta's ride. A trip with him across the island has something of a triumphal parade. Passing cars start honking wildly, pedestrians stand in line waving euphorically, and from every second hut a fist stretches out in greeting: 'Hail Muta! Bless Rasta!' Mutabaruka has long been much more than a Reggae star. In Jamaica, he is regarded as a social conscience, moral authority, and – even if he would probably reject this eloquently – a cultural and socio-political *institution*.

In the stop-and-go traffic on the dusty dirt road to Alligator Pond, all attention belongs to him. Although he shuns too much attention. When he's not holding a microphone, standing on a stage in front of thousands of listeners, addressing (large parts of) the nation on his weekly radio talk shows *Cutting Edge* and *Steppin Razor* or on television, he prefers to keep to himself and talk very little. Star hype – especially of the demanding *yard variety* – is anathema to him. Even Rastas he doesn't know, who are eager to shake his hand, are quickly brushed off. Understandably so. Anyone who knows Jamaica knows about one of the rarest local resources: privacy. Only the friendly greeting of a passing Bobo *donman* on his racing bike (by tapping twice on the hood of Muta's jeep) is returned with an outstretched fist.[11] Quickly, the *militant* Bobo disappears with *Rude Boy habitus* in a cloud of dust on his yellow Ninja, apparently in tune with his yellow turban, trusting that the pedestrians will vanish into thin air or at least jump aside in awe.

'Yes man! That is Rebel Salute! Strictly Rasta, from all walks of life,' Muta turns back to his passengers. Suddenly his joy dwindles, and his facial expression darkens. He starts gesticulating and honking. At first, it looks as if the traffic jam after the Rebel Salute annoys him, and he wants to copy the Bobo on his Ninja. Only when he manages to get on the same level with the taxi driver in front of him, the emotional outburst clears up: 'Yo, driver! Tell your customers not to pollute the landscape. You're not in the city here!' Startled, the driver and all the passengers submissively apologize to the Rastafari in his righteous anger. The taxi stops and a young lad hops out of a backseat and, at Muta's behest, starts collecting all the plastic and paper rubbish that had been thrown out of the window.

This episode characterizes Mutabaruka's personality. This man indeed walks the talk, and lives by the rules he proclaims so passionately and eloquently in public. Sadly, this is not at all common in Jamaica, according to Jamaican critics. Even some Rastas indulge in long monologues about the power of creation and the necessity of a nature-loving way of life, only to dispose of the empty tetra pack of a box juice in the nearest river the next moment or to give a passing crab a deadly kick without even realizing the contradiction.[12] For Muta, there are no exceptions in his respect for nature and life. *Ital livity* to him is no vain buzzword, but a matter of course he has followed all his life. Sometimes he jokingly quotes fellow Jamaicans, who ridicule his vegan lifestyle in this (or similar) manner: 'Muta, you eat like a rabbit!'

The Man Many Love and Some Love to Hate

Muta abhors short-sighted thinking and contradictory courses of action. His critical mind never switches to pause, in contrast to many self-appointed moral preachers globally. Rather, he probes every mindset, ideology, or religious 'truth' for reasons and rational arguments, consequences, and connections. There could be no more apt name for his weekly talk show on Irie FM than *Cutting Edge*. For more than three decades (since March 1992), he has occupied four hours of Wednesday nights with his provocative social analyses. And with so much success that in 2013 he also got an afternoon talk show (*Steppin Razor*) from 2:00 p.m. to 6:00 p.m. on Irie FM each Thursday. In countless Jamaican households from Kingston to the remotest hill of the country, the programme is on, regardless of whether the recipients agree or disagree with the Rasta *agent provocateur*. Apparently, even his sometimes-bitter opponents love to take offence at his biting comments. Mutabaruka is regarded by many as the people's hero personified. For some, especially from the upper strata of society, the small financial and political elite, he is at least *the Rasta folk hero they love to hate.*

It is no coincidence that the renowned sociologist Barry Chevannes appointed him 'folk philosopher' at The University of the West Indies. It's no great dare to say that hardly anyone has influenced the formation of Black and African consciousness in Jamaica more than Muta over a period spanning the last three to four decades, even and especially within the Rasta and Reggae universe. Once he has taken aim at somebody or some institution, there is no cover for his target: 'Run for cover, rebel Muta is taking over,' so to speak. Sometimes even successful Jamaican Reggae artistes come under fire, when they offer *fool fool lyrics* according to his standards – lyrics that are at odds with Black consciousness. With words as sharp as razor blades, such texts are then publicly dissected.

Major Mackerel's rather promising career in the early 1990s almost ended in a Muta rant: 'How dare the little bwoy denigrate Shaka Zulu with his mindless babble as ugly! And Shaka Zulu is one of the greatest rulers in Black history, who even came victorious of the British army in South Africa's Zululand!' To an assembled Bobo congregation from the *Ethiopian African Black International Congress Church of Salvation* defending its doctrine of the impurity of women during and after menstruation at a Rastafari conference at The University of the West Indies, he hurled the verbal hand grenade, to the dismay of the priests and prophets from the congregation: 'Where do you think you come from? Ah not from your mama?' *Lickshot*! That hit home. Muta's wife, witnessing the event, can recall it for a good half hour, shaking with laughter about the uproar that ensued.

'You Should Not Stay in a Whiteman Country Too Long'

We don't want to create any false impression, elevating Mutabaruka to some sort of *Warrior God*. His preparedness for disputes in the form of necessary social debates, glossed over by many other media, is but one side to his personality. Muta can be extremely respectful and endearing when his respective addressee deserves it, or the situation – according to his criteria, of course – dictates it. Anyone who has witnessed how he manages to beg back an apparently stolen purse during a Reggae festival in Jamaica will know what is meant. As MC on stage during East Fest 2008 he achieved nothing less than the (seemingly) impossible.[13] How did he do it? He applied his moral conviction trained in Rasta congregations that he describes in his biographical outline (see chapter 1) and in numerous moral lectures on air, providing at the same time a face-saver for the presumed thief, addressed as a straight-shooter returning the lost purse. When the 'finder' showed up, he earned the award of Muta's sarcastic humour based on his self-ascribed rhetorical *licence to kill*: 'Brethren, we all thank you for "finding the wallet" with only 100 Jamaican dollars missing. I guess that was storage fee and finder's fee combined.' The laughter of twenty thousand Reggae *heads* appeared as just punishment for the soft-hearted thief. But anyone who deliberately messes with Muta, or tries to match his astute analyses, must dress warmly.

That, of course, applies to anthropologists like Werner Zips as well, who wrote quite a few books on subjects such as the legal and political sphere of the Jamaican Maroons and their historic struggle of freedom. For the Austrian professor's obvious sympathy for this unique victory of a *David against Goliath*, Muta has fine mockery ever ready: 'To the great intellectual Mr. Professor Zip (he always drops the 's' at the end of the name), the Maroons are glorious rebels with a glamorous history. To me, the enslaved African in Jamaica, they are just Africans like me, who think they are better.'[14]

On another occasion, when the same professor invited him as keynote speaker at the Caribbean conference at the University of Vienna in 2001, he expressed his gratefulness in this way, during his evening poetry performance in front of a large audience: 'There is an important university professor in Austria who believes he is a Rasta from Jamaica and talks to me in a Patois that is more Jamaican than I can understand. We thank him for showing how powerful Rasta has become – on a universal level.'[15] The outpour of laughter from many students was perhaps not just punishment for repeated acts of 'cultural appropriation,' but also his way of expressing sympathy.

However, the professor had a good laugh as well. As already briefly mentioned, he first learned about Mutabaruka through a Jamaican Rasta by the name of Emsley Smith, who was something like the most important 'Rasta influencer' in Vienna. Himself a friend of Peter Tosh and a Twelve Tribes Rastafari since the early days, he ran a record shop in Vienna, which in time turned into some kind of *Rasta mission house* – without intention, of course. Emsley provided the early addicts of Reggae music in Austria with deep insights into Rasta *livity* in the late 1970s and early 1980s.

Mutabaruka's first album *Check It!* from 1983 did indeed need a special instruction manual. It was a major international success of a subgenre most often categorized as *Dub Poetry*. Although the album was musically diverse, spanning different musical genres, it sounded quite different from the brand of Roots Reggae the international Reggae community was familiar with at the time. Apart from this genre-spanning variety, this was due to Muta's incomparable voice, the sounds and power of *hardcore Jamaican talk,* and the bitterly ironic indictment of the system without regard for loss. It intrigued many early Reggae enthusiasts, and made those in Austria aware of other poets, such as Michael Smith, Oku Onuora, Sister Breeze, or Linton Kwesi Johnson. Even the graffiti-like cover artwork with the painted portrait of Muta breaking through the walls of *Babylon*, illustrating the blood-red album title was nothing less than striking. And yes, indeed, the future professor, then just a student, had to *check it*. In Jamaica, where else? A year later, equipped with his dissertation topic ('Black Resistance and its legal claims'), Werner Zips experienced Mutabaruka live for the first time at the Reggae Sunsplash 1984 in Montego Bay.

Dressed all in white, Mutabaruka gave an electrifying performance at the legendary festival, and he was the topic of conversation in minibuses and shared taxis for weeks. He polarized like no other artiste before. Some thought he was simply a *madman*, as he himself had anticipated on the album. And not just because they saw him walking barefoot in long African robes through *MoBay* (as locals call Montego Bay) once a week to sell his home-knit tams. 'You shouldn't stay in a whiteman country too long?'[16] Anyone who seriously claimed such a thing in Jamaica in the early 1980s earned only incredulous amazement. Outside of Rasta circles, there was hardly a Jamaican who didn't dream of New York, Miami, or at least London. Others saw him as a visionary of Reggae, much like his great role model Louise 'Miss Lou' Bennett in literature.[17]

But only a small minority – almost exclusively Nyahbinghi Rastas – recognized in him the philosopher whose rhetorical skills would prevail consistently. They were also the only ones who knew that the chosen name *Mutabaruka* figuratively means 'the eternally victorious' in Rwandan language.[18] When he dropped the name of his birth, Allan Roy Hope, as a 'slave name' and changed his name, he could hear a lot of sceptical responses. According to Muta: 'In Jamaica, there are people called Chin, Chang, Mr. Jap, Zhan, and the likes. But if you call yourself Mutabaruka, they cry out: 'My God, what kind of name is that. You got that in Africa?' It's a funny thing. Bloodbath, Jamaican identities are totally crazy.'[19]

The *Anchorman* of Self and Social Criticism

A poster in a stall selling Rasta souvenirs at the above-mentioned Reggae Sunsplash 1984 announced the grand opening of the *Pitfour Nyahbinghi Center*, not far from Montego Bay and Muta's then home in Johns Hall at the foot of Cockpit Country. Honorary speaker at the opening: Mutabaruka, said the poster. A great opportunity to encounter Mutabaruka off a live Reggae stage. Indeed, a Nyahbinghi setting has little or nothing in common with a Reggae party. Most of the leading elders of the *Nyahbinghi Order* came to Pitfour on this important day. Their whole appearance commanded awe. These locks were truly *dread*, hair matted into life-size mats. Their words and eyes burnt as they pontificated on Babylon in its various manifestations. Comparatively, any contemporary *fire man* of Reggae would appear like a Shango costume at the Trinidad Carnival.

When Muta grabbed the microphone around midnight in Pitfour, everyone gathered in front of him. His *reasoning* about Rasta and the further development of this diverse culture lasted over an hour. The poet, who was just thirty-one years old at the time, did not spare self-criticism: 'Take these dreadlocked Haile Selassie pictures off the walls. Haile Selassie I. never had *dreadlocks*. This means creating false images. I and I should not repeat what the Christians do, creating God in their own image.' Then followed another attack on the Bible-affiliation of some Rastas and a warning against the foreshortening of African identity by the 'Judeo-Christian worldview,' as Muta still likes to paraphrase it today.

When he left the small stage of the *Pitfour Nyahbinghi Center* after his uninterrupted 'words, sounds, and power,' a rather puzzled and frozen looking Rasta congregation was left behind. No wonder since there was hardly a Rasta *yard* void of Haile Selassie paintings with imaginary *dreadlocks* at the time. His ongoing deconstruction of the Bible recalls equally ambivalent responses, as the Old Testament remains the key focal point in many Rasta reasonings. This Rastafari speaks his mind, regardless of expectations and preconceived ideas of conformity. In his own words in the first chapter of this book, he will emphasize the freedom of individual conceptions against outsider ideas of uniformity.

Mutabaruka clearly distinguishes the need for unity from misconceived notions of uniformity. Even in the context of Nyahbinghi, he enters the lion's den like Daniel with his intransigence personified. Speaking of the high-grade Rasta identification with the *African King of the savannah*, visible in the ubiquitous lion imagery in Rasta households, he could not resist a comment on this very occasion:

> Okay, the lion is a powerful animal in Africa. I and I think
> we are powerful too, and our *locks* look like a lion's mane.

> But be careful! Don't follow false icons and prophets! Lions
> kill and eat meat. Rastas live ital. This is crucial! If we live
> like lions, we will die like lions: toothless and far too soon.

The Return to the Motherland

All these experiences were not exactly the ideal preparation for a
relaxed first personal meeting of Werner Zips (then still a student) with
Mutabaruka. This only came about a few years later at the Sunsplash
festival in Wiesen 1989 in the Austrian federal state of Burgenland.
To cut a long story short: to each of his supposedly open interview
questions Muta answered with a decided 'No' as an introduction to a
detailed rebuttal. The message was quite clear: white academics should
please not believe that they could contribute anything substantial
to Black history, philosophy, and certainly not to the indispensable
struggle for freedom. In this respect, Werner Zips's expectations were
not too high when he met Muta again in the summer of 1997, at the
third Panafest in Elmina and Cape Coast, Ghana.

But this time there was one small and decisive difference: on the
one hand, it apparently commanded his respect that such a white
academic (by then university lecturer) would travel all the way to
Ghana to document a festival dedicated to the cause of postcolonial
liberation; on the other hand, Zips was accompanied by a film team
from Austrian television. It is important to know that Muta loves
films and sees feature films and documentaries as his most important
media of information. Thus, he considered it as a more than welcome
opportunity to record this pivotal point in his life, as he recollects later
in this chapter. The slave castle in Cape Coast is as much a symbol for
transatlantic enslavement, as the return to this location, often coined
'the place of no return,' signifies freedom.

After all, Panafest deals with nothing less than the reappraisal of five
hundred years of slavery, colonialism, and all other forms of injustice
applied to Africa and its people over many generations. Muta knew
this location very well through film, without ever having experienced
it physically before. He had played a leading role in the film *Sankofa*,
directed by the Ethiopian filmmaker Haile Gerima (1993).[20] This classic

movie on the African and diasporan experiences of the transatlantic slave trade was partly set in the Cape Coast castle. But Muta's part was shot in the Caribbean (Jamaica), which made his personal return to the motherland even more significant.

It was for this reason that Muta responded enthusiastically to record his various performances for posterity and, particularly, to inform Jamaican people at home, unable to visit Panafest or Ghana, on African realities. In addition, he proposed to film a personal visit of the slave dungeons with his wife *Empress Amba* and his daughter. That's how two ends can meet: Muta found an entire film crew 'free of charge' to his disposal, and Werner Zips found an opportunity he would never have dreamed of fourteen years earlier in Emsley Smith's record shop. Over the entire period of three weeks, the film crew followed Mutabaruka, the official top act of the now legendary *3rd Pan-African Historical Theatre Festival*, Panafest 1997.

Before that, his revolutionary poems accompanied by a heavy tapestry of sound had taken him practically all around the world. But no performance ever equalled this return to Africa, homeland of his ancestors. Moreover, this 1997 Panafest had taken the original idea of reuniting the displaced African family very seriously and invited congregations from the entire diaspora. The cultural festival first dedicated to theatre performances had extended into all performing arts pursuing pan-African ideas in the spirit of Marcus Garvey. These three weeks covering various historic locations, where the abduction across the Atlantic began five hundred years ago, were Mutabaruka's personal re-encounter with his stolen but reclaimed identity. In his own words, filmed six years later in Jamaica, and included in a DVD edited by Werner Zips in cooperation with Mutabaruka:

> You cannot pay for this experience. To know that a lot of these poems that I used to write over the years were leading me to that. It was leading us to: Here we are now, these are the poems, all of these poems, this is the point where it stops. This is the fulfilment of this poetry. And to see that I get the opportunity to read the poems in the place where the poems were relating to, it brings tears to my eyes, you know. I actually cried. If someone had told me, 'Mutabaruka, you're going to write poems that will take

you to the place you're writing about,' I just wouldn't have believed it.[21]

Film captured the moment: There he stood, cordless mike in hand, in the glow of lit torches, raising his striking voice in denunciation of slavery, colonialism, and neocolonialism. In the middle of the courtyard of the Cape Coast slave castle, he recited his poems a cappella, accompanied only by the irregular breaking of the waves, which incessantly crash against the rocks in front of the massive structure – a stone history marker of perhaps the greatest, but certainly the longest crime in human history. In groups, often leaning on each other, people from Suriname, Brazil, the US, Guyana, Jamaica, and other Caribbean islands left the dungeons, where their ancestors were kept under inconceivable conditions. Many had tears in their eyes, sometimes from sadness, mostly from boundless rage. They were greeted by the power of words of the African poet from Jamaica, who dug into the wounds of the past, as if it were a matter of drowning the enemies in their own blood. In front of him, incense rose from a vessel – perhaps a symbol of the simultaneous desecration of the tomb of former British governors and the consecration of a memorial as a place of return, after five centuries of being the place of final farewell to the motherland Africa, the *point of no return* par excellence.

At this moment, the television camera rather exposed the Austrian film team. Thousands of clenched fists stretched into the night sky as Mutabaruka raised his poignant voice: 'We want to tell you in Ghana that we are still enslaved. This place represents the blood, sweat, urine and flesh of our ancestors.'[22] Many witnessing this moment in time, including the members of the film team, will recall it as one of the most intense experiences in their life. What it meant for Muta testifies the following passage recorded on film:

> After that drumming experience and the poetry experience to actually go into these slave dungeons, it was unbelievable. I heard some people saying that they heard ghosts in there. I never heard nothing like that. I never heard nobody. I just sat down in there and tried to experience it. I tried to figure it out because the ground you walk on is not really clay. You walk on flesh, blood, shit, piss. Because this is like the dungeons where the slaves were locked up. This is a place

which was maybe washed out once a year. It's all mixed into this ground. It almost became like concrete. It really grabs me that all my poems were really for that experience. It's almost like I can no longer bother about writing more poems about that subject again. Because that meant the sealing of years of writing about slavery. That experience in my career as a poet was THE experience, THE moment. If I would have never performed again after that, I wouldn't care. There's no other moment that I can recall, that had such an impact on what I feel I achieved.[23]

Global Justice as a Common Thread

The Jamaican artiste and Reggae anchorman has been invited as guest lecturer on several occasions at the University of Vienna. Apart from his participation at the Caribbean Conference in 2001, as mentioned earlier, he was part of a two-day programme during Werner Zips's course on Caribbean studies at the Department of Social and Cultural Anthropology in December 2011. This was the second time when author Sebastian Schwager, then still a student, met Mutabaruka in person, but the first time to see him as a speaker in front of people, namely a few hundred anthropology students. As soon as Muta marched into the lecture hall – barefoot of course – he was surrounded by a certain aura. With charisma, humour, and yet enlightening seriousness, he told the students, who were listening intently, about his own *Rasta experience*.

He mentioned the different *Rasta Houses* and their special features, as well as explained the history of the ark of the covenant and the importance of this for Rastafari.[24] In a second lecture, after the socio-economically critical documentary film *Life and Debt* by Stephanie Black (2001) had been shown, he addressed – similar to his radio programmes – globalization and the resulting difficulties for countries like Jamaica.[25] On the same evening of this powerful lecture hall performance, the other film *Mutabaruka: Return to the Motherland* by Zips (2011a) was first presented with a live performance in the presence of Mutabaruka in Vienna's *Volksgarten*, a prominent venue for Reggae music over the years. The concert's a cappella performances of poems and sarcastic talks about the Christmas tree and Santa Claus had a striking effect on Sebastian Schwager and became an initial motivation for his future master's thesis about Mutabaruka and his impact as a radio presenter.

These short introductory remarks on the protagonist of this book and the two other (Austrian) authors mark a shared motivation: namely, to contribute to revised intercultural relations based on the Rasta imperative 'equal rights and justice.' This means to tackle the (at least) five-hundred-year history of injustice committed on crude assumptions of a fictitious colour divide based on conceptions of white supremacy and Black inferiority. Such an effort draws inspiration from many Black masterminds, such as Haile Selassie I. and his visionary address to the United Nations General Assembly on October 4, 1963:

> Last May, in Addis Ababa, I convened a meeting of Heads of African States and Governments. In three days, the thirty-two nations represented at that Conference demonstrated to the world that when the will and the determination exist, nations and peoples of diverse backgrounds can and will work together in unity, to the achievement of common goals and the assurance of that equality and brotherhood which we desire. On the question of racial discrimination, the Addis Ababa Conference taught, to those who will learn, this further lesson: that until the philosophy which holds one race superior and another inferior is finally and permanently discredited and abandoned; that until there are no longer first-class and second-class citizens of any nation; that until the colour of a man's skin is of no more significance than the colour of his eyes; that until the basic human rights are equally guaranteed to all without regard to race; that until that day, the dream of lasting peace and world citizenship and the rule of international morality will remain but a fleeting illusion, to be pursued but never attained. And until the ignoble and unhappy regimes that hold our brothers in Angola, in Mozambique and in South Africa in subhuman bondage have been toppled and destroyed; until bigotry and prejudice and malicious and inhuman self-interest have been replaced by understanding and tolerance and goodwill; until all Africans stand and speak as free beings, equal in the eyes of all men, as they are in the eyes of heaven; until that day, the African continent will not know peace. We Africans will fight, if necessary, and we know that we shall win, as we are confident in the victory of good over evil.[26]

This extract of Haile Selassie's speech was immortalized by Bob Marley and the Wailers in their famous song 'War' (1976). In this regard, Mutabaruka never tires – on and off the radio – to remind his white audiences including the two Austrian co-authors on the indissoluble connection between this revolutionary message of Haile Selassie as mediated by Bob Marley and the much more accessible slogan of 'one love.' He emphasizes incessantly the 'until' being the keyword in the brilliant speech and its inherent call for collective and individual action. Until the obvious but so long denied equality of all (skin) colours is finally achieved, racism and racialism of all sorts demand attention and resistance. Notwithstanding, the meaninglessness of skin colours and other physical differences as divisive factors of the one human 'race' is envisioned by a great number of Reggae songs.[27] Nelson Mandela's famous imperative to 'forgive but not forget,' therefore needs specification within the popular *One Love* theme of the global Reggae community.[28] During our 2022 online reasoning, Muta clarified his position towards white Rastas and their role in the universal struggle, which we wish to quote at length because of its importance for the international Reggae community, and not least for the joint effort of this book:

> Bob Marley talked about 'One Love.' People gravitate towards that more than to 'Babylon system is the vampire, sucking the blood of the sufferers, building church and university, deceiving the people continually. Me say them graduatin' thieves and murderers' (Bob Marley & The Wailers – *Babylon System*, 1979; authors' note). ... So, a white youth comes now and sights Rasta. But he sees it from a religious perspective. I say that Rasta is a Black Power movement with a spiritual nucleus. And you cannot separate the nucleus from what it is, or, you cannot separate what it is from Haile Selassie. ... Black people are fighting for their liberation through an understanding that they create around Haile Selassie. When you come with the Bible now, it poses a problem to the liberation. Because people are going to say: 'Well, we can just accept the religious part and leave out the liberation.' The liberation is the main thing. A white youth who takes up this responsibility and says that he is a Rasta, wearing dreadlocks and praising Jah, he has a work to do. The work that he has to do is to

go amongst white people and declare what it means when Black people in Jamaica said: 'Rastafari, Black liberation, Black redemption!' That is what he must do. Because when he gets up and preaches Reggae music, 'One love, one heart, let's get together and be alright,' and then smokes a chalice and a spliff, bawls out 'Jah Rastafari' and reads his Bible – what is that? And many miss the essence of what I just said. What is it that a white youth wants when he declares Rastafari? He wants Black people to liberate him? Or he wants to say to just love each other and we are all one? His Majesty said it and Bob Marley sang it over: 'Until the philosophy that holds one race superior and the other inferior, and until the colour of a man's skin is of no more significance than the colour of his eyes, we Africans will fight if it is necessary, because we are confident in the victory of good over evil.' What is the philosophy which holds one superior and the other inferior? Racism. White supremacy. All these things. Haile Selassie talked about it. He didn't say 'until the philosophy which holds the French, British, Spanish or Germans inferior.' He said, 'African People!' That is the voice of the Rastaman! Until! This is the claim, we just are going to fight.[29]

We do not interpret this passage as a rejection of *One Love* philosophy, but rather a renunciation of apolitical pretensions of harmony and nonreflective calls for harmonization, curtailing the necessary acts of transformation, i.e., repatriation, reparations, restitutions, compensations, remission of financial debts, and sincere attempts of cooperation. The following passage from the same reasoning appears to underline this:

It is 'one love and one heart', yeah! But look now, Black people are in a serious mess! Look at Africa! Look at the Caribbean! Black people are in a mess! ... It is religion that most white people hold on to. Yes, Reggae is for love. We all must be together and be as one and smoke the chalice, and then have to go home and they (Black people) don't even have a home. ... What confronts me in a former slave plantation island doesn't confront people in Europe. It is not the same lifestyle. So let's bring it to a level where we can say: 'One love, one heart, let's get together and be alright.' It's almost like that I have to apologize when I defend my people. Why do I have to apologize? I don't want to offend any white people here. No! Why do I say that? Look how long they have offended us with their Christian religion. In the Bible it says that no flat nose person can enter the tabernacle. They say that neither Black people nor the native Americans can go to heaven. They don't apologize. The Ku Klux Klan, the biggest racist organization on earth in America that lynches Black people, still exists after so many years. They didn't apologize for nothing. And when America is bombing the people in Yemen, they don't apologize for that. So, I don't apologize because of a white youth who says he is a Rasta and developed a religion for himself. Religion is what brought Black people into that problem. And I do not turn Rastafari into a religion. ... I know that I am Rasta, and I am not religious. I don't get up every day, quote the Bible and say: 'Look here, the Bible says this and that.' I passed this stage. I never only read the Bible, I read about Buddha, Confucius, about all sort of things. And I moved away from the religion. Right now, we are talking about liberation. Liberation we work with. I say: 'White youth, if you are really interested in Rasta, talk about the plight of African people in history and now.'[30]

Therefore, white Rastafari and Reggae artistes, who perform this duty of 'international morality,' quoting one of Haile Selassie's most important imperatives, in their artistic work and social actions, work already for the common cause of global justice, with its mandatory repercussions for Africa and the future of African people in the motherland and the diaspora. They recognize implicitly or explicitly that freedom is indivisible on the level of global mankind, just like justice, as will be discussed later. Once more, this is made clear by Muta himself:

Liberation is for every human being. And right now, Black people are at the lowest bottom of everything. Africa is the richest continent and the poorest continent. Who caused that? The French, the British, the Portuguese, the Spaniards – all of them came to rob and rape Africa. That is where I expect a white youth to take action when he talks about Rasta. Not just to smoke a lot of ganja and say 'Jah Rastafari'. There is a serious thing that they are missing. They are missing the point: It is about racism that was placed on us as African people, the philosophy that holds one race superior. It is not me and my people holding Europe inferior. It is Europe holding me, my family, and my ancestors inferior. That stigma must be removed! And the only way it can be removed is to tell it to the people whose ancestors perpetuated this slavery mentality. Yes, that is what it is really about.[31]

As mentioned above, both Austrian authors see themselves as students of Mutabaruka, not only because he is the elder in their relationship, but because he is a centre of knowledge transmission relating to this history of racial violence he refers to. This is not to say that we are fans of his music and keen listeners of his radio shows, which we certainly are, but rather feel united in an ongoing universal struggle for a united mankind. This refers as much to making a modest contribution in unveiling the skin tricks played by people of white skin complexion on all others, thereby 'othering' the greater part of mankind for their own benefits. In the current crucial times of cumulative crises, the philosophical and socio-political stance Muta has brought to the Reggae table over the years has global dimensions, not only setting the historical record straight but straightening out the menace for mankind in its entirety, if not too late. Its key message could hardly be better expressed than by his poem/song 'Skins' (1989):

Black is the colour of my skin

But there is more of me to see within

Skins have played many tricks on me

Skins, yes skins is what they see

But I am made with bones and skin like you

Doin' hopin' for the same things you do

For justice peace and a place on earth

For life existence and what its worth

So stop playin' your skin tricks on me

If my skin ain't free neither will we be

Stop playin' your skin tricks I say

Tomorrow is a brand-new day

For every skin that's here on earth

Came to existence through a child's birth

The blood that moulds is always red

Life continues even when skin is dead

Skin for you, skins for me

When skins are black and in slavery

No skin can truly say its free

So stop playin' your skin tricks on me

There is much more of me to see

Stop playin' that skin trick I say

Tomorrow is a brand-new day

Open your eyes, and be wise

Take you awake and realize

Life is blood we all possess

Blood is where life existence rest

The blood that moulds is always red

Life continues even when skin is dead

Skin is black, skin is white

We live through the day

We live through the night

Skin is black, skin is white

The colour of skin is not the right to might

So stop playin' that skin trick on me

There is much more of me to see

Stop playin' that skin trick I say

Tomorrow is a brand-new day[32]

NOTES

1.   Since it is important to precipitate an awareness of the atrocities that slavery has brought upon people from Africa or of African descent in terms of subordination and discrimination, in this book 'Black' is written with a capital B (as opposed to 'white').

2.   See his own biographical outline on his gravitating towards Rastafari, particularly the *livity* and philosophy of Nyahbinghi, in chapter 1 of this book. Christian Habekost's books *Verbal Riddim – The Politics & Aesthetics of African-Caribbean Dub Poetry* (1993) as well as Julie Pearn's dissertation *Poetry as a Performing Art in the English-Speaking Caribbean* (1985) offer a great contextualization and analysis of Dub Poetry per se (with references to Mutabaruka).

3.   Zips (2011a). Note: See the interview/reasoning with Mutabaruka, partially published in written form in this book in chapter 1, in Kingston, December 29, 2007, first released by Werner Zips (2011a) in the film *From the Cutting Edge: Mutabaruka on Mutabaruka* on the DVD *Mutabaruka: The Return to the Motherland*.

4.   Rae Town is a community on Kingston's waterfront where the so-called *Rae Town Old Hits* party was established in 1982. The regular event on Sunday evening is known for its showcase of Jamaican and international musical classics from the 1950s to 1980s. Nowadays, the session is held next to the Kingston Cricket Club in Sabina Park.

5.   Interview 6 (2022). Note: The quotations throughout the book try to come close to the original. We provide an English translation or paraphrase of the Jamaican *Patois* (or *Patwah*), which is the Creole language of the Jamaican majority and used by Mutabaruka in his radio shows and interviews. Hence, we ask the reader to not be irritated by seeming misspellings or grammatical errors (as one may think of in the terms of English) in the radio and interview quotations. The anglophone Jamaican Patois features African influences but is close to the English language, see also Cassidy (2007, 2f.). For more information on the socio-political background and development of Creole languages in the Caribbean see Cassidy (2007, 10–25) and Mühleisen (2002, 58–64). It should also be noticed that Mutabaruka likes to use the plural form and often says *we/us* instead of *I/me*. In certain speeches addressing the general public, he predominantly uses the masculine form, which is meant inclusive in line with his gender equality stance.

6.   It is possible to re-listen to the *Steppin Razor* broadcast with the last-mentioned interview here: https://youtu.be/dSuGewMCMvM (uploaded on November 23, 2018).

7.   Hattori Hanzō was a famous Samurai of feudal Japan. As a historic figure, he was the leader of the Ninjas from Iga. Furthermore, Ninjas belong to the most referenced foreign pop icons in Jamaican Reggae,

owing their popularity to the abundance of Ninja movies in Jamaican cinemas.

8. Rebel Salute is one of the most important Reggae festivals in Jamaica. It has been held annually in January since 1994, around the birthday of its founder Tony Rebel, and strives not only to preach Rasta-*livity*, but also to practice it. In terms of musical orientation, emphasis is placed on artistes and content that is largely based on the ideas of Rastafari *conscious music.* Furthermore, there is neither alcohol nor meat for sale.

9. The key notion *ital* stands for the natural lifestyle of Rastafari. Combining the words vital and I, it has a complex variety of meanings that distinguish Rastafari *livity* from all other, particularly Western ways of life. Corruption, capitalism, over-consumption, exploitation, and environmental destruction are just a few buzzwords marking the latter in extensive Rasta reasonings. See also Interview 1 (2018) and Roberts (2014, 190).

10. Alligator Pond is the next larger place, whose name probably also suggests the (former) distribution of crocodiles.

11. Besides Nyahbinghi and the Twelve Tribes of Israel, the so-called Bobo Shanti is one of the most popular Rastafari organizations, made famous by Reggae stars like Sizzla and Anthony B, who embody the grouping's tenets in their lyrics and their looks.

12. Crabs, like other crustaceans, are considered scavengers and therefore inferior creatures.

13. East Fest was an annual open air Reggae concert initiated by the Reggae group Morgan Heritage. It also featured mostly *Rasta artistes.*

14. Cf. Mutabaruka (2011) for details of his view of the Maroon freedom struggle as part of the all-African resistance, which is not so different from Zips's perspective as he himself apparently assumes and which appeared as an epilogue in Zips's book *Nanny's Asafo Warriors* (2011b) not least for this reason.

15. His keynote speech was transcribed and published in the conference proceedings, cf. Mutabaruka (2006a).

16. The homonymous poem on the aforementioned *Check It!* LP from 1983 is still one of his most famous poems. In the Jamaican and international press, it has earned him the label of one of Reggae's most controversial artistes and left a racist impression on some listeners. From Muta's point of view – as told in a personal conversation – it deals with the experiences of some of his closest relatives who settled in London as migrants, completely alienated from their origins in the process, without ever coming close to gaining a foothold.

17. The late Miss Lou, to whom Mutabaruka dedicated a sensitive poem of the same name, was the pioneer of a literature written in *Jamaican* ('*nation language*'). Before that, the unofficial national language was considered 'bad English' or dialect, equated with illiteracy and backwardness, and at best tolerated in spoken everyday language.

18. Hollington (2015, 195): 'In Rwanda, Mutabaruka is a special name which is given to people who survived a war and returned home. It can also be given to a child of a mother who experienced hardship and destruction in a war, or to a person who encountered very difficult situations and risked his life and survived without being harmed or having problems.'

19. Zips (2011a). Note: *Bloodbath* (literally 'blood bath') is one of Muta's neologisms replacing Jamaican swear words such as *bloodclaat* or *raasclaat*, which are associated with intimate body parts and therefore have sexist connotations.

20. The movie *Sankofa* (125 minutes) was restored in 4K and re-released by ARRAY in 2021.

21. Interview/reasoning with Mutabaruka at Treasure Beach/Jamaica on August 18, 2003, released on the DVD *Mutabaruka: The Return to the Motherland* edited by Zips (2011a).

22. See also Mutabaruka/Zips (2008) on the significance of the Panafest for the historical reappraisal of slavery and its aftermath as well as for the pan-African idea.

23. Zips (2011a).

24. Basically, a *Rasta House* means a distinctive organization or rather loose grouping of Rastafari. Barry Chevannes (1998, 16) specifies the origin of the House as following: 'The concept of House seemed to have originated in the second phase of the movement's development (at around 1955; authors' note) when, as a result of the reform activities of the emerging Dreadlocks, the movement split into two orders or Houses: the House of Dreadlocks and the House of Combsomes, that is, those who comb their hair.' The most popular Houses are Bobo Shanti, Nyahbinghi, and Twelve Tribes of Israel.

25. The film *Life and Debt* explores Jamaica's economic and social situation as the International Monetary Fund (IMF) and the World Bank have made structural adjustments.

26. Selassie (1963).

27. Including the particularly striking tune of immortal Lucky Dube, written under the experience of apartheid: 'Different Colours, One People' (1993).

28. Mandela (1999).

29. Interview 6 (2022).

30. Ibid.

31. Ibid.

32. Please note that each poem and song excerpt in this book is quoted directly from the original source. Thus, don't mind any misspellings and the special formatting.

ACKNOWLEDGEMENTS

Mutabaruka, Sebastian Schwager, and Werner Zips

Mutabaruka:

I would like to thank those who have contributed to the radio programmes since its inception.

Special mention:

Karl Young
Chad Young
Ka'Bu Ma'at Kheru
Debbian Dewar
Jacqueline Hope

Past hosts:

Tony Rebel
Kshema Francis
Carolyn Cooper
Robert Williams
Miguel Lorne
Jalani Niaah
Flow O'Conner
Mitzie Williams
Barbara Blake Hannah
Ibo Cooper
Franklyn Mcknight
Mark Wignal

Digital Chris
Amber Crowl
Louis Moyston
Leahcim Semaj

Producers:

Joy Morgan
Samantha Mittoo
Tonian Lindo
Tracy Ann Morris
Shamara Preston
Saundrie Shaw
Simone Brown Keise

Technical operators:

Wilbert Wisdomn
Dj Neil
Dj Bryan
Dayne Young
Dj Kemar
Shane Clarke
Nigel Durrant
Nicholas Francis

Sebastian Schwager:

Sincere thanks are given to our interview and conversational partners in Jamaica for the provision of their time and exciting narratives and to my Jamaican friends for the love and hospitality they have shown me over the years. I would like to thank Errol Hamilton and Armin Herbinger, who both have been door openers for my research, especially in Kingston. I also thank Christian Moll for his company during my last fieldwork in Jamaica (and for providing two interviews for this book) and my former fellow students Stephie and Rudolf for the exchange of ideas and inspiration.

I thank my parents for the gift of life; their new partners for their solidarity; my brother and his family for their support in difficult times; and my own, still young family: my wife Phiona and our lovely daughter Iyana. I deeply appreciate the wonderful bond among the three of us. It was your backup and flexibility that gave me the energy and opportunity to work on this book project.

In particular, I devote the book to Sevana Leona, our beloved firstborn daughter, who unfortunately left this side of the universe way too soon.

Werner Zips:

I want to thank the late Emsley Smith heartically for shining the light of Rastafari in Vienna and Austria. I particularly thank him for two wonderful trips to the African heartlands in Tanzania, where he found his personal salvation and, in fact, brought the Jamaican African experiences and musical expressions back to the motherland, as a sound operator, DJ, and radio jock.

A big thank you goes out to Mr Leon Hill and family from Maroon Town, St James, for basically adopting me in his family and teaching me the means, linguistically and otherwise, to even come close to grasping the sense of Mutabaruka's statements or *highalogues*. By extension, my thanks go out to a great number of Jamaicans showing me love, understanding, and allowing me to experience bits and pieces of the cultural universe.

Finally, I wish to thank the Department of Social and Cultural Anthropology in Vienna for supporting this project. And particularly its former members, Karl R. Wernhart and Manfred Kremser, for their relentless support and for promoting research on the Caribbean.

We all thank the Queenmother of Reggae Studies, Carolyn Cooper, for her readiness to contribute the foreword. Last, not least, we wish to thank the entire staff at Ian Randle Publishers for all the prudent work to bring this book to light.

CHAPTER 1

WORDS, SOUNDS, AND POWER
Mutabaruka on Mutabaruka[1]

1.1. The Movie Days

If I want to psych out myself, movies made an impression on me in my youth days. When you grow bigger, you understand now. … You see the whole thing comes out revealing itself to you in the perspective of history. … *The Ten Commandments* – mostly white people acted in this film. The Pharaoh was white, played by Yul Brynner. Moses was white, too, played by Charlton Heston. Everybody was white in that movie except the people who were enslaved. All of it refers to certain things historically.

When you watch *Solomon and Sheba*, everyone was white in that movie, and you start to put the movies into perspective. Because it is the visual that makes me remember them. You know that a picture speaks more than a thousand words. When I am talking in a radio programme, it is through the visual that I remember those things and I can relate back to it. This resonated in my mind for years. When I am talking now and people ask me where I know all those things from, I am telling them that it comes from movies! All this *Star Wars* and *Matrix* phenomenon, this is where the minds are going to and they understand it from this perspective. You are watching the movie and you feel that it is just fiction! Most things in movies that were made twenty or thirty years ago, we see it right now as a real thing. We never knew about computers thirty years ago, and in the movies they used computers. These are things which we used to see in a science fiction movie, and these things help. Especially when you are connected, because the best thing is not just to have the information but to use the information and to connect the information with what is going on.

When we used to watch movies, I saw politicians being involved in the corruption, like in drugs and other things. You as a youth you feel that people like you wouldn't be involved in such corruption. And now you grow up and you realize that in the American system you have big politicians who run your life but are also involved in paedophiliac and all kinds of deviant behaviours.

1.2.   The Rise of the Poet

I remember a teacher by the name of Misses Pusey. Misses Pusey was an English teacher and taught writing in the class. She asked us to write a poem – the class learned to write a poem. So I wrote a poem, and everybody was supposed to read the poem in front of the class. I wrote a poem about birds, the first I ever wrote in my life: 'Birds are lovely things to see, just to see them flying free. Birds with many colours, it's wonderful to see them flying for hours.' This was like something else. The teacher gave me a big mark for it. I think that motivated the poetry aspect and the creativity in me.

After that, I started to write poems that were related to social commentary, and I put them in the magazine of Marcus Garvey Jr, who had his magazine at that time. There was another magazine by the name of *Swing*. *Swing* magazine was the equivalent to the American *Ebony* magazine in Jamaica. It showed you what was happening in Jamaica. I used to send my poems to them. You know, as a youth you want to be heard, so you send the poems all over the places to see if anybody would publish them. And they published one. They eventually asked me, if I could put some in it every month, because it was a monthly publication.

So I started to put poems in *Swing* every month, and they came to me and asked: 'Why don't you just publish the poems in a book?' And I said: 'Yeah man!' As a youth if you hear that you have a book, it is a big thing. Because we didn't hear about a young poet who had books, you know. Most of the poets that we read were from English literature: Shakespeare, Keats, Chaucer, Milton, and all these people. To actually write some poems yourself as a youth going to school, I see it as a big publication. It was really something else. They published a book with me named *Outcry*. These same poems are the poems now that people know me for, and they were written from school. Most of the poems that I have recorded over the years, I wrote them in school. Some of the people they don't believe me; they think that I am Rastafari and Black Power. But the poems from *Outcry* – the second album was also called *Outcry* – were written when I was in school. And a lot of the other poems were written when I was in school. So they published the book and, in those days, everybody was kind of politically conscious. Politics was like ... everybody was on the Left. It was the era of the rise of communism, socialism, and the Black Power Movement.[2]

In America you had the Black Panther Movement, Martin Luther King, Malcom X, and all these guys. And then you had poets like Gil Scott-Heron, Sonia Sanchez, Amiri Baraka, and Nikki Giovanni. I started to read them, too. Because I realized that I am also a poet, so I started to read these poets and I started to listen to them. Because poets like The Last Poets used to record their poems, so most of the time I actually never read the poets, we rather used to listen to them.[3] So all these American poets were very much into what we called social change and Black Power consciousness, and this was what we used to read. And then we had books like *The Autobiography of Malcolm X*, *The Philosophy and Opinions of Marcus Garvey*, or Frantz Fanon's *The Wretched of the Earth*. All these books helped to shape my whole mindset, and we started to move amongst that kind of mindset.

1.3. Marcus Garvey and the Black Power Movement in Jamaica

In Jamaica, a lot of us were influenced by what was taking place within the Black Power Movement in America. You had men like Malcom X and Stokely Carmichael. And then you had the mentioned books. Those books were banned, they couldn't be found. The prime minister at the time banned any book which was dealing with Black things. It was like fighting with the ganja. When a police officer would find you with a Malcom X book, they would lock you up. You know, that is how it was. But as a youth we used to move amongst these people who were in the Black Power Movement, and some of the teachers at the Kingston Technical High School were part of that movement, too.

A brethren named Locksley Comrie was the first person who introduced me to Malcom X, on record. He had a lot of records in his office at school. We used to go into his office and listen to the Malcom X records.[4] And then we started to get books. *The Autobiography of Malcolm X* was one of the first books in my life I read all the way through. Usually, I read books and stop, but this book was the first book I ever actually read. And in those days, too, you had to hide the book when you go to school. We used to tear up the cover of the book and put another cover on the book – like a schoolbook cover – and paste it up. So, when you opened it, it looked like a schoolbook. Then we knew a brethren named Marcus Garvey Jr, who was Marcus Garvey's son and used to teach at Kingston Technical High School. He was very much involved in Black Power, because he came after his father, and he formed an organization. We started to join the organization and out of that we started to develop this sense of Black consciousness.

We used to go to Amy Jacques Garvey's house. She was Marcus Garvey's wife and used to live in Mona Road. We used to go up there, sit down, and have conversations. As a school youth, we were radical, even more than people who claimed they were Black Power. They dealt with certain things, but we didn't work with these things. They would be called moderate. For some reason we were more like the Malcom X kind of vibes, you know. We were into the Malcolm X kind of thinking, 'by any means necessary.' 'The ballot or the bullet' – those kinds of vibes. After, we even started to write the poems like that.

So we went through, and the Black Power Movement got big in Jamaica, politically. People were very motivated on the Left. But as a youth, I was never on the Left; I was never into the socialism and communism. We still saw Marx as a white man, and we didn't follow Marx. We followed Marcus Garvey. We sat down and had social meetings, and we used to run some little projects for children. But we started to recognize that socialism and communism don't work. We as young people, who came into this thing, we said that something else must be there. And it was then at school when we started to juggle because we had some youths at school who smoked herbs and they said 'Rasta!' But we were not yet into the Rasta thing; we were Black Power. We had Black Power business. We had to plan to do a revolution.

I was never a socialist because at socialists' meetings all you hear was Marx, Marx, Marx. We didn't hear them saying Marcus Garvey. And as a matter of fact, they looked down on Marcus Garvey because of the *Back to Africa* thing. They said that Rastafari is escapist. They said that the Rasta movement wants to escape from here and just tries to go to Africa. Their focus was like Marx, Lenin, and all these things. We never worked with that. Over a period of time, we read, and we read, and we read, and we started to hear the youths at school. The youths actually mentioned certain passages of the Bible, and they related those to Rastafari. We went to a certain meeting and a Rastaman got up and talked; we listened to them still as youths coming up. He took out the Bible, and I looked in the Bible and said: 'Rhaatid! Sam and all these things relate to Africa and Ethiopia. Rhaatid! I wondered if all these things have any validity in what Rastaman said about Selassie.'[5] So that made me try to figure it out and I said: 'Maybe this thing has some serious thing to it because Rastaman talks about Blackness, but them also talk about God.' What we were really missing from the Black Power Movement was the spirituality. It never had any. It was a socio-political movement.

For some reason that idea connected us: You can be political and social but still spiritual. I want to say that the movement that people in Jamaica named Rastafari maintained that socio-political thinking, but it had that spirituality, that we were missing from the Black Power Movement. So we started a kind of shift in our thinking. The Black Power Movement now got more left. They were more into the Marxist thing. We would work with Marcus Garvey. Garvey would tell you about 'Africa for the Africans.' The Marxists never told you about that. They told you about proletariat, bourgeoisie, and their big words. As youths we were never into those big words. We were just into African freedom, liberation, and revolution. We now started to examine the Rasta vibes.

1.4.   Rasta By Experience: From Twelve Tribes to Nyahbinghi

Rastafari shaped my thinking more and more. The more I examined it, is the more we were going to it and the more we realized. And we never left out the socio-political, but we added something else to the thinking. … Marcus Garvey became like a pivotal part of my consciousness, also because of Marcus Garvey Jr., his son. Rastafari came into the whole picture, and we decided to join an organization, the Twelve Tribes of Israel. Inside the Twelve Tribes we read the Bible, and we started to see certain things where I wasn't in line with the Twelve Tribes. So we started to go to Nyahbinghi. And when I joined them, back then the Twelve Tribes didn't want me to go to Nyahbinghi because Nyahbinghi is totally contrary to Twelve Tribes. The Nyahbinghi say: 'Bun Jesus Christ!' And the Twelve Tribes say: 'Greetings in the name of our Lord and Saviour named Jesus Christ!'

The Nyahbinghi took the Bible and threw it in the fire and didn't care. And a man went to the Twelve Tribes and told them that a Rastaman burned the Bible and this and that. Nyahbinghi are talking about ital food, whereas Twelve Tribes eat chicken and curry goat. The Nyahbinghi men would throw away pot, pan, and all those things. It was almost like a contradiction. Every time we would go to the Nyahbinghi, the Twelve Tribes people would be vexed. And I started to eat ital food. It wasn't a part of Twelve Tribes thinking to eat ital. You had a few youths in there who were also on that level, so we sticked together and became like a clique inside the Twelve Tribes. You had ital youths versus meat eaters and such things, so it became a problem.

Eventually, we had to leave the Twelve Tribes. It was kind of too binding; it was never open. We saw it as a Christian thing. Coming from the Black Power thinking, we couldn't work with the Christian thinking. They are saying Haile Selassie and Jesus, and we never worked with that neither. We bun Jesus and God. So eventually we left Twelve Tribes, and we just sticked to Nyahbinghi. Then I went up in the hills in St James, because in Kingston – we lived in St Andrew – we moved up and down and I said: 'Bwoy! I really want to leave Kingston

and go to the countryside to live, plant food, and all these ways.' …
And we stayed down there for 15 years. In those times, we stopped
with the political agenda claiming 'left is right.' We saw Rastafari more
important now. …

Eventually, I started to move in the country areas. I would traverse
from one hill to the next hill, where the Rasta were – all over
Westmoreland, Hanover, and all those places. We started to move into
the mountains, and we started to meet the Rastafari. Those hill Rasta
vibes were different than what we used to hear in Kingston. We heard
a man saying he is a Rasta, but he didn't like Haile Selassie. We heard
a man saying he is a Rasta, and he didn't eat cooked food. We heard a
man saying he is a Rasta, and he didn't smoke herbs. Different things
started to appear because we saw different things, and we were not
exposed to these things until we went up the hills and experienced it.
We saw the Rastas living a different way. We wouldn't know about it in
Kingston. So we kind of gravitated towards that.

We did the *Binghi* (short for Nyahbinghi), but the Binghi was
limitation, too. In the hills of Jamaica, I saw these Rastas who didn't
go to a Binghi. There were some Rastas who got up every day and just
planted food, planted food, planted food, and didn't go to a market.
They didn't use pot and knife. You know, they didn't use nothing, just
natural things such as a coconut shell. We went and lived like that.
We eventually got going in that mindset, and it was just about Haile
Selassie and nothing else. We didn't add nothing; we didn't subtract
nothing from the name; we didn't talk nothing else. And the *livity* was
in that space there. No fire, no burning of herbs. We used to have
this thing where you say: 'If you would love the herbs, you wouldn't
burn them, because Rome burned. Don't burn herbs.' People who
love ganja, why would they burn it? Sounded like police. Anyone who
would come smoke herbs, we told them: 'No, sir. A man can't plant
herbs and you burn it, are you the police?' All those little things we
used to develop in our mindset: 'No, the herbs are too nice. It is better
if you just eat them. Burn nothing. Burn hashish? That comes like a
police force going to your cane piece and burn down your ganja.' So
most of us had other vibes. We were just ital. No shoes, no top on our

heads; we just trod trough. We developed a philosophy which I kept to this day. …

Nobody can truly say that I never made use of my life. Because I think that most things people said that you cannot achieve with that mindset, we achieved it. Most people in Jamaica would give up when they are thinking to achieve these things, but we never gave it up. We went the same way, continued, and moved in that direction. And all things, whether materially or spiritually, where people would say you have to do other things to get these things, we stayed in it and got it. That to me is an achievement itself. To know that we never bowed, and we never suffered. Even though we started to suffer the same humiliation: 'Hey Rasta, you are *dutty*... Rasta, you are nasty!' People despised us and said we don't have no sense. Now we have come a long way and we haven't changed the thinking and we see people, even when they don't like you, they must respect it. Because you have sticked with it. We went through, you know?

We are still going through the same thing, and we still have the same vision we have experienced over time. We have carried ourselves through, and we have inspired other people. Because it is not something we just read in a book and learned, it is something that we live. So, when we tell somebody something, we don't base it on what Charles Darwin said, or someone else. I know that this can work, so it goes; like if somebody has a cut and I suggest taking some bird pepper and putting it on the cut. I didn't read that in no book. I know that it works because I used it on my children. The normal Jamaican doesn't eat raw ackee. But I know that you can eat it because I have eaten that for twenty-odd years. I fed my children with it, and it worked. It is not like reading or learning things, but it is an *experience*. And I think now that the experience is what makes you firmer in the tradition. The diversion is not something that you think about, because it is your way of life. … I wonder if someone could ever turn Christian, because they pray for you all the time. They are praying for me, so that I change. They come on the radio and talk these things. I say: 'Yah, pray for me, go on pray for me, man!' But the *livity* what I hear a lot of people talking about as Rasta, we see it manifesting itself in front of us.

1.5. Twelve Tribes – Bobo Shanti – Nyahbinghi: Unity vs Uniformity in Rastafari

We see the evolution of these things in the different Rastafari movements: in the Twelve Tribes, the Bobo Shanti, and the Nyahbinghi. The only reason why we stuck to the Nyahbinghi is because the Nyahbinghi do not conform. It is not a conform space. It is not an organization, so you have different kinds of thinking there. Even though you have people in there who try to put it into uniformity, it tends not to keep into that uniformity because it is so loose. It is not like a House. You know that people say 'Nyahbinghi House,' but it is not really a House. It is just people trying to put it into that frame to identify it. But the Nyahbinghi is not a House because even the Bobos would tell you about their *Nyahbinghi ceremonies* (or 'Binghis'). It is only the Twelve Tribes who don't recognize the Nyahbinghi. Because they don't see it as a uniform system. In the Nyahbinghi House you don't have a uniformity, you see. We have a Rastaman in there who just says: 'Burn God.' And you have another Rastaman in there who says that Selassie is the almighty God. But in the Twelve Tribes everybody says 'Gad' (Dr Vernon Carrington, founder of the Twelve Tribes, known as Prophet Gad; authors' note). There is no Gad in the Nyahbinghi. There is just one focus: Haile Selassie. And all the other things come now through the experience, the *livity*.

In the Twelve Tribes you don't have to experience Rasta. You can learn about Rasta and understand it from the biblical perspective that Prophet Gad shows you, but you don't have to live it. As long as you can articulate what Gad teaches and how the Twelve Tribes of Israel connect with Haile Selassie, the returned Messiah and these things, then you are safe. In the Nyahbinghi now, it is very difficult to say that you just learn it. You have men who learn it, but a man *burns* you out totally if you come with too many Bible arguments. Because even though he quotes the Bible, too, he doesn't want you to talk too much about the Bible, like if you don't have it in yourself. The Nyahbinghi man will quote the Bible and will know all the psalms and he can quote from the back to the left. But if it comes down to true *livity* now, he doesn't want you to tell him nothing about the Bible. And he tells you about Yasus Christ, but he will burn Jesus. Because he has an interpretation that goes beyond it, what you call the orthodox viewpoint.

You have many people who from that time till now will give credence to the Nyahbinghi, who even don't understand that this foundation is in the holy mountains in the land and in the gates of Zion according to Jacob, and they quote these things like I could quote it now. But within the framework of this experience, this is not what worries the Nyahbinghi man. He matters about *ital livity*, he is talking about the system coming from Africa, and he is looking upon it on a different level. He licks down white supremacy with Marcus Garvey. The Twelve Tribes do not focus on Marcus Garvey, to no fullness, you see? The Nyahbinghi man says that Marcus Garvey is the prophet. The Twelve Tribes do not work with that, they say Gad is the prophet. The Twelve Tribes are thinking that Haile Selassie is dead now. So they are working with Zere Yacobe Selassie, the grandson of Haile Selassie. The Twelve Tribes recognize him because they claim that he is the heir to the throne. They rally around him because he is next in line to the throne. The thinking is that Haile Selassie is dead, and he is next in line for the throne because they still maintain the throne as a centre. It is a different way. It does not necessarily have that *livity* in it. But you can *understand* and *articulate* it. Haile Selassie is not the centre anymore because according to the Twelve Tribes Selassie is dead, but the throne remains. The throne is what gives the continuity of King David's lineage and Zere Yacobe is in line to ascend the throne. The Binghi man still hails Haile Selassie; he still regards Haile Selassie as the centre of the whole thing.

Some Nyahbinghi Rastafari don't want to even hear nothing about pot: 'Pot? I don't have any pot in my house. Come light fire in my house? You know, fire is a destruction.' And he looks up in the sun and chants: 'The sun I live I, I, I, the sun I – Haile I Selassie I.' He gets up every morning and takes care of his herb fields and treats his herbs like a woman. And he plants the food like he would take care of a woman. So he teaches you certain vibes, and if you come amongst him, it is a different vibe. It is not that he wants to convert you, as you can see in a certain place. Most men who learned things want to convert you, like the Christians. You have Rastafari who don't have no business with conversion. He has no business if you are a Rasta or not. He deals with I I I I I, Selassie. They would come up here with that kind of vibration. We sieved it out; we sieved out a lot of them because we learned about it the same way. We started out with the Bible, and we evolved into something else.

If you compare the Twelve Tribes with the Nyahbinghi, you find that the Twelve Tribes organization is one thing; it is about Gad, Jesus Christ, and Haile Selassie. And the Nyahbinghi have different thinking even though the Nyahbinghi is not really a House as how you would classify House – like you have the Bobo House with Marcus Garvey, Prince Emmanuel, and Haile Selassie. The Nyahbinghi have different thoughts inside of it. So in the Nyahbinghi, you have someone like me, and you have a next man who says that Haile Selassie is God, and you have a next man saying Yasus Christ, and you have a next man who burns Jesus.

I say that the Nyahbinghi don't give credence to the uniformity. There is no uniformity even though people would like to have that uniformity to study it. Because sometimes in order to study something you have to have a consistency in the thing. But there is no consistency in the Nyahbinghi House. It poses a problem to persons who are studying, because they want to structure and organize every thinking and say 'This is this and this is that.' In the Nyahbinghi House it is very difficult to do that. Especially now with the Binghi youths who come up. I have a youth who comes up and thinks what I think: to bun Jesus and God same way. We do not have anything to do with Houses and all these things. But they still tell you about Nyahbinghi.

Well, to me it doesn't matter because it is already planted, and the fruit is already bearing. The idea of Haile Selassie being dead or alive, I don't think it is an important manifestation of Rastafari because when the Christians say that Jesus Christ is dead, it never stopped Christianity. But not only that, in order to make society live, Christianity raised Jesus Christ from the dead. The faith that one day he will come again in the flesh is very pivotal to the Christian faith, and that is what a lot of Rastas take up in their mindset, too. The idea of death is very weird to deal with in the Rastafari mind. But death is .... Well, if you are born you are dead one day, is not like 'wow'! That does not deviate from Rastafari, Rastafari is … I am Rastafari. So it is I creating whatever you see; it is the outcome of Rastafari. When I say 'I,' I don't mean Mutabaruka, I mean 'I, the internal.' So is I creating this idea, this consciousness. The whole *livity* of Rastafari is Rastafari created it. Without even getting any instructions from the man Haile Selassie.

The man Haile Selassie is the recognized centre of that symbol of spirituality. But it is not the behavioural centre of the spirituality. You don't behave like Haile Selassie, the man. You behave like Rastafari in the spirituality and what the spirituality manifests to you. It is not a religious structure that you can study from that viewpoint, when a man says that he studies Rasta. Because he gets confused. It is confusing for the outsider to hear different sayings of Rasta. But it is not a confusion. People just want the uniformity instead of the unity. You see an army is in the same uniform, but it is not in the same way unified. So we have to separate what is unification and what is uniformity. In Rastafari, there is no uniformity because different Rastas tell you different things and it will confuse the outsider.

I guess it is the same thing with Hinduism, too. Hinduism isn't a structured thing because different Gods represent different behaviours. In Rastafari, the way of life decides how you articulate. The environment in which you see the thing, and you come up in the thing, that is how you articulate the experience. Rastafari is responding to its environment and the perception that is gathered in that environment. A Chiney man comes and says that he is a Rasta, and a white man comes and says he is a Rasta. This is very difficult to understand for a Rastaman, who recognizes that this is a Black Liberation Movement searching for Black identity through the Haile Selassie consciousness. But the white man is recognizing in his environment an experience that he can identify with the centre of this Rastafari force. He creates that out of his environment and his experience, and he comes up and says that he is a Rasta, too.

1.6. Rastafari as Philosophy of Liberation

This is kind of weird because what Rastafari tries to do is to awaken that other side of the colonized and to ask: 'Look here man, where is your culture?' Because religions come out of culture; it is not the other way around. People have culture before they have religion. The way of life of the people is distinct and then you develop certain things. So, for instance, you have like Judaism which never started out as a religion. It is just a set of people who live in a certain way. And in order to put them into a perspective, a religion came out of it. It is a very political religion because Moses was one of the greatest politicians of all times. Moses was able to structure something that made the Israelites rally around it. And what was that thing? His idea of a Jahwe and the idea of a box named the ark of the covenant. He himself created laws for his tribe, the tribe of the Levites, in this thing that they call tabernacle.

They built a tabernacle and put this box inside the tabernacle, and only Moses's tribe could go inside there. He was from the tribe of Levites, so all the Levites became priests. It became what you call a theocratic mindset where there is nobody that is saying anything to them inside the tabernacle. They created the doctrine and came outside of the tabernacle to say: 'Just save the Lord.' Who was saying that? Not the Lord himself, it was Moses and the tribe of the Levites. They gave these laws and regulations to these people who were nobodies in order to keep them structured, to keep them unified. But it wasn't a religion. It was just a way to unify the people. He put all these things in regulation to unify the people. That is what Rasta is. Rastafari is a response to slavery and colonialism. It was started to make Black people aware of what they have been surrounded by – politically, socially, and spiritually. So that they can move forward. The spirituality that they found – Rastafari – is not unique to Rasta. It is a universal truth. So people can relate to that.

We have come around to white people who can see it as a truth and relate to it. The response to slavery and colonialism by these Black people gave rise to a spirituality that is universal. They wouldn't see that through Christianity. Even though you might go to the eastern part of the world, like to India, China, and Japan, you see the same thinking in the spirituality. If it wasn't for Rasta, these colonized people would have never seen that. Christianity doesn't offer that freedom and liberation outside of the Roman thinking that refers to the Pope or Jesus. What Rastafari has been able to do is to connect a universal truth with a domiciled ex-slave group of people that would not have been able to see it without that Rastafari mindset. And that is a wonderful thing to me; even looking at it as an outsider, not from the perspective of Rastafari. But look at Christianity, though. Christianity has helped to enslave these people. It has helped to build the structure on which the oppression was based upon. All the people that were saying this thing, they set up this structure. Because the same Roman Senate that structured the political order of the Western world, the democracy that we speak of, started right in the Senate of Rome. The political structure is Roman, and the structure of the religion is Roman.

How are these people who are domiciled in this colonial thinking going to escape when the political, social, and religious structures are based on the same people who oppress them continuously? They find a socio-political understanding through Africa, Marcus Garvey and Haile Selassie. Then they connected it to a spirituality outside of the Roman Empire. And you get to defy the Roman Empire because we choose to go outside of that Empire now and look for the universal truth. You have no Roman truth because you have the Roman truth that dominates the whole Western world. I have the universal truth that Romans, Indians, Japanese, and people anywhere can relate to, that is life now: nature. That is what the Rastaman brings to the table, to the people who never have had the opportunity to see further than that. He brings the nature thing, the 'pagan mindset' to the table now. People don't like the word 'pagan,' but pagan is not a bad thing. It's just that the Christians made it bad. People believed pagans were poor people in Europe, farmers who lived life day by day, recognizing it for what it is.

The Rastaman brings that life connection to the whole religious belief thing. And everybody can relate to it. But we still declare that as a liberation for Black people! Rastafari comes to liberate Black people. It never came to liberate the world. But there are aspects of it to which the world can relate. The aspect of it is the spirituality, the connection with life, nature, earth, the moon, the stars, heat, air, and water. That is the connection that Rastafari brings to it. And you can't go in the church and tell people you study about the sky. You can't get in and tell people about Mother Earth. They do not recognize Mother Earth and Mother Nature, but the Rastaman comes with that.

'Inna the dung, the filth, inna the shit they would put we into,' we come with that. 'The dutty locks and the ganja smoking, who can't get no work,' being despised and all these things. And you tell a man: 'Love?' You live in the shit and a man passes you and you tell him: 'Love?' You call a woman, who has never seen a palace yet, a *queen* and *empress*. The man who lives in the shit, lives in the piss, and who can't get any work, and people despise him, looks at his woman and says: 'She is a queen!' You can't get better than that. I do not care what a man says; you can't get better *than that* because Rasta is the only set of people who bring that to the table.

No political structure – whether it is Marxist, Leninist, or the Black Power Movement – has ever brought that to the table to elevate the people in the structure. So even though you have nothing, you still have something. You look at your queen and you say: 'What is happening, my queen?' You see a woman and you call her 'empress.' And you see a man and you say 'king.' You don't even know if he is a murderer, you know? But you relate to the I in him and you say: 'Love brethren, how the I stay?' Whether he is a murderer or not, he must feel a way because you say LOVE. Love is a powerful source, a powerful thing. I don't know anybody else in Jamaica who brings that to the table. And looking from outside – I must keep saying it because you have to understand this – being a Rasta, it sounds like you want to uplift Rasta, but looking at it and if you want to be truthful to yourself, it is only Rasta that brings that to the table. No other person. I don't see Christians walking on the road, hailing other Christians and telling them: 'Love!' And I see no Christian looking at other Christians telling them: 'Oh, this lady is an empress; she is a royal queen.'

I listened to the gospel songs, and what all of them are doing is to big up one man: Jesus. How do you want to say that you love God, and you can't love who you can see? You must love who you can see first and that is what the Rastaman brings to the table. If you love me, you love God. You can see God, and you can see me and love me because I am a manifestation of God. That is really what it is all about, and that is what the Rastaman tells you. It is very difficult for the Rastaman to live up to that in this filth, shit, and Roman mindset. So even he himself gets touched by the madness. But the philosophy is true, and they know that's how it is supposed to go. They know that this is the reality of the thing, and we know of the embeddedness that exists in Rome.

I mention Rome because Rome is very powerful. You have more Roman Catholics in the world than any other Christian denominations. It's Rome running the Western world. I don't care what a man would say. Rome set it up in the Senate. The smallest country of the world, Vatican, is the richest country, which is the organization of Roman Catholics same way. So all these things adapt to what we see right here. Rome controls. We wanted to call it another name, a republic and democratic party, like the Westminster system. Rome decides who Jesus is. Rome decides what democracy is. Rome decides all these things. When people are talking about the devil, it is Rome that decides because Rome creates the devil. All these things are manifestations of the Roman system.

And the Rastaman is trying to break away from it. It is very difficult because sometimes you seem to drop, too. Like anybody else. But if you look at the philosophy and what it is supposed to do, Rastafari is real; Rastafari is every day. And you can't hear that so many people would say it. Rastafari is a way of life and not a religion. If you go to most Rastas, they will say that. It is so cliché ultimately, but if you really go into what Rasta says, it is not a religion because a religion is a uniformed behaviour. Rastafari is not a uniformed behaviour because you can see what people perceive to see. Confusion in Rasta – that is what makes it beautiful. When you look at the confusion, you see how beautiful it is. Because how good it is that me and you are Rasta. And I can think how I want to think, and you can think how you want to think, instead of one man thinks. That is what you call the individual in the unity. So even though you are an army, each individual maintains its unity, its mindset. He can best deal with the collective when the time comes. That's how I see it.

We still maintain that Rastafari is a Black Power movement with a spiritual centre. It comes to liberate Black people from white supremacy, colonialism, and Western mindset. It is not unique in its spirituality because spirituality can't be unique. Spirituality is for life, and the order of life cannot be unique to people or an individual person. Like a man says: 'One way Jesus.' We don't give credence to that. But to: 'So many leaves are one tree. And so many rivers are one sea.' So it goes!

NOTES

1. This interview with Mutabaruka was recorded by Werner Zips and Manuela Zips-Mairitsch in Kingston/Jamaica on January 28, 2008. The entire reasoning was published on the DVD *Mutabaruka: The Return to the Motherland* edited by Zips (2011a).

2. In one of his radio shows (SR24, 2016) he resumed how this manifested in his lifestyle: 'I was a Soul boy in my school days. Afro, Dashiki bell foot pants, and all these things. Black Power business, you know!

3. The Last Poets are often considered to be the forefathers of Hip-Hop. The group is still active and celebrated its fiftieth anniversary with the album *Understand What Black Is* released in May 2018, cf. Bengal (2018).

4. Locksley Comrie was chairman of the *Kingston Technical High School Board* and, according to Mutabaruka, very much into the Black Panther movement. He introduced the young Mutabaruka to texts dealing with the Black Liberation struggle, such as Malcolm X *Message to the Grass Roots* (1965), an audio album that features the famous speech of the same title by Malcolm X; or Amy Jacques Garvey's *The Philosophy and Opinions of Marcus Garvey* (1986); Walter Rodney's *How Europe Underdeveloped Africa* (1972); Franz Fanon's *Black Skin, White Masks* (1966) and *The Wretched of the Earth* (1963); C.L.R. James' *The Black Jacobins* (1938); and Carmichael's and Hamilton's *Black Power* (1967).

5. According to Urban Dictionary, *rhaatid* is a Jamaican expression of surprise and irritation. See https://www.urbandictionary.com/define. php?term=Rhaatid.

CHAPTER 2

MUTABARUKA'S RADIO SHOWS
Cutting Edge and *Steppin Razor*

> When you live in Jamaica, there are so many things
> happening that you really have to deal with it on a level.
> And we are not in parliament, and we never vote, but we
> have a voice on the radio. We use a microphone to express
> whatsoever we want to express. We hope that the people
> gravitate to it and listen.
>
> Mutabaruka: *Steppin Razor*, March 30 (2017)[1]

> I'm like a stepping razor
> Don't you watch my size
> I'm dangerous, dangerous
>
> Peter Tosh (1977b)

2.1. Black Liberation Struggle Gone Global

When one thinks of Jamaica and especially of the music and arts
coming from this *likkle* Caribbean Island, one may associate it with
Reggae and Rastafari immediately.[2] Reggae artistes have consistently
been an inspiration for myriads of people worldwide, surprisingly from
all walks of life, given the Black Liberation stance of the music by and
large. Acknowledging this sustained global outreach, the UNESCO
inscribed Reggae on the World Heritage List. The inclusion explicitly
referred to Reggae's 'contribution to international discourse on issues
of injustice, resistance, love and humanity.'[3]

Mutabaruka is rarely mentioned in name droppings of the founding
fathers (and of course mothers) of Reggae. But arguably, there are
only few artistes who wielded a more persistent influence on the rise of

Black consciousness within Jamaica, the Caribbean and beyond. As a Rasta educating not only about Rastafari, Muta's biting commentaries may pick up any topic appearing relevant to him. No individual or organization may feel exempt from his critical revision. Referring to his weekly radio shows *Steppin Razor* and *Cutting Edge*, he may be called 'Jamaica's (foremost) Verbal Swordsman' – a true 'Voice of Thunder.' In Jamaica he is highly revered for his thoughtful deconstructions of international politics, economics, and religions. As a radio host, he gets more airtime than politicians. He never appears to get tired of raising awareness on all social issues, be it locally or on a global level.

Even more astonishing, in turn Jamaica's public does also not get tired of listening and debating his views. The conversation usually starts something like this: 'You hear wha' Muta say last night?' What may be described as a phenomenon, certainly has manifold and complex reasons, but at its core lies his unconditional advocacy for justice to people of African descent, after '500 years enslavement, colonialism, mental slavery, and suppression masked as discovery' as he will frame it in one way or the other. In the view of many Jamaicans, Muta over time evolved into a moral institution, perhaps 'the' moral institution in this mainland of Reggae and Rastafari. Even the political elite finally recognized his impact by rewarding him the 'Order of Distinction (Commander Class).' Something unthinkable in the early stages of his intellectual crusade as a *barefoot* revolutionary poet, not least to himself, as he indicates at various passages in the interviews conducted for this book.[4]

But there is yet another side to his story. His approach to communicative rationality – enshrined in the Rastafari notion of 'reasoning' or higher dialogues ('Iyahlogue') – opened doors to like-minded people globally. After all, justice is indivisible. It stands or falls universally. There is no justice for some, without regard to all. This is where his international followers – not to say fans – come into the play, not least ourselves, as the co-authors of this book. As born Austrians, we may appear as fairly strange fruits of Muta's inspirational influence. But if you consider the global dimension of justice, relentlessly rallied for by Haile Selassie I. in his struggle for international morality and collective security, it becomes much less inexplicable, why Romans join into Muta's cry for 'fire 'pon Rome,' Germans edit his poetry books, and people around the world flock to his concerts (he still tours) or tune into his radio shows, blogs, and other media of expression nowadays. For the last two decades, he has appeared not only as a performing artiste but also as an MC live on stage, using his stage time for much more than just announcing the next artiste. An example of this was his consciousness speech and unparalleled counselling of young Dancehall sensation Jahshii during the Rebel Salute Festival in January 2023.

It is nothing less than pure delight that Muta decided to celebrate his seventieth *earth strong* with a new album aptly entitled *Black Attack* (2023), produced by the legendary Mad Professor. And, on top of that, to present it live on stage (in August 2023) backed by The Robotiks in the equally legendary Rototom Sunsplash Festival, held in Benicàssim in Spain. It may be that he could have toured even a lot more (as an artiste, poet, or MC) over the years. But time and prioritization of his radio shows were probably a reason not to, even if he has also repeatedly transmitted his programmes from abroad (including the UK and Ivory Coast). Thirty years of hosting a radio show on Irie FM – open to online listeners around the globe – speak for itself. *Cutting Edge* and his later brainchild *Steppin Razor* became household points of reference for the international Reggae community.

In a nutshell, this is the main reason we asked his permission to write this book with him in a joint effort, although separated by very different personal and collective historical experiences that are usually framed in identities along the national, colour, and class divide. If nothing else, this book may therefore bear witness of the potential of someone raised in Rae Town/Kingston to reach out to far remote places (such as Austria) and to make a meaningful difference. The impact of this intellectual and cultural exchange goes far beyond the means of entertainment through music. Although Muta owes his first-time prominence to music, he never saw himself as just another Reggae artiste or, more narrowly, Dub poet, as he was and still is occasionally labelled.

2.2.   From First-time to His Current Status

Born as Allan Roy Hope on December 26, 1952, Mutabaruka became famous during the early 1980s, when he successfully started a recording career and extensive touring around the world as an avowed Rastafari and Dub/Reggae artiste. Among other pioneers, such as Linton Kwesi Johnson, Michael Smith, and Oku Onuora, he was one of the first artistes who shaped an influential subgenre of Reggae, which came to be known as 'Dub Poetry,' although he himself prefers to view his art form as just 'poetry.' As a poet, he feels perfectly free to choose any type of music to bring his poetic messages across – enhanced with sounds and power.[5]

Muta is not only a poet and performing artiste but also an actor, music *selecta*, producer, philosopher, 'development thinker,' activist, lecturer, and last but not least, a social commentator since more than three decades.[6] The aforementioned *Cutting Edge* has been on Irie FM consistently since 1992.[7] His weekly daytime radio broadcast carries the tale-telling name *Steppin Razor*. Irrespective of the medium he is working with, he well understands how to string together words to reach his listeners like a 'cutting edge.' Representing a defiant and unorthodox voice within the Jamaican media landscape, the renowned Rastafari philosopher and Black Power activist is loved by large audiences.[8] Often labelled as 'controversial' by mainstream media, he manages to challenge hegemonic ideals and values rooted in Jamaica's colonial past. Supported by his local fan base, Muta relentlessly broadens the frame of his critical reasonings to the global arena.

Whereas in the *Steppin Razor* programme Muta mostly confronts (Jamaica's) socio-political issues, he deals with rather philosophical and spiritual matters in the *Cutting Edge*. However, the themes overlap in both programmes, ranging from the socio-cultural, (geo)political, economic, historical, musical to the religious. His reflexive, mentor-like and oftentimes reprehensive arguments are presumed to be social commentaries with a huge societal significance in Jamaica and beyond. It is therefore for a reason that he is attributed the informal title 'The Great Mutabaruka.'[9]

The radio host is jointly responsible for an awareness raising even outside of the Rastafari, Reggae, and poetry community. As a well-respected public intellectual, he regularly gives guest lectures at colleges and universities worldwide, e.g., at The University of the West

Indies in Mona/Jamaica, at the Merritt College in Oakland, US, at the Stanford University in California, US, at the New College University of Toronto/Canada, at the Wits University in Johannesburg/ South Africa, or even at 'our own' University of Vienna/Austria.[10] Occasionally, he even becomes the subject of academic research, for instance at the Rastafari Studies Conference in Mona, where a presentation paper was titled 'Mutabaruka: The Icon.'[11]

It doesn't matter where one gets the chance to see or hear Mutabaruka. It is always very special regarding his appearance, aura, eloquence, righteous teaching, and philosophizing, just as Jamaican media personality and scholar Carolyn Cooper puts it concisely: 'Allan 'Mutabaruka' Hope inhabits a world of endless possibilities in which the power and authority of this extraordinary Rastaman are fully manifested.'[12] Mostly within his radio programmes, he understands to use charm, jocularity, rebelliousness, and smartness all in one to address his views and arguments in a very comprehensible and simple way that succeeds in reaching the whole (Jamaican) nation. Since his broadcasts have talk show characteristics, Muta takes his time to depict his views on all kinds of relevant discourses, from crime issues and corrupt politicians in Jamaica to the global Chinese and American influences, to notions of Rastafari empowerment.

The public philosopher is reckoned a pan-Africanist, influenced strongly by Malcolm X among other Black nationalists and freedom fighters born in the US and Africa, as well as by the legendary Jamaican pan-Africanist Marcus Mosiah Garvey, as he emphasized in his own words in chapter 1.[13] Rastafari informed his reading of Black Liberation, the Black Power Movement, and the urge for the African unity, including the entire African diaspora and the African-American as well as African-Caribbean experiences. Where contemporary movements such as *Black Lives Matter* struggle against police brutality and all forms of discrimination and inequality in the light of unabated structural racism and right-wing nationalists, Mutabaruka's life struggle incorporated far-reaching concepts such as 'Africa-CEntrism' (coined 'Afrocentrism' in the US) and a broader perspective on cultural politics that may be adequately referred to with the imperative 'Black

Lives Centre.'[14] In the limelight of current identity debates, the up-to-dateness and relevance of Mutabaruka's philosophy and opinions appear obvious. His success in music-enhanced poetry opened channels for his public appearances in media, particularly on air.

2.3. The Poetry Experience

As he emphasized in his autobiographical reflections in the previous chapter, it was at school where his motivation to consider a poetry career started. It was fuelled by his English teacher Mrs Pusey, following his first poem on the beauty of birds (see chapter 1.2). He remembered that she even encouraged him to read his first ever written poem in front of the whole class.[15] However, the work of other poets he became acquainted with at Kingston's university made little impression on him, because he strongly felt the influence of radical Black American poets:

> Many of these poems weren't exciting. It was annoying. They were monotonous, just dead. … And me and my friends used to laugh. Because we said the poems come like a Humpty Dumpty sort of thing. I mean, some were serious poems, but they never related to us as youths who were looking for something different. It was more like *The Last Poets* who struck us! You know, these Black Power poets who said that 'revolution will not be televised.' Those poets really ignited us.[16]

Mutabaruka alludes to The Last Poets as well as Gil Scott-Heron's recorded poem 'The Revolution Will Not Be Televised' (1974), whose title was a popular slogan for the Black Power Movement in the 1960s. His reminiscence of his school days provides evidence that the young poet was already strongly influenced by revolutionary notions of *Blackness* in terms of politics and poetics at an early stage in his life. An especially important and enduring inspiration he refers to is Jean-Baptiste Mutabaruka, a Rwandan poet whom he got to know through an anthology of African poems named *Writing Today in Africa* by Mphahlele (1967). When he read Jean-Baptiste Mutabaruka's poem 'Song of the Drum' in the anthology, it reminded him of his own poem 'Drum Song,' which, in his view, sounded alike.[17]

Consequently, the resemblance of his own poem to the work of the Rwandan poet amazed him to such an extent that he eventually

adopted the Rwandan poet's surname and thenceforth started to
publish his poems with that name:

> As a youth now I said: I like that name, Mutabaruka; I
> rather take that name. And, first I said Mutabaruka. Then
> I said Mazisi Mutabaruka. Eventually, over the years, I said
> just Mutabaruka again. So I started to write the poems in
> that name.[18]

It was also during that time that he developed the self-consciousness
as a revolutionary poet and subsequently started to publish his poems
and present them to a wider audience. His very first earnings for a
publication in *Swing* magazine during his school days marked a turning
point, although the financial return was quite meagre: 'That now was
really like something else, you know, to actually see one of my poems
in a magazine. It was like a big thing to see the poem. I think they gave
me four dollars.'[19]

Nevertheless, it paved the way for regular publications leading finally
to the release of a book with a collection of his early poems, called *Outcry*
(1973). It took another decade and his grounding in the philosophy
and *livity* of Rastafari, aptly summarized in the autobiographical
sketch in chapter 1, before he released his first music album *Check It!*
(1983), followed by his second album citing the title of his first official
print publication *Outcry* (1984). His transformation or rather self-
realization of Rastafari was invigorated by a thorough exploration of
Leonard Percival Howell's life and ideas. Howell is commonly credited
for starting the first *Rasta movement* by praising the Ethiopian Emperor
Haile Selassie I. in 1930.[20] He encouraged his early followers at the
now famous Rasta community of Pinnacle to worship a Black king
instead of the colonial white supremacist king of England.

After finishing high school, Muta worked for the Jamaican telephone
company and rubbed shoulders with his future first wife Yvonne
Peters. Together with Yvonne and their first daughter Ishiwawa, he
moved to Johns Hall, a rural community outside of Montego Bay in
the Jamaican parish of St James, where Yvonne gave birth to their
second daughter, Ishama. This was the time he deeply delved into
Nyahbinghi's ital *livity*, which shares some commonality with the now
popular vegan lifestyle:

> We started to find likeminded people who were interested
> in no meat. Less is more, more is less, you know. So we
> kinda shed a lot of things. We were up in the hills, and
> we saw true things, and we would reason about things. ...
> We built a little house up in the hills, way up in some bush
> like this (referring to his present residence; authors' note),
> but less modern. We were never modern; we never had a
> pipe or electricity. We never had so-called modern facilities
> up there. But we had a spring. We planted some food. We
> lived a Rasta life how we viewed it in that consciousness as
> Nyahbinghi! Ital *livity*, you know! We stopped cooking, we
> ate what people call raw food nowadays. We never knew
> about vegan. We just didn't use leather. We didn't wear
> leather clothes. ... And out of that, we decided that we are
> going to do it now! We decided that this is how we want to
> view Rasta. We wanted to view Rasta from what we call the
> ital perspective. Natural![21]

Since Muta had always been interested in diverse spiritual universes, he used his free time at his house in the hills for reading. Amongst others, he found a source of inspiration in authors such as Lobsang Rampa, who mainly published religious Tibetan tales, or the Chinese philosophers, Laozi and Confucius. He also expanded his knowledge in Japanese literature and Buddhism.[22] Until today, Muta feels strongly influenced by Asian philosophies. Furthermore, he got inspired by other Rastafari, regardless of their formal education, as he elaborated in the following interview:

> And we went amongst certain Rastas who never read the
> Bible. Some of them couldn't even read. But we saw that
> they have the same attitude towards life as the people who
> we read about, who are Buddhists living in the Himalayan
> mountains. They don't wear shoes, they don't use this,
> they don't use that. They don't even want to kill a worm,
> and they just live. And I said: 'But, this is Rasta for me!'
> It carries you on another perspective because you don't
> shed the Africanness. Because you now even see yourself
> as an African, even much more than when we used to be
> at the Twelve Tribes. Because there you read the Bible and
> see yourself as African, but it wasn't like *African*. It was
> like: 'Yeah, I am an African, but you know I am a Twelve
> Tribes.' Now you said: 'Africa we are working with. Marcus
> Garvey, Haile Selassie!' So we started to shed a lot of
> different thinking and meditation![23]

As a responsible father, he had always been aware of monetary matters for maintaining a household, catering for the children, and eventually building a house. He accepted the invitation to lecture tourists attracted by Bob Marley and the early Reggae founders on Rastafari in the fast-growing fishing village of Negril turned into a tourist centre. Little did he know back then that this experience became a training ground for his lecturing career at local and international universities perhaps also becoming an accomplished radio host. Despite considerable lack of approval among his family and some friends for his intended life journey as an artiste, Muta stayed well on track. Some may have referred to his resilience as stubbornness back then, while he himself frames it as staying in focus, quite congruent with the meaning of his Rwanda-derived name: Mutabaruka – the 'ever victorious.'

After a time of abstention from writing due to his choice of a natural life in the Jamaican hills, Muta started to compose poems again, as he 'couldn't escape the poetry thing,' in his own words.[24] Before he moved to Johns Hall, he had handed over all his poems to his friend Stafford Harrison. Some of these poems were published in a book entitled *Sun and Moon* in 1976, which is a collection of poems by Muta and his Panamanian friend Faybiene Miranda, whom he saw as his congenial counterpart: 'I am the sun, sister Faybiene is the moon.'[25] With regard to his printed books, he also alludes to his very first informal one from 1972, the so-called *Twenty-Four Poems*, which he had only sold from '… hand to hand, (as) we used to walk up and down and sell them.'[26] Another publication that opened further doors was *The First Poems* (1980b), a collection showcasing the work written between 1970 and 1979. Issued through the initiative of Paul Issa, whom Muta knew from the Negril Beach Village Hotel, this book set his career as a world-famous poet in motion.[27] Encouraged by Issa's and Harrison's publications, the young poet followed his artistic calling even more vigorously. Whenever he returned to Kingston, he would take the challenge to present his poems, most notably at a place called *Zinc Fence*:

> Anywhere the poetry there, we found ourselves there and read the poems. One place named Zinc Fence. Zinc Fence was a place owned by Third World (the famous Reggae

group; authors' note) and they used to have performances
in there. One day they had a concert in there and I was
performing a poem. The poem was 'Every Time A Ear
De Soun.' And Mortimo Planno heard this poem. He said:
'Look here, I wanna tell the Jimmy Cliff musicians to put
you on the concert that Jimmy Cliff is keeping at his home
place.' So I said: 'Okay.'[28]

Subsequently, as it was contrived by the influential Jamaican
Rastafari Mortimo Planno, Muta visited Jimmy Cliff in Somerton,
which was near by his own house in St James, for a rehearsal of the
poem put to Dub music.[29] Relating to these first steps as a performing
artiste still sparks pure joy and amazement in Muta:

I went down to Jimmy Cliff's house for rehearsal. And the
concert was kept, and we did 'Every Time A Ear De Soun.'
And the place was filled with thousands of people and I
never knew that people could react that way to poetry. ...
That was the beginning now of Mutabaruka as a Reggae
artiste![30]

As a result of this concert and through encouragement from
famous Reggae-guitarist Earl Chinna Smith, Jimmy Cliff's Oneness
band leader back then, Muta's first record was released in 1980. He
recorded the poem 'Every Time A Ear De Soun' (1980a), which,
according to Muta, was the first Dub poem that entered the Pop charts
in Jamaica.[31] Three years later, his first studio album *Check It!* (1983a),
which was released on the American blues label Alligator Records,
emerged in the footsteps of the success of his first single. Shortly after
his performance at Zinc Fence, a concert trip to Cuba with Jimmy
Cliff and a performance at the legendary Reggae Sunsplash festival in
Montego Bay in August of 1981 followed:

And the same Oneness band asked me if I can do two
poems at the Sunsplash. The Sunsplash was kept in a place
called Jarrett Park in Montego Bay. And I did 'Every Time
A Ear De Soun.' What was frightening and scary to many
people is that here was a guy without a tam, the dreadlocks
just coming and a little streak in the hair. No shoes and no
shirt, you know. Short pants, never looking like a Reggae
artiste. Raw, raw, raw, coming out of the bush. And I came
on the stage and said: 'It no good fi stay inna white man
country too long.' That was something else in the place.[32]

Muta's first Sunsplash performance well qualifies for the all-time Reggae landmarks, partly because of his self-critical, highly sarcastic song 'Whiteman Country,' considered an outrageous breach of taboo even by many Jamaicans at the time.[33] It turned into one of his biggest hits in the years to come. As a result, from his stunning appearance in Montego Bay, the young performer was booked for a live concert in California, starting his establishment as a well sought-after international Reggae artiste. Although it proved an ambivalent experience, as he reminisces:

> I went to California and coming on the stage I had a white chain around my hand. No shoes, no shirt. My dreadlocks out and I came on stage: 'It no good fi stay inna white man country too long.' I don't know, but many white people got up and walked out. But that never stopped me because we were doing it. Anytime I came off the stage, you would never know that Third World, Dennis Brown, all these artistes, were on the show. All the reporters were in the changing room trying to figure out who the hell is this man! Because they never heard about me yet. … Who is this guy coming to America and saying 'it no good fi stay inna white man country too long' and 'every time a ear de soun'? It was like a new thing to the Reggae scene. … Coming back to Jamaica, a tour was planned. And we went with the High Times Players band, and we toured about 4 weeks in America. Every show was sold out! Every show! And I came back with not one cent! I came back with nothing at all except the newspaper praise![34]

Even if years later he can laugh about the non-lucrative North American tour, it must have been the usual 'learning the harder way experience,' as with most of his contemporaries in Reggae. However, he understands those first steps in music bestowed the life as an international recording artiste upon him, as plenty of concerts, festivals, and tours followed up in the wake of his several albums, all doing well in the global Reggae market.

2.4. Blakk Muzik Days: The Rise of a Radio Host and Philosopher

The emerging lifestyle as performer and artiste gave Mutabaruka the opportunity to travel the world in the 1980s, following his critically acclaimed *Outcry* album. Whenever he found time between international tours in his countryside *retreat* in the Jamaican hillside, he continued writing more poems and lectured on his Rastafari way of life through music and other media:

> We started to tour all over the place. We were all over the world. I mean, everywhere you can think off. In the '80s, we were touring in Europe three times a year, two weeks in Germany alone. ... Five days a week we just did shows, you know. All over Europe, and when we went out there in all these big cities, we ended up back in our bush (referring to his residence in St James back then; authors' note) same way. ... And we started to write more, read more, articulate more. That now led us to be just more than a Reggae artiste! We started to articulate our *livity*. ... We started to articulate why we do this, why we don't do that. What is our reason for this, our reason for that, and all these things. So people started to find it very interesting, too.[35]

Paving the way for himself as an acknowledged 'folk philosopher' and media personality, Muta started a sound system by the name of *Blakk Muzik*, according to him 'the first sound system in Jamaica that played CDs.'[36] He eventually became an ambassador of so-called World Music and Black Music, primarily collecting and *selecting* African music made in Africa, i.e., the likes of Salif Keita, Fela Kuti, and Muta's label mates at Shanachie Records, Ladysmith Black Mambazo and Lucky Dube. His CD collection grew steadily by promotional albums from various labels or extensive shopping tours in record stores during his own concert tours. At Zinc Fence, he introduced Black music from near and far to his Jamaican audience. He interspersed it with selective Reggae music from Jamaican artistes such as Black Uhuru and Burning Spear, and he constantly played with his sound system at the socializing Zinc Fence sessions.[37]

After his marriage with his second and current wife Jackie Cohen (also known as *Empress Amba*), he had made a name for himself as a music collector and *selecta*. In 1992, the relatively newly founded Jamaican radio station Irie FM offered a proposal to Muta:

> About two years into the radio station, one of the programme managers came to me and said that they wanted me to do a programme on the radio, to play Reggae

> from around the world. Because they realized that I have
> the music. So I said: 'Yeah, we do it, Reggae from around
> the world.' We went on the station, and we played Reggae
> from around the world. But, unfortunately or fortunately,
> I couldn't just play pure music for four hours. I had to
> say something! I couldn't just play music like the ordinary
> DJs. I had a thinking, a Rasta and Black Power thinking.
> Marcus Garvey inspired me, so I had to expound that in
> the programme. Well, I started to do it in the programme
> and apparently the people started to love and hate it. So I
> became the man they love to hate.[38]

In this quote, Muta addresses his provocative way of hosting
the broadcast; he had quickly realized that his first weekly radio
programme *Cutting Edge* caused heated debates and considerable
controversy. As the programme became 'more talk than music, and
more philosophical,' according to him, people were constantly riveted
by his social comments and discourses. In retrospect, he emphasizes
that right from the beginning many listeners have maintained a love-
hate relationship with him and his broadcast:

> Apparently, more people hated what I said, but they were
> almost masochistically listening to the programme like it
> hurt them, but they still felt the pain and they would come
> back for more pain every week. … They really wanted to
> stop listening to me, but they would say: 'Alright, he can't get
> worse.' And when they listened to me and I got worse, they
> would say that I am a mad guy, and they would still listen:
> 'I really want to hear what he is telling this week.' They
> kept listening, listening, and listening. So the programme
> became a phenomenon in Jamaica. The *Cutting Edge* is
> there, and it has stayed.[39]

As Muta looks back at the programme's beginnings, he recalls stories
from listeners who reported that they were even beaten by their parents
for listening to his programme. Essentially, the *Cutting Edge* show was
an exciting innovation on Jamaican radio and, despite its controversy,
became an enormous success. Since Muta still hosts the show today,
his decision to join the radio crew and launch *Cutting Edge* in March
1992 had a lasting effect. In 2013, he started his second programme
named *Steppin Razor – The Art of War*. Since then, he has been the host

of two shows: *Cutting Edge* on Wednesday nights and *Steppin Razor* on Thursday afternoons.

2.5. The Pinnacle of a Great Edutainer's Career

Despite representing an ever provocative and uncomfortable voice to many people, Mutabaruka has steadily continued to articulate his perspectives, perceptions, and philosophical reasonings live on air. He speaks in favour of the poor and oppressed, particularly Black people, and has become the 'voice of a nation,' an attribution *Kingdom Nubia Radio* gave him on its website.[40] Yet Muta regards himself as being a voice for the common people rather than the 'voice of a nation,' as he elucidates:

> I talk for the people because they don't have the radio, they don't have the means to project themselves. I listen to what the people are saying, and I go back on the radio and say it. It is like I am a spy for the people. You know, I am moving in different circles, so I am listening to what these guys would say about the people. And I am listening to what the people are saying that they really require. So I go on the radio and say it. Of course, it sounds like a voice of the nation. But it is not something that I walk with. ... But one would say it because of what I say. You know, people say 'the Great Mutabaruka.' That's what they say. I say I am going to start to believe that now, you know, like Great is my first name. ... Because everywhere I go, politicians, preachers, beggars, or thieves, they say: 'Whappen, the Great Mutabaruka, man.'[41]

Over the years, the outspoken Rastafari has become an *institution* in the Jamaican media and entertainment scene, not only hosting his two radio programmes, but also presenting a TV show named *Simply Muta* and moderating many music and poetry festivals in Jamaica and other countries;[42] his wide appeal made him a role model for upcoming entertainers, in fact globally.[43] Beyond that, he has never stopped touring as a poet, Dub/Reggae artiste or philosopher who *edutains* – as the now common combination of the words education and entertaining indicates. He unapologetically voices his notions on multifaceted matters and particularly creates space for Black issues. Above all, he played the rebellious slave Shango in Haile Gerima's drama movie *Sankofa* (1993) and was the protagonist in the documentary film *Mutabaruka: The Return to the Motherland* (2011a).[44] There are seemingly endless indicators for his attribution as the *Great* Mutabaruka. Whilst we suggest listening to his radio shows or watching a live performance to really appreciate his achievements, others may refer to official honours. Some of his formal awards are listed below:

- *Best Dub Poet* of the Jamaican Music Awards, repeatedly awarded[45]
- Award for *over 30 years of outstanding work in the field of the arts* by the National Centre for Youth Development (NCYD) and the Rotaract Club of Mandeville (Jamaica) in 2010[46]
- *Pan-Afrikan Grand-Master* award by the Alkebu-Lan Revivalist Movement along with Best Kept Secret Spoken Word Collective in London[47]
- *Order Of Distinction (Commander Class)* from the Jamaican government in 2016
- *Lifetime Achievement Award* at the Black Royalty African Heritage Expo in Connecticut (US) in 2018[48]
- *Lifetime Achievement Award* by Irie FM in March 2019.[49]

2.6.   Music and Words: *The Art of War*

> Music goes with radio, you don't understand? So, we cannot just do the talking and don't play music. And we cannot just play pure music and don't talk. Because there are so many things socially which confront us, that it is necessary for us to give our opinion! And not only give our opinion but find a way how we can get the people involved in their own community and develop a certain pride! Pride is what we are working with now!
>
> Mutabaruka: *Steppin Razor*, January 20 (2016)

'This is the *Steppin Razor, The Art of War*! We are here with you on another Thursday!'[50] The jingle for Irie FM's Thursday afternoon programme at 2:00 p.m. says it all. Here comes Mutabaruka with his charismatic voice finding its way into many radio sets, pimped-up car speakers, and peoples' headphones on the entire island of Jamaica. Since Irie FM provides a live stream on its website, Muta's 'art of war' receives a transnational dimension as it attracts many international listeners, too.[51] Whenever he speaks his introductory words, one knows once again, Mutabaruka will take his time to reason, listen, and entertain for the next four hours. This also applies to Wednesday nights when people listen to his trademark (first) programme at 10:00 p.m. and are greeted with the following words: 'Good night! This is the *Cutting Edge* on Irie FM on a next Wednesday night!'[52]

In the following, we provide an overview of these two popular weekly broadcasts on Irie FM with behind-the-curtain reflections of Mutabaruka (taken from interviews conducted in Jamaica) on his intentions and perceived impact of both weekly shows. This is based on transliterations of selected broadcasts analysed in the following chapters (chapters 3–6), in which one may become a *listener* of his reasonings. The current and subsequent chapters (2.7–2.10) present the talk shows in content and format. They also provide background information on the broadcast procedure(s), his team as well as some (statistical) information about the shows' popularity and range of influence.

The radio programmes offer, in principle, casual and unorthodox procedures in form and content. The four-hour long broadcasts mix talk show and music, according to Muta's own choice. Since he is the host, he decides on the topics he wants to talk about: 'Most of the time, I put the programme how I want to put it. I don't have anybody to tell me what to do.'[53] The same applies to the songs he plays, which, for the most part, come from his own repertoire of *conscious* Reggae and African music. 'Sweet, sweet Reggae music, man! I tell you, man!' as he promotes his selection.[54] In his playlist, one comes across artistes such as Abdel Wright, Asantewaa, Black Uhuru, Bob Andy, Brimstone, Bugle, Bunny Rugs, Burning Spear, Busy Signal, Damian Marley, Dennis Alcapone, Dub Nation, Fabine, Hugh Masekela, I Saba Tooth, Iba Mahr, J Boog, Jah9, Justin Hinds, Kabaka Pyramid, Konshens, Ladysmith Black Mambazo, Lavaska, Lee Scratch Perry, Lucky Dube, Macka B, Michael Fabulous, Queen Ifrica, Ras Penco, Ras Takura, Ray Darwin, Santa Davis, Serano Walker, Sizzla, Stewart Nelson,

Tarrus Riley, Third World, Xana Romeo, and Xylophone to name but a few. Occasionally he also plays tunes requested by listeners.[55]

Although the programmes' formal procedure may be easy-going, their topics and Muta's narratives and social commentaries are anything but comfortable. As the name of his most recent broadcast reveals, the radio host operates like a 'steppin' razor' when he philosophizes according to his razor-sharp views, unbashfully reprehending politicians, church leaders, Dancehall artistes, oppressors, white supremacists, scammers, or even other radio DJs.[56] Usually, Muta delivers off-the-cuff speeches, as he discloses in interview: 'Many people believe that I have a script in front of me whilst doing the programme. I have no script; I just say it!'[57]

In the *Steppin Razor* programme, his speeches refer to national issues and/or international news, ranging from Jamaica's crime situation to Donald Trump's latest coup. Comments and sometimes extensive reasonings are never one-dimensional, since he always tries to include the sociocultural, (geo)political and historical background. Through his critical analyses, which stretch from the dissection of a certain political system's state to questions of people's happiness or rather dissatisfactions, he makes his position clear using the Jamaican vernacular as his means of expression.[58] In the second half of the broadcast, there is usually a call-in component as Irie FM provides a direct telephone line to the Rastafari presenter. Sometimes, the callers pick up Muta's preceding considerations or come up with a new subject to discuss with him. Many callers also ask him for advice concerning personal matters, e.g., to find a missing person, or they call in need of a shoulder to cry on. Moreover, some of them use the radio as a public stage to raise certain issues, such as Rohan Marley, one of Bob Marley's sons, who called to rectify the dispute with Bunny Wailer.[59]

Steppin Razor is an interactive 'talkback' radio in which everyone is free to express her or his views. Thus, whilst providing a forum for his callers, Mutabaruka takes the time to reply and talk freely. Sometimes his introductory reasoning takes thirty minutes nonstop, or he talks to someone on the phone up to twenty-five minutes. In a radio show from March 2016, he points out the elemental power of *talking*:

> We don't stop talking. … Talking is good! I don't have nothing against a man who talks a lot! Even the dumb and

> ignorant have a story, you know! So when a man is talking about that 'you are talking now (but) what are you going to do?' Talking! That is what I am doing! I am talking! And people listen! Most of the people who start wars in the world, they never go first to shoot anybody, you know! They talk and sign papers and make people kill one another. So I have nothing against sitting down and talk! Because out of that talking, you will be best able to construct your way forward! Everything that is done started with speaking! And we don't have nothing against that! I have a microphone in front of me. I speak![60]

Muta assumes that open conversation and debate is the fundament for further actions, namely people's actions. To avoid any misconception, his reference to the 'art of war' as the show's subtitle is meant tongue-in-cheek and doesn't advertise the use of violence. In some ways, it elevates the art of war in Dancehall circles to philosophical and moral disputes. Besides, *The Art of War* epithet (or subtitle) discloses a perception of war that is meant as a celebration of 'straightening things out,' as he explains the choice of the show's mission statement with a reference to Sun Tzu's book *The Art of War*:

> The message in *The Art of War* is very revealing. ... It's a Chinese philosophy about how you go to war, how you defeat the enemy sometimes without even firing bullets, you know. So we just say, 'the art of war.' Many people ask why I don't say 'the art of peace'? But I explain: 'Yeah, we could say that, but we come from a philosophy, a Chinese philosophy that says *The Art of War*, which leads to peace.'[61]

Indeed, Sun Tzu's ancient book suggests various strategies for 'breaking the enemy's resistance without fighting.'[62] One quintessence of the Chinese author is to outthink enemies rather than fight them. Whereas the twenty-five-hundred-year-old book is considered a directive for generals and commanders of armies, it may also provide rhetorical lessons in other domains such as politics, business, and sports. The connection between Mutabaruka and this Chinese philosophy clearly shows when he tries to break the resistance of his antagonists. In a figurative sense, he attempts to conquer them with a critical mindset and *outtalk* them with his harsh words in the space of the radio broadcast(s). In Jamaica, there is a common saying referring to Muta that reads such: 'Bwoy, Muta nuh easy, you know!'

However, his adversaries are mostly politicians and other elite members or so-called 'opinion leaders' that he considers corrupt(ed) and oppressive. According to Sun Tzu's principle 'attack him (the opponent; authors' note) where he is unprepared, appear where you are not expected,' Muta takes advantage of his weekly shows on the radio as he is able to address conscious music and offer challenging thoughts to people.[63] On such a public platform, one hardly faces a Rastafari speaking up against injustice and reprimanding various people. He confronts his counterparts and potential opponents with counteractive reports, statistics, stories, and realities about society's status quo, and not least rebellious music. In the end, the *Steppin Razor* – similar to Sun Tzu's *The Art of War* – serves as a medium that uses certain oratorical strategies to defeat an adversary without fighting. The show delivers guidelines for actions to help suppressed people reclaim their self-esteem, self-respect, and *pride* as cited at the outset. In doing so, Muta can help to outthink the powerful, often feeding on (Jamaica's) deprived people, in a 'very serious way, steppin'!'[64]

His two different programmes are not detached from each other but rather epitomize a complementation. On the *Steppin Razor* show, for example, he regularly picks up topics from the *Cutting Edge* programme the night before. Also, the *Cutting Edge* broadcast has procedures and elements similar to those of its daytime counterpart. Whilst *Steppin Razor's* focus is on socio-political argumentation, *Cutting Edge* deals mainly with philosophical and religious facets, according to Muta.[65] However, the legendary late-night programme has changed and evolved over the many years, as he explains in an interview:

> The *Cutting Edge* has become more talk than music and more philosophical, … The development of the show is really interesting. We used to play a lot of lecture tapes by Black scholars in the early days. Yosef Ben-Jochannan, lecturing about books and African history. In one show we would play a one-and-a-half-hour lecture tape and intersperse it with my talking and my philosophy. We would speak a lot about Africa and religion, and then a next time we would play a tape by somebody who has a PhD. When I say it, is one thing, but when the listeners hear somebody who has a PhD saying it, it is a next thing. When they hear a

Doctor from Cornell University, they would listen more. If you listen to *Cutting Edge* of the '90s and early 2000s, you will hear a lot of lectures and less of me talking. Then we started to talk a lot, and still play the tapes. The evolution of it now was when we play the African music. Then the talking and tapes were resonating. A lot of people have never heard a programme on the radio that plays pure African music. That was like a treat. Even though people say: 'Muta, I don't understand what they are saying.' But we still keep on playing it. Like Ladysmith Black Mambazo, who was one of the favourites of a lot of Jamaicans. And they used to love Lucky Dube, because he was a Reggae heart and sounds like Peter Tosh. So we have developed a programme known for a different kind of music and the lecture tapes on religion or Black consciousness. That is what it still is, just that we play less of the long tapes nowadays. We hardly play any one-and-a-half-hour tape because the radio station is now filled with advertisement. … Now I just play shorter tapes. You have people who send things to me on WhatsApp. We go through it, and if we feel that it is justified to hear, we play it. And then we talk. We talk a lot, and sometimes we interview people.[66]

In the course of the same interview, he told us that long before the YouTube era, cassettes containing recorded *Cutting Edge* programmes were even sold in England, Germany, and Italy, as he experienced on site. This clearly shows the success of this long-running radio show from Jamaica, which received international attention early on, as Muta confirms:

Many people know me as the *Cutting Edge* radio man, but not as a poet. When I go to England, the audience rams up the place because of my radio shows. But mostly because of the *Cutting Edge* as it is the longer one. It is really something else![67]

An essential aspect of his night programme is definitely what Muta calls the '*Cutting Edge* University,' a regular section in the show to make his listeners aware of various aspects of history and how it relates to African people. This usually very *biting* part also often involves audio tapes as mentioned in his quote above.[68]

2.7. A Public Platform and Weekly Stage

Between talks, music, and incoming calls, the host frequently plays audio tapes of speeches, for example from Jamaican politicians, pan-Africanists such as John Henrik Clarke, Yosef Ben-Jochannan and Umar Johnson, or inspiring speakers such as Indian yogi Sadhguru and Hollywood actor Denzel Washington.[69] This applies to both, the *Steppin Razor* and *Cutting Edge* broadcasts. He also plays audio clips of other media reports with Black history background, such as the story of Congo and Belgian King Leopold II., discrimination against Haitians in the Dominican Republic, Robert Mugabe's 'rebellion against white supremacy,' or clips referring to important personalities like Marcus Garvey.[70] Those tapes and clips serve as the basis for reasoning and, additionally, as evidence for Muta's views on the subject or as the 'vegetable of the matter,' as he would call it.[71] Sometimes the Rastafari anchorman offers a eulogy for a prominent personality, considered influential for the Black Liberation struggle. For instance, one comes across reports and debates on the life and achievements of Marcus Garvey Junior, the firstborn son of Jamaica's national hero Marcus Garvey, or American boxer Muhammad Ali, who (according to Muta) was not only the greatest boxer, but also 'a beacon for Black people right around the world.'[72]

In addition, Muta conducts extensive telephone interviews or studio interviews live at Irie FM station with a large variety of individuals: crime victims, police officers, lawyers, local politicians, politics analysts, activists, representatives of organizations, Black Power leaders, University professors, festival organizers, clerics, farmers, midwives, Reggae and Dancehall artistes, Rastafari, other actors in the realm of civil society, and even anthropologists like the co-authors. The interviews are predominantly connected with current national/global events, issues, or gossip.

Well-known personalities appeared in Muta's broadcasts, i.e., Jamaican scholars Michael Barnett, Carolyn Cooper, Herbert Gayle, and Verene Shepherd; Reggae artistes Dennis Alcapone, Dean Fraser, Marcia Griffiths, Brigadier Jerry, Beenie Man, Tony Rebel, and U-Roy; legendary DJ Ricky Trooper; international singer/actor Grace Jones; Haile Selassie's grandson Prince Ermias Sahle-Selassie; renowned

Rastafari elder Mortimo Planno; pan-Africanists James Small and Malik Zulu Shabazz; Louis Farrakhan, who heads the *Nation of Islam*, and Clive Muhammad, who is the Jamaican representative of the same; Dr Ray Hagins, the spiritual leader of *The Afrikan Village* in Missouri; long term prisoner Kid Ralph; or Peter Tosh's common-law wife Andrea Brown. Evidently, the spectrum of interviewees is extremely broad.[73]

At times, Muta creates space for upcoming artistes to present their poems.[74] Amongst his most prominent call-in candidates were Catherine Howell, the daughter of the well-known *first* Rastafari Leonard Howell, as well as Reggae artiste Chronixx and Dancehall queen Lady Saw, who merely called Muta to praise him for his educational programme.[75] There are also frequent callers from the US and the UK (which shows the international appeal of both broadcasts) and regularly callers from Jamaica. Amongst the latter are gossip talker Mister Universe, journalist Mandingo, female Rasta elder Fyah Mumma, Reggae artiste I Saba Tooth, and medical herb doctor King Yahshua.[76]

Muta clearly tries to amplify the voice of people from all walks of life, including crime victims and *ghetto youths*, whose voices are otherwise neglected or overheard. But he applies no strategy of exclusion against the elite or members of the power structure, represented for instance by spokespersons and superintendents of the Jamaica Constabulary Force. This representational strategy underlines the Rastafari idea of impartiality, at least in principle, much less in content. Therefore, through the openness for oppositional voices, his listeners get a multi-perspectival, balanced, and multifaceted picture of certain issues. Obviously, this strategy allows the host to be even more resolute in voicing his views and valuations, without facing (too many) reproaches of one-sidedness. In fact, listeners are encouraged to see different perspectives that they would normally not be exposed to. Therefore, *Cutting Edge* and *Steppin Razor* – two radio shows that would be banned in most countries or not even be thinkable – may provide some of the best evidence for lived democracy in Jamaica.

The reasonings and debates constitute the nucleus of both radio shows. Given the unpredictability of talk, discourse, and reasoning,

Mutabaruka's broadcasts never stick to any fixed protocol. Flexibility is their continual order of the day demanding his masterful delivery of improvisations. Muta is conscious that this ever-lingering moment of surprise keeps his listeners' suspense and, indeed, the broadcast alive over an amazing period of more than thirty years in the case of *Cutting Edge*. He maintains an interactive and untethered style of presentation that makes him incomparable to other talk show hosts. As an ardent supporter of lively, inclusive, and evolving debates rather than pre-fixed rules and norms, inclusion and diversity – two key ethical requirements of the present – became his very trademark. Most importantly, the two shows do not exclude any segment of society. According to him, he experienced such (un)democratic exclusion, when he visited the Parliament of Jamaica at Gordon House and was not allowed to answer issues he was personally involved in as a public intellectual. The following incidence made him realize that politics follow strict protocol without exception:

> I went to the House the other day and they told me that I cannot talk from the gallery. Even when the man called my name down there (and) I well wanted to talk, you know. Sleepy (meaning minister Robert Montague; authors' note) talked about how I get rid of him, you know Rasta! And I well wanted to answer. The man said: 'Nobody can speak from the gallery, or we will ask him to leave.' I was there holding my bottom, holding my mouth. Everything was just tight up on me. That man down there talked about me, and I couldn't answer the man. You don't see it? It is just a terrible thing when a man talks about you, and you just wanna answer, and you cannot answer because of protocol and all these things there.[77]

Since there are always unforeseeable and amusing incidents during his broadcasts, the verbal swordsman's strikes obviously never turn into routine. To give but one example, in November 2015 four participants of the thirteenth season of the German talent show 'Germany searches for the next Superstar' (*Deutschland sucht den Superstar*) were surprisingly invited for an interview with Mutabaruka during *Steppin Razor*. Accompanied by the German show's juror H.P. Baxxter, who is best known as the lead vocalist and frontman of the legendary German Techno band Scooter, the young singers could introduce

and promote themselves on Irie FM. During this broadcast, Muta
unexpectedly revealed his love for Techno music, as he explained to
Scooter's frontman: 'I mean, I love the Techno thing, believe you me.
I love Techno! I have been performing at a lot of Techno festivals in
Europe.'[78]

To sum up, *Cutting Edge* and *Steppin Razor* serve as public platforms
for manifold interests: crying out against injustices, liberating people's
minds from the fetters of suppressive systems, rectifying news and
issues, and reporting on societal incidents and events. Furthermore,
they foster discourse on relevant sociocultural, political, religious, and
economical aspects of life in the Caribbean, Africa, and beyond. And,
specifically, they raise consciousness on anything concerning Reggae
and other Black music, provide information about Black Power,
culture, and history, and, last but not least, reason about the Rastafari
movement and Haile Selassie. The shows supply their listeners with a
space for critical evaluation, interpretation, and reflection on national
and global developments. They are Muta's weekly performance stage
to entertain, critique, rebuke, educate, and help people in various
contexts. In this sense, they have extended his former outreach through
music as a Reggae artiste and poet. The issues and stories he deals with
are often not even mentioned in the mainstream media, a fact which
Muta is very much aware of.[79] Notably, his son-in-law alludes to this
fact in an interview:

> *Cutting Edge* is a programme that delves into things that
> you don't usually hear on the regular media. It deals with
> topics that you don't kinda delve into. So therefore, these
> are topics that deal with Africa and bring the various social
> injustices to a forum, giving us, the considered lower class
> or lower middle-class, a voice. ... To hear that we came
> out of the colonial experience, that we tend to be caught
> up in that whole European model and look into Europe for
> everything in terms of intellect, our history, and that sort
> of things. Mutabaruka was able to shift it back to Africa.[80]

Mutabaruka provides a panel for open discussions and serious
debates, thereby offering possible solutions to social problems. He
partly challenges the callers and interviewees by asking them for
strategies or actions to avert certain negative trends, for instance the
sexually explicit development of the Jamaican Dancehall culture.[81]

In this spirit, he helps people to help understand themselves and 'overstand' at least some of their challenges. From time to time, he offers certain callers his personal mobile number to contact him for detailed information relating to their problems. When able to help a situation, he and his radio team even investigate certain cases. This shows that his programme is not only connective but also solution-oriented, as he claims:

> We don't really let things go! I hold on upon things until things rectify. You understand?! Because we need to rectify certain stuff. We cannot just keep bringing up things on the radio and then afterwards we let it go and go upon a next something, and the something what we talked about before didn't rectify! We have to keep it in the consciousness and minds of the people![82]

Without doubt, this Rastafari acts as a mediator when he unrelentingly presents his views, ideas, and judgements. However, as he complains, his proposals are hardly ever or, rather, never taken up by decision-makers: 'I am saying, it is time for them (the authorities; authors' note) to listen! Because even though it sounds like we are always aggressive, but we represent ideas. If you would have listened to the ideas, maybe it could have helped in a certain way!'[83]

2.8. A 'Dinosaur' and His 'Mosquitoes'

> I want to give thanks for Shamara, who is with us right through, and Neil, who is with us. … Young Young is here, you know. … I wanna give thanks. Because you have done a great service to this programme here. I want to hail up Kabu. … It has been an honour and a pleasure to work under you for so many years. It is wonderful. I hope your basket is never empty with fruits, and your fridge is never empty with juices. So Kabu, give thanks! All the operators outside there, whose names I cannot remember. I had to give them my own names. Black Princess, Jermain, Fluffy Diva, and Petite. We give thanks for them.
>
> Mutabaruka: *Steppin Razor*, December 28, 2017

Whereas the *Cutting Edge* show is run single-handedly by Muta, *Steppin Razor* enjoys the company of his associates during live broadcasts, consisting of engineers, programme managers, Irie FM's programme director Ka'Bu Ma'at Kheru (Kabu), and several other people from Irie FM staff, e.g., the telephone operators. During a broadcast in Irie FM's studio facility in *Ochi* (short for Ocho Rios), Mutabaruka usually sits in front of a studio microphone and uses his personal laptop to select music in real-time. One of the engineers stays next to him and offers support with technical issues. Guests sit opposite Muta in a vitreous compartment (at least this was our experience during the studio visit in November 2018). For the daytime show, his co-workers offer diverse inputs on various subjects, which implicates inter alia inter-generational dynamics. When we were invited in the broadcast, it was primarily programme manager Shamara who repeatedly entered the studio to debate the progress of the show.[84] Muta tends to lose time dimensions in serious reasonings and, at times, his colleagues remind him what was scheduled to happen next, for example, when it is time for advertisements or receiving calls. Nevertheless, the experienced radio presenter mostly acts in a highly relaxed manner and uses his charm, self-irony, and a fine sense of humour to compensate for possible detours from the subject.

Muta loves to call himself a 'dinosaur' and sometimes even a 'fossil,' whereas he ironically refers to his much younger colleagues as 'mosquitoes,' indicating their significant age difference and their constant attention.[85] In fact, he appreciates the young environment as he benefits from their multifaceted input:

> I am glad that I work with you, because I kinda learn exactly how you young people think. I know how you think, believe you me. Sometimes I sit back at my yard, and I say: 'You know, I am glad that I am working with pure little mosquitoes here in the studio.' Because I am a dinosaur, and they are mosquitoes. Believe you me.[86]

Notably, Muta has a close bond with all his colleagues. He is on amicable terms with them and obviously maintains a flat hierarchy. Speaking from personal experience, an easy-going studio atmosphere seems to be the order, not only of the day but the entire programme over the years. *Positive vibes* – as one would describe it in Jamaican terms – rule the process of broadcasting and the interaction of the whole team inside the Irie FM studio. Even on air Muta loves to banter with his workmates: 'Because nobody feels that they get enough pay, when they do nothing like Neil. He doesn't feel that he is getting enough pay, but he doesn't really do anything. He sits back here on his phone.'[87]

He may even run jokes with them during a serious debate, for example in the context of the American deportation policies: 'Most of Neil's family members are in America, illegally. So, Neil, you better call them and tell them that tonight they must come to their bed, burn some white candle, call Jamaica, and get some black candle and burn it – so that Trump doesn't win.'[88] Such cultural referencing and other skits of Jamaican oratory art, as well as proverbs, comments, and comparisons are essential and bring a lighter mood to the otherwise quite serious social and political issues highlighted in the shows.

As a committed Rastafari, who was excluded and seriously marginalized in mainstream media before the inauguration of Irie FM, Muta appreciates (or *appreciloves* as Rastas would have it) his almost unlimited artistic freedom. In an interview during his Lifetime Achievement Award ceremony, he mentioned that Irie FM's programme director Kabu has never ever stopped him from delving into any subject he brought up during the two radio shows, no matter how controversial and sensitive the content may have been.[89]

By means of an announcement at the beginning of the programme, Irie FM points out, at least in the case of *Cutting Edge*, that 'the views expressed are not necessarily those of the company.'[90] This speaks volumes for the trust that is placed in him by those in charge of Irie FM. No wonder, that a grateful Muta pays homage to Kabu, describing her as the 'driving force in Irie FM' and claiming that he is proud to work under her supervision.[91]

It should be noted at this point that Kabu is responsible for the positive image Irie FM has achieved for the last thirty-plus years. The Reggae channel became Jamaica's leading radio station with a circadian focus on music, Rastafari, and Africa-centred programmes. Besides her position as the station's programme director, she has run her own regular broadcast titled *Running African* since 1990. Kabu is a pan-Africanist and, like her friend Muta, a leading figure in Jamaica's campaign of unmasking colonial indoctrination and liberating the Black psyche.[92]

2.9.   The Programmes' Range of Influence

> The only bad feeling I have is when they put a lot of
> advertisements on my programme, and I cannot say
> anything! It is like I am talking in between the advertisements,
> like I am doing the advertisement programme and I am
> just fitting in rather than I am doing the programme.
>
> Mutabaruka, Jamaica (2018)

During the shows, the only interruptions between talks and music
are news reports, regular advertisements, and announcements of the
Supreme Ventures lottery game results. Muta resents the considerable
number of advertisements, which he believes shorten his airtime and
distract from the just course. He complains that the advertisements
contradict the content of the programme. However, Carolyn Cooper
emphasizes that the level of advertising in the *Steppin Razor* programme
offers valuable clues to the vast reach of Irie FM in general and Muta's
broadcast(s) in particular:

> It will be good to see who advertises on the programme. ...
> When I was on the *Steppin Razor*, you had like brand name
> advertisers, is big companies that are advertising. The
> advertising will tell you something about the importance
> of the show.[93]

According to Cooper (who sometimes fills in as the presenter
for Mutabaruka during his journeys abroad), an analysis of the
programme's advertising is useful in terms of indicating the outreach
of both shows, *Cutting Edge* and *Steppin Razor*. Not only does the
large number of advertisements generate high revenue for Irie FM,
but it also says a lot about the shows' importance in terms of media
penetration. In fact, Irie FM receives sponsorship from a variety of
companies. During *Steppin Razor*, Muta regularly announces sponsoring
notifications, for instance: 'The hour between two and three is brought
to you by Lime.' Or: 'The hour between four and five is sponsored by
Kirk Distributors.'[94]

Other corporations that advertise in *Steppin Razor* are Epican, ABC
Electrical Sales, and LUX. Whereas Epican, a medical marijuana
store in Kingston, and ABC Electrical Sales, a service provider in
electrical products based in Jamaica, are local companies, Unilever's

famous soap and shampoo brand LUX, the Colgate-Palmolive portfolio distributor Kirk Distributors Limited, and the Caribbean communication provider Lime (renamed as Flow in 2016) are global corporate enterprises.

This proves that Irie FM is meanwhile considered as a prime marketing outlet for major companies in Jamaica. As it occupies the leading position in Jamaica's radio landscape (see statistics further below), the radio station provides a far-reaching medium and thus a potential target audience for advertising companies. Branded sponsoring in *Steppin Razor* gives a hint on the vast scope of the broadcast and its considerable impact factor.

Ironically, political parties such as the Jamaica Labour Party (JLP) use Irie FM (including the *Steppin Razor* show) as a platform for campaigning. Given that Muta demonstrates a high level of criticism towards politics in general and many ministers of the JLP in particular, this seems to be a paradox. But, according to Muta, campaigning on Irie FM simply follows the findings of a JLP-funded poll.[95] This poll revealed that Irie FM is currently the main media used by people living in the province of St Mary, a parish in the northeast of Jamaica chosen as a sample. The pollster eventually advised the JLP to advertise on Irie FM. In this context, Muta strongly disproves any political affiliation of Irie FM:

> The JLP bombards the station with advertisement which make my programme short! Yes, every time I come here on Thursday, I can hardly talk. It's pure JLP advertisement. … St Mary people love Irie FM! I want to hail up St Mary people, not because you vote! But because you told the pollster that it is Irie FM you are listening to! And Irie FM didn't pay for that, the JLP paid for it! Irie FM is not working with the JLP, and the JLP is not working with Irie FM. It just happened that the people said Irie FM is the media that best serves your advertisement vibes.[96]

Another fundamental source for the proof of Irie FM's popularity is the *All Media Survey 2018 Executive Report* undertaken by Market Research Services Limited (2019), a Jamaican marketing research organization. The report features a study on 'media consumption patterns among Jamaicans aged 10 years and older.'[97] Its findings should be used 'by the media and advertising fraternity to help make strategic decisions about programming and advertising.'[98] The study, whose estimates hold a 95 per cent level of confidence, was conducted from October 2018 until January 2019 by sixty interviewers who undertook 1,782 interviews with Jamaicans across the country. Questionnaires targeted the respondents' listenership and viewership patterns surveying twenty-four hours of individual media consumption.[99] The resultant charts of the report provide detailed evidence for Irie FM's leading position. Irie FM held 23.4 per cent of the overall Jamaican radio listenership (including radio via Internet access) and was positioned at number one amongst twenty-seven stations. RJR 94 FM came in on second rank (13.7 per cent) and Mello FM in third place (11.5 per cent). Despite a decline compared to 2007 when Irie FM held around 34 per cent of listenership, it was still by far the most popular station. During the time of the study, Irie FM reached two hundred and seventy-six thousand people on a typical Wednesday and two hundred and sixty-three thousand people on a typical Thursday, to mention the two days which also feature Muta's programmes.[100]

Whereas Jamaica's upper and upper-middle socio-economic group preferred to listen to radio stations such as RJR 94 FM (11.7 per cent), Love 101 FM (11.4 per cent), or Kool 97 FM (10.9 per cent), the majority of the middle-income (20.2 per cent) and especially the low-middle and low-income group (26.3 per cent) listened to Irie FM.[101] In terms of gender distribution, Irie FM was the leading station for female (16.9 per cent) and male viewers (29.0 per cent). Apart from the group of adults over fifty years of age, which primarily listened to RJR 94 FM (24.2 per cent), the three remaining age groups – tweens and teens between ten and nineteen years of age (21.2 per cent), young adults (23.9 per cent) and adults between thirty-five and forty-nine years of age (19.2 per cent) – mainly listened to Irie FM. Furthermore, Irie FM had the largest listenership in all different regions, including the rural region (27.5 per cent), urban region (22.9 per cent), and the city areas of KMA (Kingston and St Andrew, Portmore, and Spanish Town) (19.5 per cent).[102] The latter result mirrors Muta's assumption about the listenership of his programmes since he mostly receives callers from the countryside: 'It is mostly country people listening to that programme. I wanna hail up all the country people who tune in to *Steppin Razor* every Thursday and don't leave their little radio out of the ears!'[103]

Among Jamaica's afternoon radio programmes from Monday to Friday (between 12:00 and 6:00 p.m.), Irie FM had the largest listenership (21.6 per cent of all radio stations on average). The same applies to evening (22.3 per cent) and night programmes (20.6 per cent) from Monday to Friday, all time segments when also Muta's shows are on air.[104] However, the number of international online listeners are not reflected in these statistics. Irie FM with both programmes, *Cutting Edge* and *Steppin Razor*, would most probably obtain even a higher percentage in such statistics if those numbers were included.[105]

According to the previous version of the report from 2016, the listenership of Muta's *Steppin Razor* programme reaches its peak between 4:30 and 6:00 p.m., with a maximum listener outreach of ninety thousand people.[106] This is when Muta usually answers incoming telephone calls. It therefore appears that *Steppin Razor*'s interactive element is highly appreciated by people. The *Cutting Edge* broadcast reaches a maximum listener outreach of seventy-nine thousand people, which is by far the most of all Jamaican radio programmes on Wednesday night.[107]

In summary, Irie FM spearheads Jamaica's radio landscape. Especially among the nation's younger population (under fifty years of age) and rural population, the Reggae radio station is very popular. But the report also shows a potential new target group for the *Cutting Edge* and *Steppin Razor* broadcasts, which until early 2019 mostly consisted of (younger) adults from rural and urban regions.[108] On average, almost fifty-one thousand people – mostly from the middle- and low-income socio-economic groups – listen to Muta's radio shows. Furthermore, the survey's version of 2016 points out that *Cutting Edge* is the most popular programme on Wednesday night amongst the general radio listenership.

As mentioned above, the international dimension (unfortunately not included in the media report) and particular forms of advertising are signs of the continual impact of Muta's programmes. Apart from that, the Rastafari presenter told us in our interview that the decision to launch a second radio show apart from *Cutting Edge* was made due to Irie FM's declining ratings at that time: 'The ratings by the station were falling at the time. … The motivation was really to jump the ratings of the station, you know! And it did that!'[109]

Accordingly, Irie FM recruited Mutabaruka to reclaim the station's high ratings. In fact, the station was able to gain more than 4 per cent (which represents around forty-one thousand listeners out of the total potential audience of 1,032,000) compared to the survey's results from 2014 (it increased from 19.30 per cent to 23.4 per cent of the overall Jamaican radio listenership within four years).[110] The launching of Muta's second broadcast, *Steppin Razor*, in 2013 may have contributed to that progression.

2.10. Radio for *I and I* Reasoning

> If the watchman sees the danger and doesn't warn the people, the blood of the people will be on his shoulder.
>
> Mutabaruka: *Steppin Razor*, January 20 (2016)

> Concerned citizen talking! So even if you don't like the messenger, check the message that he is dealing with!
>
> Mutabaruka: *Steppin Razor*, August 3 (2017)

Based on the study of seventy broadcast episodes, we have selected four major topics for the following analysis structured by some preeminent contents (chapters 3–6). It intends to provide an overview of Muta's opinions and views on these subjects, as deducted from the sample. Whereas it will not be attempted to present a coherent world view of our protagonist, we will discuss some recurring narratives, correlate them with each other, and interpret his positions in relation to other contextual sources and empirical data received in Jamaica through further interviews, personal observations, and the literature. We will consider Mutabaruka's extensive speech acts over a period of over four decades (including his pre-radio output) as an ongoing discursive practice.

Given the amount of his public appearances on air, on screen, on stage, and otherwise, this can only provide a preliminary snapshot of his practical logic and will have to be rewritten and extended over time, since – like any other human being – Muta is fully entitled to learn, broaden his wisdom by experience, and therefore reframe his thinking. But we trust that many of his attitudes and stances will stand the test of time. In fact, this reflects the general quality of Rastafari reasoning as a collective practice, based on the equality of *I and I* (or *I-n-I*).[111] It is worth quoting this core concept in Muta's own thinking at some length, as he delivered it in a keynote address during the 2001 conference of the Society for Caribbean Research (SOCARE), at the University of Vienna:

> I and I is seeing the being, the manifestation of the supreme in man and woman and in every living thing that exist. So when the Rastaman say 'I and I,' the normal Jamaican is getting complicated because he's articulating 'I and I' based on the English concept of 'I' meaning first person. So you couldn't have two first persons in the logics of the language. You couldn't have 'I and I' as two first persons. So the normal Jamaican is seeing that as semantics. The Rastaman is going beyond this semantics now, he is saying that 'I' is what you call the spirit. So 'I and I' is referring to the spirit in the man, which is the good in the man, so this is the supreme being that he is referring to, when he says 'I and I.' He is going beyond the man, that you see, and looking into the man that he should be. So the Rastaman is continually saying 'I and I.' 'I an I.' An him put 'I' on everything that is I-rie. So you have I-rie, which means all right. You know, and I-tal, which is natural. And this 'I' becomes so synonymous with Rastafari that we have a radio station that is named Irie. And it is not funny again to say 'I and I,' even politicians now get up and say 'I and I,' and don't feel any way, not knowing or understanding the term 'I and I,' how great it is and how important it is, to explain the supreme being in man, not the supernatural.[112]

Cutting Edge and *Steppin Razor*, Muta's two extensive contributions to the Irie FM station, are not just separate broadcasts but rather speak volumes of oral literature. At the same time, they prove the close connection of Irie FM – already indicated by its name – with Rastafari philosophy and thought. Muta never tires to explain that Rastafari is no doctrine like most religions, ideologies, or socio-political organizations. He is therefore very much aware that he does not speak for Rastafari but rather as a Rastafari with his individual experiences and ideas. When we proposed to him a book title referring to him as Rastafari, namely 'The Rastafari Verbal Swordsman,' thinking to attract a broader audience interested in Rastafari in general, Muta refused. He did not want to make it appear, as if he took on the role of an official spokesman. Although sometimes he seems to accept his informal leadership position, by voicing positions of Rastafari philosophy. Yet this is mostly the case, when he is certain about a broad consensus among Rastafari on a particular subject, e.g., the fight against apartheid, colonialism, and white supremacy.

This double role of Rastafari and public figure provides a guiding thread throughout the two weekly shows.[113] Instead of considering these broadcasts as one-time affairs, one should acknowledge their commonality as part and parcel of his *reasoning* with Jamaican society and beyond. Reasoning is an integral part of and common practice in Rastafari *livity*. On an everyday level, reasonings serve the purpose of 'Rastafari exchanges on historical and current happenings related to the local and global level.'[114] Rasta reasoning on a more philosophical level may be regarded as an ongoing collective search for wisdom and as the opposite pole to the Western model of discussion, a term that etymologically derives from the Latin *discutio* (to smash).[115]

Mutabaruka follows this tradition and *reasons* with his listeners on everyday occurrences as well as their underlying historical and geopolitical dimensions to reach deeper insights, based on what may be termed 'communicative rationality.'[116] Since he picks up issues from previous *Steppin Razor* broadcasts and *Cutting Edge* shows, he deals with related themes and uses iterative arguments. This means that the discourse never stops, the arguments never end, and, if you wish, democratic processes of opinion and will formation are unleashed in a manner of which the parliamentary system often enough falls short.[117] In the following chapters 3–6, reviewing mainly *Steppin Razor* broadcasts, the individual episodes are condensed to form a conglomerate of manifold narratives that ultimately coalesce into exemplary portraits of the *overarching reasoning*.

Chapter 3 deals with Muta's narratives concerning Jamaica's politics and policymakers. Chapter 4 is devoted to the radio host's attitudes towards the island's crime situation. Whereas Chapter 5 attends to his views on societal phenomena in the context of culture, music and religion, Chapter 6 presents conceptions of Rastafari, reparations, and decolonization.

NOTES

1. The radio quotes from the *Steppin Razor* broadcast are indicated with SR (+ the respective number), those from *Cutting Edge* with CE (+ number). An overview of all broadcasts quoted can be found in the bibliography (arranged chronologically by number).
2. Likkle is the Jamaican Patois word used for *little*.
3. Euronews (2018).
4. Cf. Interview 1 (2018) and Interview 6 (2022).
5. Cf. Interview 1 (2018).
6. Selecta is the Jamaican Patois synonym for selector, meaning a disc jockey who plays or *selects* tunes in a dance. A selecta is therefore the key figure in the sound system culture. See also Stolzoff (2000, 54ff.). The source for the designation as a 'development thinker' can be found at Cooke (2010).
7. Irie FM is Jamaica's most popular radio channel and featured 23.4 per cent of Jamaica's radio listenership in 2018, cf. MRSL (2019, 21). For further reading on Irie FM, its launch, and early development, cf. Mockyen (2003, 333–36).
8. Cf. Interview 1 (2018).
9. Ibid.
10. Whereas many video and audio clips of Muta's lectures can be found on YouTube, his keynote address from the Seventh Conference of the Society for Caribbean Research, which was held at the University of Vienna in July 2001, is published in the book *Rastafari: A Universal Philosophy in the Third Millennium*, cf. Mutabaruka (2006a).
11. Cooke (2010).
12. Cooper (2013, 113).
13. Cf. Interview 1 (2018). Note: We refer to the notion of pan-Africanism as outlined by Horace Campbell (1988).
14. For a general discussion of these structures see Achiume (2018), Beirich/Buchanan (2018), and FRA (2018). Monteiro-Ferreira (2014, 1–12) serves as an introduction to the topic of Afrocentrism.
15. In another interview, he elaborated that the Black Power ideology quickly turned his nature poetry into another direction: 'I think that was what motivated me to continue, because I realized that it was accepted, and this is something through which I could express myself. But it took a turn from nature poems because I was very politically motivated, Black Power motivated. So I started to write poems that were socially

conscious, were socially politicized through the Black consciousness movement' (Interview 1, 2018).

16. Interview 1 (2018). Humpty Dumpty is a character in an English nursery rhyme, mostly portrayed as an anthropomorphic egg. The name is used as an allegory for fragility, weakness, clumsiness, inaction, and indecision. It occasionally appeared in his later poetry work as the anti-thesis to political action.

17. Cf. Interview 1 (2018). To compare the two poems, see Mphahlele (1967, 145–48) and Mutabaruka (1980b, 23).

18. Interview 1 (2018).

19. Ibid.

20. For more information on Howell and his influence on the genesis of Rastafari see Lee (2003).

21. Interview 1 (2018).

22. Cf. Ibid.

23. Ibid. Note: The book *What Is Africanness?* by Charles Ngwena (2018) evolves an epistemology for constructing the hermeneutics of Africanness within a wide-ranging view.

24. Interview 1 (2018).

25. Ibid.

26. Ibid.

27. It became rereleased in 2005 in a double volume extended with a collection of newer poems called *The Next Poems*.

28. Interview 1 (2018).

29. Mortimo Planno was a well-established and influential Jamaican Rastafari and known as an advisor of Bob Marley. He even wrote some of Marley's songs, e.g., *Selassie is the Chapel* (1968). Furthermore, he left a hand-written report on Rastafari's oral traditions (1969). See also Davison (2006).

30. Interview 1 (2018).

31. Cf. Ibid. For the recording he revisited, adjusted, and rephrased his poem, but, originally – as one can find it in his poetry collection (1980b, 6f.) – it was entitled *White Sound*, serving sharp and provocative verses against white slave drivers. See also Cooke (2009). Note: We refer to Reggae charts lists that were compiled by several Reggae record shops from UK in 1981. Between May and September 1981, one could find Mutabaruka's *Every Time A Ear De Soun* in the top ten for seven weeks, next to other Reggae hits from that era, e.g., Eek-A-Mouse's *Wa-Do-Dem* (1981) and I Jah Man's *Jah Heavy Load* (1978). See: https://reggaelabelartarchives.wordpress.com/category/articles/uk-reggae-charts-1974-1987/1981-charts.

32. Interview 1 (2018).

33. Cf. Mutabaruka (1983a).

34. Interview 1 (2018). Note: The *High Times Players* was a Reggae studio and backing band, founded by bandleader and High Times label owner Earl Chinna Smith.

35. Interview 1 (2018).

36. Ibid. Note: When Mutabaruka gets booked as a *selecta*, he uses that name for his sound system until this day.

37. Cf. Ibid.

38. Ibid.

39. Ibid.

40. Kingdom Nubia Radio (KNR) is an online radio station and information provider of Black topics. For access, visit: kingdomnubia.com.

41. Interview 1 (2018).

42. In November 2009, the Jamaican TV station CVM launched Simply Muta. Muta's own TV show lasted for two seasons. Furthermore, he also appeared several times on Ian Boyne's *Religious Hard Talk* TV show, where he verbally *clashed* with the presenter and other Reverend scholars about Christianity and Rastafari.

43. Cf. Cooke (2010).

44. Cf. Zips (2011a).

45. Cf. Habekost (1993, 26).

46. Cf. Jamaica Information Service (2010).

47. On YouTube, one can rewatch the awarding: 'Mutabaruka Awarded "Pan-Afrikan Grand-Master" in London,' link: https://www.youtube.com/watch?v=5Eg-5vSw3jk (uploaded on September 5, 2018).

48. Cf. Grizzle (2018).

49. Cf. Francis-Pitt (2019).

50. SR 44 (2017).

51. On its homepage, Irie FM (2022) states: 'Listeners from Australia to Switzerland, from Seattle to Denmark are tuning in to IRIE FM. Thousands of people log on to www.iriefm.net as part of their daily routine. The website has clearly paved the way to become a reggae portal of great substance.'

52. CE 17 (2020).

53. Interview 1 (2018).

54. SR 17 (2015).

55. Cf. CE 1–20 (2013–21) and SR 1–50 (2014–17).

56. Cf. Ibid. Note: According to *urban dictionary* (2007), 'a steppin' razor' is a dangerous person that is not to be messed with, referring to the fact that they are quick to fight.' The term was made popular by Peter Tosh's recording of the homonymous song (1977b) – although it was originally written by Joe Higgs (1967) – as well as by a Peter Tosh documentary film of the same title directed by Nicholas Campbell (1992).

57. Interview 1 (2018).

58. Muta is said to be one of the authenticators of using Jamaican Patois on the radio. In cooperation with the English and Linguistics Department of the UWI, he even produced the newscasts in Patois for a short period of time. See also Mockyen (2003, 336).
59. Cf. SR 14 (2015).
60. SR 21 (2016).
61. Interview 1 (2018). For the book *The Art of War* see Sunzi/Giles (2008).
62. Sunzi/Gilles (2008, 10).
63. Ibid., 5.
64. SR 28 (2016).
65. Cf. Interview 1 (2018).
66. Ibid.
67. Ibid.
68. Cf. CE 8 (2016) and CE 13 (2017).
69. Cf. CE 3 (2014); CE 10 (2017); CE 11 (2017); SR 7 (2015); SR 20 (2016); SR 25 (2016); SR 39 (2017); SR 40 (2017).
70. Cf. CE 11 (2017); CE 13 (2017); SR 45 (2017); SR 48 (2017).
71. CE 11 (2017).
72. Cf. CE 19 (2020) and SR 24 (2016). Zips provides a demonstration of Muhammad Ali's socio-political accomplishments in the book *Nation X*, cf. Zips/Kämpfer (2001, 9–19).
73. Cf. CE 1–20 (2013–21) and SR 1–50 (2014–17). According to Muta, Interview 1 (2018): 'Kid Ralph, in the '90s. I think that was the biggest interview I ever did.'
74. Cf. SR 8 (2015) and SR 26 (2016).
75. Cf. SR 7 (2015); SR 14 (2015); SR 40 (2017).
76. Cf. CE 1–20 (2013–21) and SR 1–50 (2014–17).
77. SR 47 (2017).
78. SR 16 (2015). Muta's love for Techno is also demonstrated by his recorded Minimal Techno song 'Wata,' which resulted from the collaboration with South African producer Beat Pharmacy (cf. Beat Pharmacy/Mutabaruka 2006). During his last live appearance in Vienna, Austria, he even performed some of his poems to Techno sounds pre-recorded on a tape brought along.
79. Cf. CE 11 (2017).
80. Interview 4 (2018).
81. Cf. SR 24 (2016).
82. SR 3 (2014).
83. SR 14 (2015).
84. In general, one must imagine the Irie FM broadcasting centre in Ocho Rios as an open-door facility, since diverse people (other employees, local Reggae artistes or simply enthusiasts) gather inside the rather small building and, if permitted, enter the studio to watch the operations

and perhaps chip in with some comment. Therefore, it is a continual coming and going. For instance, together with two local artistes, we were allowed into the studio to watch legendary DJ Wayne while he ran his programme.

85. SR 30 (2016) and SR 39 (2017).
86. SR 27 (2016).
87. SR 14 (2015).
88. SR 25 (2016).
89. Cf. 'Lifetime achievement award to Mutabaruka on behalf of Irie FM Radio', 2019, link: https://www.youtube.com/watch?v=26mKgF3Ui1c (uploaded on March 28, 2019).
90. CE 9 (2017).
91. Cf. SR 35 (2017).
92. Cf. Cooper (2015) and Sweet/Olaniyan (2010: 286).
93. Interview 2 (2018).
94. SR 1–50 (2014–17).
95. Cf. SR 43 (2017).
96. SR 43 (2017).
97. MRSL (2019, 8). We regard this report as a snapshot from 2018. Therefore, results could be different at present.
98. MRSL (2019, 8).
99. Cf. MRSL (2019, 8ff).
100. Cf. MRSL (2019, 21, 23, 30).
101. Note: We adopted the market segment divisions (upper, middle, low income, etc.) as mentioned in the report.
102. For all statistical details as mentioned cf. MRSL (2019, 38ff.).
103. SR 12 (2015).
104. Cf. MRSL (2019, 34).
105. On the basis of Duke Baysee's (@DukeBaysee100) YouTube channel (with 58,800 subscribers and 23.2 million views as of May 21, 2023) one can evaluate the outreach of the *Steppin Razor* and *Cutting Edge* broadcasts. An uploaded show reaches around ten thousand to eighteen thousand views on average (sometimes even up to sixty thousand views), which means that many people (re-)listen to the programme on YouTube. Additionally, the commentaries on the YouTube uploads shed light on the broadcast's acceptance, its impact and stimulation for further debates. And there are even other YouTube channels which regularly upload the recorded programmes.
106. Cf. MRSL (2017, 120).
107. Ibid., 118f.
108. Whereas the urban region represents the parishes of St Catherine, St James, St Ann, Westmoreland, Manchester, and Clarendon, the rural area includes St Thomas, Portland, St Mary, St Elizabeth, Trelawny, and Hanover. The four remaining regions, namely Kingston, St

Andrew, Portmore and Spanish Town are considered the city region. See also MRSL (2017, 25).

109. Interview 1 (2018).
110. Cf. MRSL (2017, 22) and MRSL (2019, 22).
111. See also Mutabaruka (2006a, 37–39) on the core concept of I-n-I for the divinity of Haile Selassie in man, according to Rastafari philosophy.
112. Mutabaruka (2006a, 31). Note: 7th International Conference of the Society for Caribbean Research in Vienna, Austria (July 4–7, 2001).
113. We would refer to him as a 'public intellectual,' but are well aware from many personal conversations that Muta himself denies any special status for himself above the commoner. He strongly feels as a man of the people and for the people.
114. Barsch (2008, 119; our own translation of the German text).
115. See Zips (2006a, xii–xiii).
116. Cf. Habermas (1987).
117. We consciously borrow an epistemological tool in Jürgen Habermas' theory of discursive democracy here, because of its obvious analogies to the key Rastafari imperative of 'Equal Rights and Justice' and the legitimating power of reasoning, cf. Habermas (1987; 1996) and Zips (2011b, xxiv–xxvi).CE 12 (2017).

CHAPTER 3

'ABSOLUTE POWER CORRUPTS ABSOLUTELY'
On Jamaica's Politics

They tell you that the only way to beat the system is to join the system, that you have to go inside to make a difference. Guess what? They become a part of the system which is oppressing the people.

Mutabaruka: Cutting Edge, August 5 (2015)

These politicians are reactionary! They are so backward. … Why do I have to come on the radio and talk these things? Some simple things, you know. This is foolishness. You shouldn't talk about this on the radio. But they disgust you.

Mutabaruka: Steppin Razor, January 7 (2016)

JLP and PNP are the worst things ever happened to Jamaica! They are worse than the gunmen! I tell you, man!

Mutabaruka: Steppin Razor, January 15 (2016)

Many narratives in Mutabaruka's shows, mostly in the *Steppin Razor*, deal with politics. He steadily supplies his listeners with political analyses embedded in critical narratives. As a Rastafari familiar with his Jamaican birthplace and actual life in many regions of Africa through his extensive travelling on the continent, he is credibly able to relate the micro-level of 'politics ah yard' to macro-political structures within historical contexts. Global views are therefore never absent from his takes on Jamaica's politics and policymakers.

3.1. A Two-headed Dragon: The JLP and PNP Power Games

Since the introduction of universal adult suffrage in Jamaica (1944), Jamaica has had a democratic political system in which two parties, namely the conservative Jamaica Labour Party (JLP) and the social-democratic People's National Party (PNP), have taken almost regular turns of coming to power. The two parties have not only fought for the nation-state's leadership but have also waged a dirty struggle by means of violence and garrison politics against each other. The year 1980 marked a bloody peak in their history of animosity, as around eight hundred people were killed due to political divisions in territorial districts in the run-up to the elections. Constant battles between politically affiliated groups created an ongoing division in Jamaican society to this day. Especially in marginalized and poor communities of Kingston's, May Pen's and Spanish Town's inner-city ghettos, the so-called garrison communities, political violence has been frequent. According to Figueroa and Sives, 'a garrison, as the name suggests, is a political stronghold, a veritable fortress completely controlled by a party.'[1]

In the past, rival groups of such garrisons were armed by the respective parties in exchange for support in elections and in maintaining political dominance. 'Politicians started the gun thing in Jamaica,' as Muta resents.[2] Reciprocal accusations of foreign involvements (e.g., the CIA in the case of JLP) or Cuban alliances (in the case of PNP) were exchanged in mirroring last century Cold War.[3] Recent developments in 2022 threaten to see a revival after the hot war between Russia and the Ukraine supported by a Western alliance through sanctions and other means started to reform the Cold War divisions. Although Jamaican gangs are not necessarily tied to parties any longer and have their own sources of income nowadays, as will be discussed later, the parties still offer political protection in exchange for votes.[4]

Mutabaruka repeatedly reports on the pervasive politically motivated hardships for Jamaican society at large, what he calls the 'two tribalist political parties (which) really deject and reject the people.'[5] In an episode from November 2017, he addresses the genesis of garrison communities and unveils his own experience with ghetto structures of homogenous affiliation and voting, setting the people of similar social status against each other:

> I hear this prime minister (Andrew Holness; authors' note) wants to get rid of the garrison, and I see that he makes more garrisons! Because Mount Salem to me is how garrisons are made. Nobody doesn't want to take promises in Mount Salem. It is a political party that makes a garrison. It means that years down the line, everybody votes for the party that came in there and does what they were telling to do. So it goes! Nobody cannot tell me no difference! Garrison Tivoli Gardens is a good example of how it is made. Now they are going to mash down zinc fence, fix road, and make people pay light bill. And then, what other choice do you have apart from voting for them? When the next election comes, they have gone to Denham Town. Tivoli Gardens is here, Denham Town is there. We know that at this place the dons have gone straight up already. Around Payneland and all these places there. … It is a war between the two (parties)! When they go to a dance, they look out for one another and shoot one another. It is only the women who can go up and down the road.[6]

When Muta elaborates on the socio-political structure of Jamaican ghetto communities, he cautions against police interventions, such as the so-called *ZOSO (Zone of Special Operation)*, which was introduced by the Jamaican government to curb criminal activities in Montego Bay's community of Mount Salem in 2017.[7] Muta thinks that such interventions are first steps towards establishing a highly politicized community, ready-made to release its political tensions into eruptions of violence. In this context, he draws on negative examples from the past; for example, the garrisons of Tivoli Gardens and Denham Town, two neighbourhoods in Western Kingston that were formed through government-sponsored housing schemes. An important means of co-optation that eventually evolved into a proxy civil war fought between gangs from the respective rival areas for decades.[8]

In general, the radio host reviews and often condemns Jamaica's existing political culture and landscape. He reproaches the reciprocity of violence and partisan politics and of monies and clientelism, which amounts to absolute (forced) loyalties of the electorate in garrison communities to one political party. Muta makes his listeners aware of this systemic corruption. Calling it a *one campaign election* and *one box voting*. He wonders about the perseverance of these rigid structures:

> How can they not lose? That's why it is a one campaign election and a one box vote. They count one box and just declare the winner. ... One gets six thousand votes, and one gets like one hundred. These dons know that they are going to win there, because of the garrison![9]

Muta is enraged about the dubious election results from the St Andrew South Western constituency in 2017 where Angela Brown-Burke (PNP) received 6,324 from 6,659 votes counted.[10] Such occurrences clearly show the questionable political structure in Jamaica and the country's ongoing incidents of political corruption by and large. In his broadcasts, Muta illuminates the political racketeering and appeals to people from the affected constituencies to become aware of the dazzled conditions.[11] In fact, he wants them to assume responsibility and self-empowerment: 'If the people lead, the leaders will follow! And so it must go. The people must lead so that the leaders follow.'[12] Muta states that politicians only care for the citizens during election campaign periods to gain voters. He unambiguously prompts his listeners to get rid of their own ignorance:

> The time when you know that Jamaican people are ignorant is the time when election comes round. When election comes round, politicians rent coaster (Toyota Coaster bus; authors' note), put the poor people on it and give them T-shirts to put on and Kentucky (*Kentucky Fried Chicken* fast food chain; authors' note), and a 5,000 Jamaican dollar bill, and they pack up the arena. They pack up the squares. And when the politicians behave like they are entertainers, too, you know. Believe you me, they could perform at Sting! When they lick their face and say certain things, and the people jump up. And then the soundman plays the right tune, and they are getting a frenzy. It is like a church! It is like a church and Sting in one! And then, look here now, when election is finished, those same people there come on TV and say that after they voted for Mister this and that, they haven't seen him come to the area again. They don't want him back around here. They want Mister other

man now. You don't see that it is a two-headed dragon in
Jamaica?! When you cut off one of the heads, one head is
left, but of the same body. The two heads are working from
the same body! The PNP and the JLP are defending the
same thing. It is like you are doing the same thing the same
way all the while and expect to get a different result.[13]

Here, Mutabaruka addresses a common political practice during
Jamaica's election campaigns: Parties provide bus tours for their
supporters and attract citizens with give-away articles such as shirts,
money, drinks, and food.[14] In this context, he sarcastically advises
politicians to take part in the legendary Dancehall-festival, Sting,
since politicians behave like entertainers or church preachers when
they hold their open-air rallies. To illustrate the political model of
the Caribbean state, he alludes to a two-headed dragon analogy that
emblematizes the country's two-party system and the insignificance of
the incumbent's party affiliation since there would always be the same
corrupt and unsatisfactory outcomes.

Omar Hawthorne, a Jamaican researcher on corruption and
global security, speaks of 'the view that party comes before country.'[15]
This attitude lends to a mentality commonly shared by Jamaica's
politicians that has unfortunately led to partisanship instead of a sense
of responsibility for the citizens. To make it worse, this principle has
become entrenched in the mind of the public, almost as part of a
national habitus.

'A promise is a comfort to a fool,' Muta broaches the empty promises
of corrupt politicians.[16] He doesn't only blame the political entity for
villainous conditions, but also the citizens, as they continuously fall
for the authorities and their promising agenda like a 'lamb to the
slaughter, … and they want shepherd to lead them.'[17] Most notably,
the opposition party in Jamaica vehemently pretends to be better and
more caring than the incumbent party.

In July 2017, reports about then-finance minister Audley Shaw's
(JLP) high cell phone bill became a hot issue in the media.[18] Shaw's
bill amounted to J$8.34 million (approx. €55,000) from March 2016 to
February 2017, and he had a J$4.2 million bill in October 2016 alone.
According to the ministry, the bill was that high due to Shaw's overseas

travels. Muta pays attention to such political scandals, signifying them as 'scamming at its highest level.'[19] Furthermore, he includes other interesting facets of such stories in his argumentation, for instance, reminding his audience of a newspaper article from October 2014, containing data about PNP minister Arnaldo Brown and a J$1.09 million phone bill:

> Hey! Watch yah, Jamaican people! I don't want you to take this thing here lightly, you understand?! The former government under the PNP chucked up a hefty phone bill from one of his junior ministers, and the JLP opposition criticized them terribly! And three years after, the next government under the JLP comes and chucks up a hefty phone bill. ... They get away with too many things! We have to put this on every news, every paper, and it cannot come off the headline. ... You know that cock mout' kill cock. Cock mout' kill cock![20]

The Rastafari philosopher deepens the debate by reminding of the former PNP minister's telephone bill and the subsequent critique by the JLP opposition in 2014, which he describes with the Jamaican proverb *Cock mout' kill cock.*[21] This phrase conveys the meaning to be more careful with one's own words as they may be harmful: 'Cock mout' kill cock! The cock never knew that its mouth would reach there so. Because he looked for votes; it is all about getting votes!'[22] Through this proverb, Mutabaruka tries to foreground that the two parties constantly malign each other but ultimately defeat themselves with their own arguments, an example being this very saga about high cell phone bills. It exemplifies Muta's analogy of the two-headed dragon: When the respective candidates run the country, they act similarly to (if not even worse than) their opponent predecessors.

Muta argues that such incidents badly undermine the government's credibility, integrity, and accountability. He ironically pretends to wonder why politicians don't follow their usual role model, namely the former *colonial motherland* England[23]:

> In England that couldn't happen! And it is England that we are trying to follow! These little house slaves are trying to follow the colonial master who now have become neocolonialist. In the house slave mentality, the house slave becomes like the master! And when the master leaves the

> plantation, the house slave is there to help sustaining the plantation, and he oppresses the field slave! Because the field slaves behave like idiots, like they are stupid people. But the field slave is the one who just burnt down the plantation and doesn't feel no way about it, because he doesn't lose nothing anyway. The house slave sits down in the house and behaves like the master.[24]

At this point, Muta communicates a critical stance and uses the distinctive house-and-field slave analogy inherited from the likes such as Malcolm X as a metonymic reference to Jamaica's political system. Whereas the field slave in this scathing analogy represents the suppressed citizen who risks his or her life for rebellion, the house slave embodies the privileged and (seemingly) superordinate politician who merely serves as a henchman for the former colonial power. Repeatedly, Muta takes on the role of an alternative media anchorman accentuating political news by attributing their legacy to the colonial aftermath. By means of such like analogies, his listeners receive a more accurate critical picture of common social structures from the past and they may recognize the continuity of such practices and structures in the present. During a broadcast from December 2017, he uses a similar image of slavery:

> You don't need to wear coat and tie in Jamaica in summer. Coat and tie are for colder climates. You must be free, make your body breathe. These boasy slaves who behave worse than the slave masters, worse than the white men who used to slave us down here, they don't know what clock is ticking.[25]

Mutabaruka – himself dressed in African robes and clothes, walking the land, any land, that is, ever-barefoot – consistently ridicules the dress code of Jamaica's politicians.[26] He prefers to wear long smocks of many colours and made of African fabrics (or, at least, with African looks) and a head cloth in which he usually covers his dreadlocks. His early socialization in the philosophy of Rastafari from the House of Nyahbinghi and perhaps also his extensive readings in Buddhism determine his outward appearance. But this only reflects the symbolic distancing from what he refers to as the *boasy* appearance and behaviour of political representatives, meaning a demeanour rooted in colonial mentality.

Whilst devaluing politician's Italian ties and shoes, he continuously makes his listenership aware of the enslaving system the politicians still perpetuate, even 'worse than the white man who used to slave us down here.'[27] Such a rhetoric reminds of revolutionary philosopher Frantz Fanon, who also wrote about 'Blacks who are whiter than the Whites.'[28]

Muta finds the reference to national heroes made during speeches of Jamaican politicians such as Peter Murcott Bunting (PNP) and Robert Montague (JLP) rather contradictory. With his uncompromising stance and sharp tongue, the dissident Rastafari destroys the ministers' predications and presents an intellectual pastime reflecting on the status of the national heroes:

> Why do these politicians get up and talk about Paul Bogle and Sam Sharpe as national heroes, when it is a known fact that Bogle and Sharpe rose up against the elected government of the time and broke the law by killing people and upsetting the equilibrium of the Jamaican society? Burning down plantations, chopping off people's fingers and all these things! How is it that Mister Bunting would stand up now and say that these men are really legitimate national heroes when in fact they were really outlaws of the state? They were enemies of the state because they were fighting against a system that they thought is unjust! They rose up physically against the system! And they were charged and hanged! ... If a Paul Bogle rises up today or if a Sam Sharpe rises up today, would Mister Bunting recognize the Paul Bogle or Sam Sharpe in them? Or would they just be common criminals that are fighting against the legitimate order of the society? Or would they say that the Paul Bogle and Sam Sharpe spirit in this time is an illegal, unlawful spirit and must be crushed at any cause?! Because you know that in this time here, the system that gave rise to Bogle and Sharpe still maintains itself! Even though the face and the colour of the oppressors have changed, the oppression still exists! ... The same people who make Bogle and Sharpe a national hero, knowing that Bogle and Sharpe were enemies of the state, would fight against the spirit of Bogle and Sharpe today! They would call parliament, the police commissioner, and the police to organize against criminal activities put on by some people in the spirit of Bogle and Sharpe who are looking for justice! Justice for the Jamaican

people against the present oppressive system that is now confronting Jamaican people in Jamaica! So these people are hypocrites! And they are worse than the British![29]

As already pointed out before, Mutabaruka is proficient in analysing political structures and practices within a historical and socio-political context. His tongue is razorblade, like a Samurai sword, which we refer to with the book title. He tries to highlight the discrepancy of politicians' reference to Paul Bogle and Samuel Sharpe, two of Jamaica's national heroes who fought against the same political system that the present-day leaders now try to maintain.[30] Yet by being allowed to do that, he also proves that freedom of expression remains clearly unrestricted in Jamaica. It is important to note that this key quality of a political system is becoming increasingly scarce globally. Mutabaruka's weekly eight hours on air provide perhaps evidence for the vitality of democracy in Jamaica. Against all odds emphasized by the protagonist of 'the cutting edge.'

3.2.   Out of Many, One People ... Suffers

Jamaican politics have been entangled with clientelist structures, crime, party-tribalism, and -paternalism for more than six decades.[31] Therein lies one of the main reasons for the tremendous obstacles to tackle sustainable development and political progress. Furthermore, Jamaican policymaking is deeply embedded in the society's colour-class stratification that has shaped the country for a long time. Based on the intersection of class and skin colour, the policy design becomes visible not only because 'the political evolution of the black middle class in Jamaican politics ... has been determined by a history of black subordination to light-skinned players,' as political scientist Rupert Lewis describes it, but also because *whiteness* (and light skin) have long been regarded superior and 'privileged' in the social hierarchy.[32] Thus, the biological categories of *Black* and *white* become categories of, in the most literal sense, social complexions.[33]

Being considered as 'white- or lighter-skinned' may still facilitate access to benefits, such as better jobs, more convenient living conditions, higher education and, above all, reduces chances of falling target for political power games. By taking the materially rich community Cherry Gardens in the parish of St Andrew as an example, the forthright radio presenter harshly argues against such segregating socio-political conditions and publicly debates the subject of 'colourism,' often considered a tacit taboo:

> The politicians know that when they go in a certain area! Here, a certain people have less education. Hey! They cannot go to Cherry Gardens and stay mean like how they do there. You see any brown people jumping up and down with them? Unless the brown people play on the stage. You see any Chiney people, who they call 'out of many one'? Out of many one only implies when you have certain things, like National Heritage Week, you know. But when it comes on to politics, I am telling you, Rasta! You see any coaster full with Indians holding up their green and orange (flags; authors' note)?! But it is 'out of many one.' But it is one people being in the streets, one people eating out of the garbage heap, one people walking in the rain, one people cutting the sugar cane. … It is like they mesmerize the people, like some white magic put them under one spell! Because that is the only thing I could say. It is like the people are under a spell for these two political parties! And the politicians they are there, you know! They know that they are playing with the ignorance of the people, and they continue! Because they know that if the people were educated, trust me man, all of them would have to go to hospital! Believe you me.[34]

Most of the time, political campaigning takes place in the garrison communities where one hardly encounters light-skinned people or people of Asian descent, as Muta points out. By using the derogatory but extremely common Jamaican paraphrase *Chiney people*, he refers to the fairly large group of Asian (mostly Chinese and Indian) descendants living in Jamaica. That is the reason why he questions the Jamaican national motto *Out of Many, One People* as a form of embellishment or 'fair-washing.' Given that it is rather the African-Jamaican (or Black) population that suffers the most and is manipulated by the *spell* of the politicians, the slogan used as a national motto doesn't match to Jamaica's social reality, in his view. Simply because its appeal to unity obviously does not equally affect all ethnic compositions within the nation. Muta clarifies that it is, out of many, *one people that suffers*. He sees this discrimination as a vestige of the centuries-long colonial politics that can be traced back to the social structures during the times of slavery and forced plantation work in the Caribbean.[35]

The following common saying from the days of colonialism and segregation is still incorporated in Jamaican society's thinking and practices to some extent: 'If you're white, you're all right. If you're brown, stick around. If you're black, get back.'[36] In Muta's perspective, this is the 'cutting edge' dividing up society that he refers to in his talk shows and, of course, in the programme's title. The acceptance of such ideas of inherent inferiority (which comes along with a belief in a Eurocentric beauty ideal, including, e.g., length and texture of a woman's hair or the shape of noses) is arguably still widespread in Jamaica. Especially amongst the lower socio-economic part of the population (which is also the largest), this mindset caused skin bleaching to become a trend. People with darker skin colour use certain substances and techniques (e.g., applying *cake soap* to their skin) to bleach highly pigmented parts of their body or face and gain a 'fair' complexion.[37] Muta calls this phenomenon by its name: unfairness.[38]

With all these social structures in mind, Muta presents stories from the deprived part of society as an antithesis of the gruelling power games played by political parties and other (religious) sectors of society. He highlights the non-progressive and biased character of the political landscape and accuses the government of only attending to what he calls the *likkle part of the pyramid*:

> They are not on any ground! Because I am going to tell this government the same thing what I told the previous government. Why do you say things are moving forward? Do you really see the people conditions, Rasta?! Do you really realize that you just talk to a top end of things, and not the level or the big part of the pyramid!? It is the likkle part of the pyramid you are talking to! Because, really and truly, when we look at the situation in Jamaica, since the past PNP was in power, right now the thing hasn't gotten any different in terms of people looking more prosperous![39]

What Muta tags as the 'little (*likkle*) part' (on the top of the pyramid) includes business leaders, financial institutions, and the wealthy class in general, whereas the ordinary and indigent people represent the big part of the pyramid, as he explains in another broadcast.[40] This categorization also correlates with the politics of (skin) colour and class. In contemporary postcolonial Jamaica, the majority of the Black or dark-skinned population (who are of African origin and make up more than 90 per cent of the population) is poor, unemployed, or underemployed, whereas the small percentage of lighter-skinned people (consisting of whites, Jews, Lebanese, Syrians, Chinese, and light-coloured Jamaicans) is predominantly at the top of the socio-economic hierarchy.[41]

It is therefore hardly surprising that lighter-skinned Jamaicans are represented above average amongst the nation's cabinet members. Alongside socio-economic structures, the political hierarchy is heavily affected by the conceptualization of colour, the construction of 'race' as the tacit key to inclusion in exclusive circles. Mutabaruka refers to these 'inconsistent consistencies' in the face of an egalitarian constitution and national motto but uses an idiom that every Jamaican citizen can easily understand. The implications of colourism obviously create an imbalance and social tensions when it comes to the negotiations of identity, especially when such unequal structures are consolidated by the policymakers.

Since Mutabaruka experienced an unprivileged childhood and adolescence in Jamaica's ghetto communities himself, he knows how it is to belong to the lower class of society deemed voiceless by those in power – except during the short election time (Muta refers to so often).[42] Thus, it seems as if occupying a position for this particular societal segment comes straight from his heart. Music and his international success in this artistic field allowed him to transcend class and ethnic boundaries. He has now the means to sit and reason with presidents, prime ministers, and other leaders, as he once told one of the authors during the aforementioned visit to the Cape Coast slave castle in Ghana (while shooting the film *Mutabaruka: The Return to the Motherland*).[43]

However, Muta's own position in the colour-class structure is extraordinary: He reverses or rather *inverts* the hierarchy by assuming a higher-ranked position in media outreach, even though he has always acknowledged his African heritage and Black identity. His cultural capital as informal leader of the people has never been institutionalized in the form of academic titles but is based on accumulation of public appeal and approval. His uncompromising stance for Afrocentric self-education and *experience* has generated noteworthy social and economic capital, as he points out.[44] The support of the common people forms his symbolic capital, which has finally been acknowledged by the government officials through awarding him the Order of Distinction.

His high living standard, the affiliation with the intellectual community, equal exchanges with leaders of all thinkable social fields and his status as a 'superstar' in Jamaica and beyond are powerful signs of social elevation. He is increasingly seen as part of 'high society,' a perception that was widely spread among many interviewees. This is, of course, counter-balanced by his relentless vindication of the common people he once belonged to. He uses this tension between his modest background and his broad-based success for motivation of the so-called ghetto people. Muta's supposedly inferior Africa-centred perspective has been his fundamental asset in life. Legions of Reggae musicians and other artistes as well as activists have learned this lesson and refer to him as a guiding star. Effectively, he has carried out a conversion that the eminent Jamaican cultural scholar Rex Nettleford called for:

> The paradox of Caribbean life is that the more things change the more they have remained the same. The vault-like ascent by the society from slavery into freedom and then from colonialism into constitutional independence is yet to be matched within the society by a corresponding progress from cultural inferiority of the vast majority to cultural self-confidence.[45]

Mutabaruka's lifeworld is a prime example of cultural self-confidence. Such a bold consciousness complies with the Rastafari stance on proudly representing and endorsing *Blackness*. His juxtaposition of Black experiences with the official position of a non-racial society reflects Jamaican realities on the ground and calls attention to the complex postcolonial and hierarchical societal structure.[46] Putting his tongue on the 'cutting edge' – in the trickster figure of the 'steppin' razor' – explores the ambiguities and double standards stressed by the elite(s). For this reason, it is necessary to emphasize this dichotomy between Black experiences with white supremacy and its postcolonial heritage. As a voice of and for the marginalized, Muta points to colour divisions 'without any apology,' and irrespective of any personal consequences, as he readily highlights.[47]

However, as suggested by British scholar Paul Gilroy, colour identities need to be scrutinized for their constructivist racialization but shouldn't be perpetuated as essentialist, reductionist, and homogenous entities.[48] Muta himself would rather refer to Haile Selassie's famous 'until the colour of a man's skin' speech in front of the UN General Assembly (on October 4, 1963), as mentioned in the preface. At the same occasion, Haile Selassie answered a journalist during an interview in this way:

> I must say that black and white, as forms of speech, and as a means of judging mankind, should be eliminated from human society. Human beings are precisely the same whatever colour, race, creed, or national origin they may be.[49]

3.3. Effective Politics Instead of *Politricks*

Muta does not merely draw attention to the suffering of the socially disadvantaged, he also offers radical suggestions for effective politics. Seen from a social science perspective, he offers a political barometer for decision- and policymakers, free of charge. Given that the political elite merely creates a 'devastation lifestyle for the people,' according to him, he sues the standstill of political inactivity facing poverty-reduction and other minimal social services.[50] As a moral judge by popular vote, he calls for serious consequences for ministers and other so-called leaders who are not prepared to do their work conscientiously:

> I would suggest, even as radical it may be, that when a party wins power in Jamaica, all of the ministers and the counsellors should write a memorandum of understanding to the people, that this is what they are going to achieve in the next five years before the next election. Write it down on paper, make it a law, make it stick to them and legislate it in the house that you are going to do this! If they don't do it, they must get locked up! Because you see if they know that they are going to jail, they don't make some highfalutin statement before they win. ... Marcus Garvey suggested

> that you must give them big money, make them feel good,
> make them and their wives and family go out, and they must
> do the duty! If they refuse to do the duty or they are not
> able to do the duty, you should call them and 'stone them to
> death'! ... They must write down what they are going to do
> for the community, and if they don't do it, they should be
> held accountable by jail house or imprisonment![51]

In this quite ruthless statement, not to be (mis)taken verbally, Marcus Garvey's influence on Muta becomes evident in his suggestions for consequential measures against the maladministration of the state. In the essay 'Governing the Ideal State,' Garvey argued that the reformation of a corrupt and unsatisfying government must happen through the introduction of a president with absolute authority and an approval of 'a salary and other accommodations so large and sufficient as to make it reasonably impossible for him, or those dependent upon him, to desire more during his administration.'[52] In turn, following Garvey, this would provide the foundation for dutiful, honest policymaking. If the president and the administrators, however, misused their power and were held responsible for acts of injustice and favouritism, they and their families should be publicly disgraced and 'stoned to death.'[53]

Even in Garvey's days this was not to be taken literally, but rather as a speech act calling for accountable, responsible, and socially sustainable governance. Muta therefore clearly distances himself from a potential literal misreading as he states any such action of physical punishment as 'archaic and primitive.'[54] Nevertheless, he draws upon Garvey's rhetorical skills in his suggestions of dire consequences for politicians who don't serve the people's interest and instead renege on their 'election-time promises.' He regards political accountability as a precautionary principle to avoid chaos and crime in society, given that these components are intertwined with politician's misdemeanour: 'When you take poor people and promise them something and they don't see it happen, they get vicious and turn against each other!'[55]

Muta passionately debates solutions for ongoing political hassles in Jamaica and threatens politicians to improve governance for better performance in the entire political landscape. As a Rastafari on air, he reminds the members of parliament of their responsibility to be role models for the citizens. When ministers curse at each other in the House of Representatives, he requests more than just media coverage and suggests monetary penalties.[56] Thereby Irie FM, the Reggae channel giving voice to Rastafari morality in Jamaica, relentlessly calls for new, postcolonial moral standards. Decolonization of the mind and self-liberation from mental slavery – a long-established Rasta claim picked up by Bob Marley and many other Reggae artistes – are the key issues at stake. As Muta constantly reminds his audience:

> Slavery is not just a chain around your foot. The wickedest slavery is when a man tries to wash your brain and you get brainwashed. Textbook colonialism disappeared, but that doesn't mean that colonialism is not there. Because you have nations who sneakingly colonize us. We don't believe it until one day when we wake up and realize that we don't have land.[57]

Once again, the parallel to Garvey's approach is obvious. This corresponds to civic society activities, for instance, the reconstitution of Liberty Hall, the original location of Marcus Garvey's UNIA on 76 King Street, in Kingston. The original building of this presently extremely active and influential institution was bought by government in celebration of Garvey's centenary in 1987 and re-opened in October 2003 on Jamaica's National Heroes Day. It provides not just an excellent small museum, but offers space for conferences, talks, and performative arts related to 'The Legacy of Marcus Garvey.'[58]

In his broadcasts, Muta provides practical recommendations for policies as well, for example, funding road works, as there are many pothole-ridden roads that call for repaving. Whereas the road to the prime minister's house is 'smoother than a baby bottom,' in his polemical remarks, solving the pothole issue doesn't appear on the government's main agenda.[59] He regularly laments the road conditions and their miserable maintenance. Furthermore, he requests a sponsored infrastructure to reuse rainwater, speaks about the need for an appropriate support of the Jamaican craft markets, or advocates the legalization of marijuana.[60] Although he has allegedly never smoked it himself, he regards 'the herbs as very important to the whole cultural aspect of Rastafari.'[61] Referring to the economic realm of self-reliance, he sees affirmative legalization as a potential source of revenue for the people and government. Another major concern for Muta is the construction of an 'official hall to represent music in all its splendour and glory, (since) music has done so much for Jamaica.'[62]

Even though he was specifically asked by some of his radio listeners to run for political office, this is no option for Muta. He smartly states his age as prohibitive reason and instead humorously encourages his younger radio colleagues, since it is up to the younger generation to accomplish change in the country, according to his view. Defiantly, he openly proclaims that he has never voted for any of the Jamaican parties.[63] His unwillingness to be considered for political functions and his refusal to vote clearly represent his Rastafari attitude to politics. Many Rastafari regard politics as *politricks* and hence don't vote in elections.[64] The term *politricks*, as many Rasta Houses label governmental action, derives from the supposition that politicians play 'tricks' on the citizens in order to achieve and maintain a privileged position.[65]

Michael Barnett also describes the concept of *Babylon* as a term that is oftentimes used by Rastas to denominate political institutions as suppressing the people.[66] Against this backdrop, Muta debates politicians' hypocrisy in his broadcasts and refers to a common saying in traditional African political systems, exemplified by many traditional state symbols, e.g., among the Akan nation in Ghana: 'Power corrupts, and absolute power corrupts absolutely.' There is an African history of this warning against autocrats in traditional kingship systems that runs back at least three centuries.[67]

Therefore the famous remark credited to Lord Acton, a nineteenth-century English historian and politician, who once stated that 'power tends to corrupt and absolute power corrupts absolutely,' may have had African forebears, glossed over by historical transmission.[68] This African reminder to the importance of rule of law and Acton's popular dictum implies that power of rulers needs to be restrained by checks and balances. This applies to all countries including Jamaica, which has a tradition of power and neglect of common people interests. Corruption and privileging self-interests by Jamaican parliamentarians and local officials have been exposed by the media, amplified by Reggae, by and large.

Whereas Muta doesn't necessarily regard all politicians as 'black-hearted people,' he argues that 'the political landscape of Jamaica brings out the worst in good people, and it makes good people do bad things.'[69] In this regard, he warns young and promising politicians not to get caught in a numb system of decision-makers where certain thought patterns are hegemonic and thus hard to overcome. Muta introduces the proverb 'you cyaan teach old dawg new trick,' meaning that it is not easy to convince long-established statesmen to rethink their political practices, since their habitus is difficult to alter.[70]

Mutabaruka detects and dissects this persistence in hour-long tirades, broadcasted live and direct. However, this does not serve the mere purpose of self-aggrandizement, as he gives voice to hope for the future rise of a new generation of politicians, open to the people's pleas. He counts on much greater inclusion of female representatives in Jamaica's parliament. This recent trend of a growing ratio of women in leadership positions as politicians and CEOs is for instance reflected by a study of the UN-affiliated *International Labour Organization* in 2018 on Jamaica. Accordingly, this Caribbean Island had a percentage of 59 per cent female managers and thus a higher proportion than any other country in the world.[71]

In academia, more women than men enrol in tertiary education, with an approximate 70:30 ratio.[72] In government, there was a record number of women elected in the general elections in September 2020.[73] These numbers indicate an ongoing development of Jamaican society at large. Although Jamaica may still be the androcentric society, as publicly deplored in many *Cutting Edge* commentaries by Mutabaruka, it seems that women themselves progressively succeed to break the walls of the male system. These trailblazers shape new gender roles and draw inherited structures of economic dependence, educational disadvantages, and political marginalization into question. The patriarchal ideology (un)consciously embodied in males and females, as the eminent Dancehall analyst Donna Hope remarked in *Inna Di Dancehall: Popular Culture and the Politics of Identity in Jamaica* in 2006, does not remain unchallenged almost two decades later.[74]

This appears fully in line with Muta's consistent rally for more respect for women, what he often refers to as 'the feminine energy.' The following statement on stage during his last live appearance in Austria at Vienna's Volksgarten ('people's garden') Club speaks volumes in this regard:

> I don't know of any God in the sky. The only place I know where God is, is in anyone inside here. Especially the females. Any religion I know comes from men. So religions were created by insecure men to oppress women. All religions oppress women, whether you are in Africa, Asia, or Europe. Religion was created by men because they are afraid of their mother, Mother Earth, Mother Nature. It is the feminine that creates and not the masculine. This is a serious thing. Because among indigenous people of the world, they understand the balance of earth to prevail between the male and the female. It is only in the Western world that people neglect the female energy or the feminine energy. So if you are a real man in your spirit and in your soul, I want you to turn to the nearest woman beside you inside here and say: 'I am sorry for fucking up the world.' You see, it is very difficult to say that. Yes, because if you look to the problems in the society today, it is created by men: all these weapons of mass destruction, these drones, and this and that. Where is our mother, where is our sister, and our grandmother? Our girlfriend, wife, and sweetheart? We need to awaken the feminine energy in the earth. The earth needs some feminine energy. That is why the earth is crying out its soul with all these wars and rumours of wars and nations rising against nations. And I never heard that a woman started a war yet. Every time me and my wife have a problem, I behave like I don't care and only when I go by myself, I figure out by myself: 'Bloodbath, I know that I am wrong.' But we are still scared to say that we are wrong because we are men. We must wake up because this thing gets wicked. This thing gets terrible out there and gave us a thing named religion, especially Christianity. This is where the problem started. We in the Caribbean got this Christianity.

This quote cited at some length exemplifies perhaps the range of influence on the international level. But it has tremendous relevance when aired consistently on the local and regional level as well. Except for some likeminded expressions of so-called Roots Reggae and the newer developments branded as Revival Reggae, gender equality, and a serious critique of male chauvinism are rarely the subject in Reggae and Dancehall music. Therefore, his self-critical questioning of moralities impacts on the self-understanding of masculinities and the empowerment of women at the same time.

As a radio presenter, Mutabaruka uses humour and intentional taboo breaking as means to bring his social and political criticism across. Carolyn Cooper, the Grande Dame of Reggae studies, calls him 'an organic media practitioner with native wit, (who is) able to get across his ideas lucidly.'[75] Although Muta never received training in the field of media representation, his early experiences in performing poems at school and his lecturing activities at Negril Beach Village, discussed in earlier chapters, shaped his skills to address large audiences, as many students at the University of Vienna, to choose our home turf as but one example, will happily confirm. Tony Rebel, himself a Reggae star and promoter of the famous Rebel Salute festival in Jamaica, emphasizes that the combination of Muta's humorous nature and comprehensive knowledge is what makes him truly special: 'Muta always gives the impression as if you are a weak heart and you can't come near. ... But if you get a chance to talk to him, he can be fun. He is a man who cracks some serious jokes, and he is somebody who you could see does a lot of research. He has a lot of knowledge.'[76]

The examples from his radio shows demonstrate his art of entertaining, hidden behind his self-ironically foregrounded (rhetorical) 'art of war.'

3.4. Selling Out Jamaica to Foreigners: About Imperceptible Funds and Chinese Investments

Chapter 3.1–3.2 examined Mutabaruka's radio suits against political power games of the JLP and the PNP. This showed how Jamaican *politricks* intersect with a corrupt, garrison-related, colour-class-associated, and neocolonial field. Now our focus turns towards another hotly debated topic in politics, namely Jamaica's use of resources and grants from foreign financial institutions, such as the International Monetary Fund (IMF) or powerful national investors like China.[77]

The structural dependence on monetary aid from abroad has a long history in Jamaica and is a frequent point of attack in Muta's narratives.[78] He doesn't see a notable and positive transformation of living conditions for 'the normal Jamaican citizen' and isn't impressed at all by the government's proclamations that IMF requirements were met successfully and that further financial assistance will be received.[79] Muta's impression rather correlates with Gallup-Healthways' *Global Well-Being Report* of 2014, which ranked Jamaica to position 115 (out of 145 countries) in the subcategory *Financial Well-Being* and thus placed the island last in the Caribbean region (even behind grief-stricken Haiti), and just between the challenged African countries of Ethiopia and Gabon.[80] Muta makes no effort to cover his frustration that Haiti is at a higher ranked position than Jamaica and, thus, alerts Jamaica's politicians: 'I don't know if the politicians take those reports serious!? ... Taking into consideration our perception of Haiti, one would never believe that the financial perception of Jamaican people is lower than Haitian perception of financial security.'[81]

Although international financial institutions declare that 'Jamaica has shown a macroeconomic turnaround that is quite extraordinary,' according to Muta the IMF's monetary support has been invisible on social terms and has not changed Jamaica's precarious situation, considering the high crime rate, the abysmal road conditions, or the influx of unhealthy food.[82] Generally, as a critic of global dependency, Muta doesn't appreciate IMF's financial support. It appears all too evident to him that it only caters for the private sector and some chosen people favoured by nepotism. He encourages his listeners to rebel against this corrupt system and insists on improvement and tangible benefits for the indigent masses of all Jamaicans:

> We don't talk about jacket and tie people who own place, own business, or this and that. We are talking about the people! The normal man on the road whom nobody asks no question what he thinks! These people you should look out for! ... The IMF still soaks up the people, and our government is telling you: 'Look here, don't worry, man, things are going to get better, you see it?! You see that we there on the right track.' Show me a country that borrows from the IMF and now gets all these things raised to a level where it can see the people living comfortably?!'[83]

The radio presenter recurrently uses his public platform to call for a perceptible implementation of foreign funds. This makes it quite understandable why he changed his medium of choice from Reggae to radio. With several hours per week, he has adequate means at hand to question the current state of affairs, in terms of prosperity distribution and stability measures facilitated through IMF funding. Muta is well aware of the experiences in numerous other so-called 'developing countries,' in which the implementation of IMF-guided adjustment schemes failed (or merely showed marginal achievements), for instance, in Argentina, Greece, and many African countries.[84] IMF advocates, by contrast, draw attention to Turkey, Brazil, Poland, and Tanzania as presumably successful examples in their publication *Successes of the International Monetary Fund*.[85]

More than a decade after this report, the sustainability of these efforts may be seriously questioned. Not just for the Jamaican radio analyst, it remains always debatable how long-lasting effects can be guaranteed, in contrast to the inflicted austerity measures that are demanded from recipient nations in return. It is a complex endeavour to lift a country out of economic recession, and there is not one copy and paste formula a state may follow, due to different geopolitical, economical, ecological, and social circumstances. Nevertheless, as Mutabaruka tries to examine, it often seems as if the IMF-guided structural adjustment programmes lead to forced policy adaptions, which include the reduction of public welfare expenditures. As a result, these regimes create financial instability, more unemployment, and social tensions, due to a rise in poverty and inequality as opposed to the overtly set goal, which is to induce economic recovery.

Due to a 'faith in market fundamentalism rather than programme outcomes,' the IMF usually demands labour market liberalization and privatization.[86] Critics argue that such policy implementations and adaptations – which are not only demanded by the IMF but also by other international institutions such as the World Bank and the World Trade Organization – mainly serve Western corporations, which then gain free access to precious natural resources (or raw materials) and regional markets.[87] Political scientist Jeffrey Harrod names other stakeholders (e.g., trade unions) that also play a crucial role in this often one-sided benefit plan once international corporations are involved:

> Multi-national corporations provide some of the most powerful bonds within the world market economy, but as these expand their operations in less developed countries, trade unions in the advanced countries where corporations have their headquarters follow the corporations abroad to try, through alliances with local groups, to influence the foreign environment. These emerging transnational structures take decisions of great consequence for the less developed countries in which they operate.[88]

In this regard, Muta's radio dissection of transnational economic policies appear quite in line with critical social science. Both highlight a tendency to serve imperialist and neocolonial interests of rich and powerful countries such as the US (although the interests are usually whitewashed as neoliberal actions). Transnational financial institutions like the IMF appear to rather contribute to the economical and geopolitical devastation of borrowing (and *developing*) countries than to aid them, and thus force those countries into a long-lasting bond that makes it nearly impossible to escape from. In his song 'Life And Debt,' Mutabaruka voices his concerns about financial aid:

> Too much importin' debt increase
>
> Country deh 'pon lease
>
> Politicians a fraud
>
> De people draw bad card
>
> Tings nuh cool
>
> Dem tek wi fi fool
>
> Gun shot in de street
>
> Blood 'pon sheet
>
> Sour nuh sweet
>
> Is life and debt all a wi a fret
>
> Life and debt freedom not yet[8]

In Jamaica, the IMF issue already begun in the late 1970s and has been a predicament for the Caribbean nation ever since.[90] The country's former prime minister Michael Manley was an advocate of self-reliance and an ardent critic of the hierarchical economic world order, deeply rooted in inequality and colonialism. In 1977, due to severe domestic economic difficulties, he unwillingly agreed to a short-term IMF loan. The loan's austerity agreements (reduction in public expenditure, removal of tariffs on imports, and privatization policies) badly affected Jamaica, primarily its working class and the great number of the unemployed. In the aftermath of Manley's support for Cuba during Angola's struggle for independence in 1975, the US-affiliated IMF wasn't willing to follow any long-term solutions for Jamaica, according to socialist voices.[91] Muta reminds his audience of these incidents as a form of economic power abuse by not only the IMF but also influential American policymakers:

> I saw them doing it in Jamaica in the 1970s, when everybody talked about Michael Manley running to Cuba and socialism and communism taking over. We saw America coming in with their things, and we saw poison flour there at the place. We saw coconuts dying, we saw old food at the supermarkets, and we saw everybody running for five flights a day to Miami. And America just did its things, and then changed Jamaica back the way it wanted.[92]

In the geopolitical Cold War antagonism, Manley's pro-Castro stance and his embrace of democratic socialism was not welcomed by some powerful actors in the West, especially the US. Allegedly, the CIA supported Manley's opposing candidate Edward Seaga and the pro-US Jamaica Labour Party by means of financial support and covert shipment of arms, in order to destabilize Manley's social policies and regain (US-American) control of Jamaica.[93]

Apart from the implications of this 'system of global destabilization,' as one caller in Muta's broadcast depicts Jamaica's situation concerning the IMF, the government obviously lacked discipline in managing its economic and finance system during the loan periods.[94] This could be another contributing factor to failed long-term results of the funding, as Muta points out:

> If you do some mathematics with the ratio what certain people get per week, in relationship to how much the government gets in loans and grants, you realize, 'but wait, these people have their PhD, but they lack intelligence,

man!' But they don't say that they have no intelligence, because they are going to tell you: 'Bwoy, right now the people don't understand economics.' Nobody doesn't understand economics like a woman who sells scallion, thyme, and ice. I know a woman whose ice cream sale made it possible to send her child to university. Ice! Can you believe that?[95]

Muta thereby deconstructs the government's agency pertaining to mismanagement and misappropriation. Since he is always pragmatic, he recommends decision-makers to seek advice from Jamaica's market vendors – mostly women or 'ooman' as he calls them in Jamaican talk – who really and truly comprehend economics from practice. Most notably, he lauds a female ice (cream) seller who enabled her child to attend university by selling her product. For years, Jamaica became struck in a vicious cycle of repayments. Hence, current loans go to the IMF as refunds for previous debts.[96] In fact, ongoing debts complicate the country's situation as institutions such as the IMF have the upper hand on the country's monetary status and, consequently, its domestic affairs. Mutabaruka addresses this 'foreign takeover' and embeds Jamaica's financial and economic situation in a broader social discourse:

> You have to sacrifice what is going on in Jamaica with Jamaican women, who sacrifice themselves for their children. Because when they go home every time and see their children bawling, they realize and say: 'Bwoy, right now anything to make the children survive!' And they end up in a very serious, precarious position. Sometimes you hear a man saying: 'Dutty gyal this, dutty that.' But sometimes the dirtiness there is helping a little youth, and we don't tell any woman about prostitution or whoredom, you know. It is not because they degrade and downplay themselves, but because they take the interest of a next life at heart! She knows that her little children don't have a father who brings them to school. They don't get food and clothes. And she is the only one who provides that! So I am just saying that the government helps to perpetuate such things! The government helps to make these things continuing and then sits down there like a pimp! Yes, I say it! Who doesn't like it, buss! … They make Jamaican people prostitute themselves, and they sell out the country

> to foreigners! And the people don't have nothing to get out
> of it! Nothing! … They soon want to sell the people, too![97]

Speech acts like this touch the heart of many Jamaicans who may not dare to frame their situation like this. In this talk about the experiential realm of Jamaican everyday life, particularly for single-household mothers, the outspoken radio presenter debates the sad but common situation in which many Jamaican women find themselves stuck. It is not unusual that – out of desperation and as a last option to feed their children – women see no other option than becoming sex-workers.[98] Muta regards Jamaica's leaders as the real procurers of this social ill since they seemingly consign the country to foreign financial institutions and thus to powerful stakeholders in bilateral arrangements.

The situation became even more serious in recent times because Jamaica doesn't only depend on financial backing from the IMF but also on funding from various foreign investors, especially from China. The latter super-power is already the biggest source of foreign direct investments for Jamaica. In fact, there is an ongoing trend of Chinese investments in the Caribbean.[99] One of 'the most striking sign(s) that the Chinese treasure ship has arrived in the Caribbean' was the financing of Jamaica's new highway construction, employing hundreds of Chinese workers.[100] In return, the Jamaican government handed over twelve hundred acres of land to China. Mutabaruka sarcastically comments on this arrangement as follows:

> I feel that we should just make the Chinese build all the
> roads and give them a portion of the land. Just give them
> most of Jamaica, like Portland and St Ann. All of the
> land, just give it to them. Because it is inevitable. You sold
> out all the beach land already to the Spaniards and some
> other people. You know, it is like there is a need to sell out
> Jamaica to foreigners. It is like this government follows the
> government before them. We see that's going on.[101]

Although Muta considers infrastructure development as 'a symbol of progress,' he is sceptical of the large number of road constructions and buildings sponsored by the Chinese government.[102] During the past decade, road constructions and road-rehabilitation projects happened all over the island. Since Jamaica is referred to not only by

Muta as a 'pothole country,' improvement and maintenance of roads is certainly important. The question, however, remains: At what cost comes such seemingly positive progress? Like the IMF issue, foreign funding provides Jamaica with an ever-growing debt and dependency. In April 2019, Jamaica signed a memorandum of understanding on the so-called *Belt and Road Initiative* (BRI) with China, enabling the Asian investor to strengthen its economic and geopolitical power even more.[103] Given that the Jamaican government forces vendors to move from their market stalls due to road constructions, as in the case of the Constant Spring market, Muta advises his fellow citizens to investigate their situation:

> Yes, lots of development. And in deposit of developing, it inconveniences the normal Jamaican people. ... Tivoli Gardens people, Muta tell you this! They are going to rejuvenate and re-establish Kingston as the centre. And they cannot afford that certain places stay like how they stay and operate now. You might just see some very strange activity going on. You really have to open your eye wide and wonder what is taking place. I am saying it. They don't know which part to sell. Constant Spring market. ... And we are talking about movement of people outside of their environment where they have been for years, from before I was born! So we are going to watch what is going on. I don't say development doesn't take place, you know. But when development takes place, and you make the masses of the people feel uncomfortable about this development because they own no land. And if you don't own land, you have no power. Land is the basis of power. ... Most Jamaican people don't have land. So the government can come in and move you and tell you: 'Right now you are here for many years, but now we have the authority to build road there. No matter if you own it or not, we can just give you money, mash it down and just do what we want to do.' It is a weird situation. We are watching it.[104]

Muta hereby addresses a common occurrence in global infrastructure developments: People are forcefully removed from the land in their possession to become internally displaced regardless of their legal entitlement of occupancy. Forced resettlement is the political activity of displacement that puts people into hardship, as was the case in

Jamaica during the 1960s when thousands of Rastafari had been forcibly removed from the Rastafari community formerly known as Back O' Wall.[105] Nowadays, similar developments are looming, and thus Muta emphasizes the importance of land ownership, as it stands for power. Above all, he views the Chinese actions as a new form of land-grabbing close to informal colonization and expresses his anger thereover:

> We get colonized slowly but surely. But you see how the leaders here don't understand colonialism and how colonialism creep in upon. Because a man doesn't need to whip you, lash you, and put you in slavery to colonize your place, you know. They have different means and methods to colonize countries. Yes! And these leaders, these boasy slaves, they see everything as development. They see everything as investment.[106]

In his *Cutting Edge* and *Steppin Razor* broadcasts, Muta regularly expresses his belief that Jamaica's politicians still perpetuate the unjust system of slavery, particularly when they accept bilateral deals with the most powerful nations like the US and China.

This section has considered Mutabaruka's talks about Jamaica's long-standing foreign financial dependency and its disregard of the common citizen. It provided evidence on his overt scepticism towards foreign grants. In contrast, he consistently pleads for policies more attached and relevant to the people and to social justice in Jamaica, such as at least a fair distribution of the IMF funds and accountable discipline in managing the country's finances. A dramatic side effect of the current mismanagement is a miserable and unequal situation for Jamaica's class-characterized society. In this context, a strongly politicized environment contributes even more to social tensions and, subsequently, a high crime rate, as we will debate in the next chapter.

NOTES

1. Figueroa/Sives (2003, 65).
2. CE 12 (2017).
3. The background that eventually led to the CIA's interference is clarified in chapter 3.4.

4.   Cf. Edie (2011, 3, 24f.); Edmonds (2016); Figueroa/Sives (2003); Leslie (2010, 12f.); Zips (2015, 141–66).

5.   SR 6 (2015).

6.   SR 43 (2017). Note: In the garrison communities, a gang leader is called *don*. See also Edmonds (2016, 60).

7.   Cf. *Jamaica Observer* (2017a).

8.   Cf. Arias (2017, 87–89) and Edmonds (2016, 59f).

9.   SR 43 (2017).

10.   Cf. *Jamaica Observer* (2017b).

11.   Cf. CE 12 (2017); SR 17 (2015); SR 43 (2017).

12.   SR 42 (2017).

13.   SR 17 (2015).

14.   In this connection, cf. Edie (2011, 13–21).

15.   Hawthorne (2018, 109).

16.   SR 49 (2017).

17.   Ibid.

18.   Cf. Radio Jamaica News (2017).

19.   SR 40 (2017). This, of course, is a pun intended on the now-common practice of telephone scamming celebrated by some Dancehall artistes who openly celebrate their fame and fortune made by scamming, cf. Chung (2020, 50–55).

20.   SR 40 (2017).

21.   English translation: *Cock's mouth kills the cock.*

22.   SR 40 (2017).

23.   In fact, the British monarchy with King Charles III as head of state is part of the Parliament of Jamaica, represented by the Governor-General of Jamaica.

24.   SR 40 (2017).

25.   Ibid.

26.   During an on-air conversation with a caller, Muta says that he will wear shoes for the concert tour in the US as he is old and 'cannot walk naked in the cold now' SR 6 (2015).

27.   Cf. SR 14 (2015).

28.   Fanon (1963, 144).

29.   SR 6 (2015).

30.   Being largely modelled on the British honours system, the well-established Jamaican honours system has been in place since 1969 as a result of the National Honours and Awards Act. It allots six different orders, reaching from the Order of Distinction to the Order of National Hero, cf. National Honours and Awards Act (2002). Hitherto, only a small group of seven people have fulfilled the conditions to receive the order, who are: the Maroons leader Nanny, the rebellious insurrectionist Samuel Sharpe, the instigator of the Morant Bay rebellion Paul Bogle, the anti-colonial politician George William Gordon, the legendary

pan-Africanist Marcus Mosiah Garvey, the JLP founder Sir Alexander Bustamante, and the PNP co-founder Norman Washington Manley.

31. Cf. inter alia Charles (2004); Charles and Beckford (2012); Figueroa and Sives (2002); Meeks (2008); Rapley (2003); Zips (2011b).

32. Lewis (2001, 136f).

33. Cf. Hope (2006, 38f); Paul (2009); Robinson-Walcott (2009: 107–12).

34. SR 17 (2015). Note: Muta smartly quotes his lyrics from the tune *Out Of Many One* (1994b) in this speech.

35. Cf. Smith (1988).

36. Robinson-Walcott (2009, 107).

37. According to the *Jamaica Health and Lifestyle Survey III (2016–2017)*, approximately 11 per cent of Jamaicans bleach(ed) their skin, that is about three hundred thousand people, cf. Ministry of Health and Wellness (2018, 3).

38. See also Hope (2006, 36–45) and Hope (2011, 167, 183).

39. SR 39 (2017).

40. Cf. SR 9 (2015).

41. Cf. Hope (2006, 7, 9) and Nettleford (1979, 9f).

42. Theoretical anthropology has this to say on the quality of belonging, the true prophet requires for adequate representation of the people: A shared habitus, shaped by common experiences and a similar upbringing is essential to create bonding between a prophet (in this case represented through Muta) and his/her audience, in famous sociologist Pierre Bourdieu (2013, 81) words:

   The habitus is precisely this immanent law, *lex insita*, laid down in each agent by his earliest upbringing, which is the precondition not only for the co-ordination of practices but also for practices of co-ordination, since the corrections and adjustments the agents themselves consciously carry out presuppose their mastery of a common code and since undertakings of collective mobilization cannot succeed without a minimum of concordance between the habitus of the mobilizing agents (e.g., prophet, party leader, etc.) and the dispositions of those whose aspirations and world-view they express.

43. Cf. Zips (2006c); see also the DVD 'Mutabaruka: The Return to the Motherland' by Zips (2011a).

44. Cf. Mutabaruka (2006a).

45. Nettleford (1979, 3).

46. On the postcolonial critique see: Mbembe (2001); Eriksen (2015, 45f); Sulikowski/Khittel (2011); and Rapport/Overing (2000, 12f, 16, 98).

47. One of our interviewees had indeed quite a negative opinion about Mutabaruka due to his skin colour-related distinctions. The elderly Jamaican, himself married to a white American woman, demanded that Muta shouldn't divide that strong between Black and white, but establish a foundation to help deprived people.

48. Cf. Gilroy (1993, 1–15).

49. Cf. 'H.I.M. Haile Selassie I squashes the argument: Meet the Press, October 1963' on YouTube: https://www.youtube.com/watch?v=hh7I-pYn4-4.
50. SR 2 (2014).
51. SR 40 (2017).
52. Garvey (1987, 30).
53. Ibid., 30f.
54. SR 40 (2017).
55. Ibid.
56. Cf. SR 20 (2016). Sometimes Jamaican politicians even use murder-imagery, as it was the case with Joylan Silvera (PNP) and his statement about associate Lisa Hanna (PNP). In order to defend his female comrade, he announced that anyone who would trouble Lisa Hanna would die. Muta analyses the situation as follows: 'Murder in Jamaica gets so prevalent now. When a politician gets up and says, 'anybody who touches the queen is going to be dead,' that is supposed to bring outrage to the people. But so many other things are going on, that people just pass that!' (SR 12: 2)
57. CE 14 (2017).
58. Black resistance and separatism from white supremacy and systemic racism in postcolonial systems are constant themes, as for instance in the 2022 Call for Papers for the Journal of Liberty Hall on the theme 'Race First: Resistance and its Limitation,' cf. Liberty Hall (2022).
59. SR 1 (2014).
60. Cf. SR 30 (2016); SR 32 (2016); SR 46 (2017). Note: Since 2015, marijuana has already been decriminalized in Jamaica.
61. SR 15 (2015).
62. SR 14 (2015).
63. Cf. SR 17 (2015) and SR 43 (2017).
64. Rastafari had not always turned away from political engagement or withheld their votes at elections. General scepticism toward politics arose in the 1940s after they felt betrayed by the politicians. See also Barnett (2012, 29f.) and Chevannes (1994, 146–51).
65. Cf. Edmonds (2003, 49f).
66. Cf. Barnett (2018, 77f).
67. Cf. Zips (2007, 123–30; 2011b, 104–183), who relates the Maroon political and legal systems to its African heritage.
68. Dalberg-Acton (1887, 9).
69. SR 20 (2016).
70. SR 32 (2016). Note: *Habitus* in social science refers to the persistence of internalized, inherited attitudes, practices, and lines of thought. On the political level this allows for a historical analysis of its deeper roots in colonial structures. Pierre Bourdieu (1990, 60f.) describes such deep-rooted schemes of the habitus: '… the *habitus* tends to ensure its own

constancy and its defence against change through the selection it makes within new information by rejecting information capable of calling into question its accumulated information, if exposed to it accidentally or by force, and especially by avoiding exposure to such information.'

71. Cf. International Labour Organization (2018, 34f).
72. Cf. University Office of Planning (2018, 6).
73. Cf. McLeod (2020).
74. Cf. Hope (2006, 37).
75. Interview 2 (2018).
76. Ibid.
77. Jamaica also receives funds from the European Union's European Development Fund (EDF) and the World Bank. However, those are only mentioned in passing in Muta's programmes. See also Reynolds-Baker (2014) and World Bank (2014).
78. Cf. Girvan (1971, 99–161).
79. SR 31 (2016). For a detailed explanation of the IMF testing and its procedure cf. Haughton (2016).
80. Cf. Gallup-Healthways (2015, 5–7).
81. SR 11 (2015).
82. Trotsenburg (2019); also cf. SR 11 (2015).
83. SR 9 (2015).
84. Cf. Friederich/Harb (2018); Mohashin (2017); Mussa (2002).
85. Cf. Brau/MacDonald (2009). Note: This publication was edited by former IMF staff members in order to counter the negative and controversial image of the IMF and its funding schemes.
86. Mohashin (2017, 678).
87. Cf. Africa W (2015).
88. Harrod (1972, xvii).
89. This powerful poem by Mutabaruka (2002) performed on a Reggae riddim was chosen as the theme song for the documentary film by the same title *Life and Debt* of Stephanie Black (2001). Even more than two decades later it is worth watching and over time it became a historic document in itself, featuring many knowledgeable political actors such as the late Michael Manley, prime minister during the first IMF sanctioned periods in the 1970s until the 1990s.
90. Cf. Edmonds (2016) and Henke (2000).
91. Cf. Bakan (2007) and Meeks (2017). Note: A first-hand insight of Jamaica's financial crisis at that time is provided by Michael Manley's book *Up the Down Escalator* (1987) and the documentary film *Life and Debt* (2001).
92. SR 45 (2017).
93. Cf. Edmonds (2016, 61–67).
94. SR 31 (2016).
95. SR 1 (2014).

96. As of September 30, 2019, Jamaica had an outstanding loan in the amount of SDR 470.17 million (equivalent to about €581 million), cf. International Monetary Fund (2019).
97. SR 1 (2014).
98. Cf. Henry (2016).
99. For further information and detailed figures of Chinese investments in Jamaica and the Caribbean cf. Bernal (2016).
100. Laville (2015).
101. SR 50 (2017).
102. Ibid.
103. Cf. Clarke (2019).
104. SR 50 (2017). Also cf. *Jamaica Observer* (2019).
105. Cf. Edmonds (2003, 84).
106. SR 32 (2016).

Muta Live at Reggae Sunsplash, Montego Bay, Jamaica 1984
Photo: Werner Zips

Muta Live at Reggae Sunsplash, Montego Bay, Jamaica 1984
Photo: Werner Zips

*Muta with a Jamaican delegation of Rasta elders in
Baltimore, USA late 1980s*

Photo: Mutabaruka private archive

Filmmaker Haile Gerima and Winnie Mandela with Muta, South Africa

Photo: Mutabaruka private archive

Muta with family, Cape Coast Castle, Ghana 1997
Photo: Werner Zips

Muta with Ghanaba at Panafest, Cape Coast Castle, Ghana 1997
Photo: Werner Zips

Muta with Ghanaba at Panafest, Cape Coast Castle, Ghana 1997
Photo: Werner Zips

Muta, Treasure Beach, Jamaica 2003
Photo: Werner Zips

Muta with the Rastafari community in Shashamane, Ethiopia 2005
Photo: Mutabaruka private archive

Muta with Baby I and Bongo Rocky in Shashamane, Ethiopia 2005
Photo: Mutabaruka private archive

Muta, St. Andrew, Jamaica 2007
Photo: Mutabaruka private archive

Muta at New Style Radio, Birmingham, UK 2007
Photo: Mutabaruka private archive

CHAPTER 4

'LIKE WE ARE IN A CIVIL WAR'
On Jamaica's Crime Situation

One hundred-odd people murdered in one month, and we are not in a war! This is not Syria, Iraq, or Afghanistan. And that is what they know about. Next month they find somebody they haven't found yet.

Mutabaruka: *Cutting Edge*, September 7 (2017)

Jamaica people must recognize how serious it is! When you live in a country and one thousand-odd people get murdered in one year, and we are not in a civil war! Rhaatid! … This is how Jamaica stays now. You have to be paranoid; you must get dizzy! You cannot walk and just keep your head straight. You have to turn your head 360 degrees, like the girl in 'The Exorcist' film who takes a spin.

Mutabaruka: *Steppin Razor*, January 7 (2016)

We really want to recognise that the government doesn't seem to know what to do as it relates to the crime. We see that they are calling meetings in Montego Bay, and meanwhile the police decides that they are going on some sick leave, you know. I mean it's weird. The violence keeps going on and on. I don't know if them know, but take me serious! The whole country is traumatized! Yes, literally traumatized with what is going on!

Mutabaruka: *Steppin Razor*, December 21 (2017)

These excerpts decidedly show how bewildering everyday violence is considered by Mutabaruka. He raises this subject at all possible occasions. We witnessed a similar public speech given at the famous Rebel Salute festival in 2007, when the crime rate shot up to frightening heights. Besides politics, Jamaica's crime situation is Mutabaruka's second most debated topic in the *Cutting Edge* and *Steppin Razor* programmes. The country was once called the 'murder capital of the world.'[1] Apart from having experienced one of the highest murder rates worldwide for many years, there remain other worrying policing issues.[2] The Caribbean island seems to be an ideal stopover for drug trafficking from South to North America and currently faces a hype of lottery scamming, which further triggers a souring associated crime rate on the Northwest coast of Jamaica.[3] The prevalent scamming practice depends on 'phone solicitation to deceive Americans into wiring large sums of money to Jamaica' and leads to an entire informal value chain of criminality, including extortion, prostitution, and gang violence.[4]

What is commonly referred to as 'tribal warfare' in Jamaica has haunted the Western part of the island, turning the former tourist region around Montego Bay into a trouble zone.[5] Mutabaruka does not concede to sweep this issue under the table, because it might affect tourism. He frequently zooms in on the scamming dilemma and sheds light on the complexity of Jamaica's present crime problems. We therefore examine the emergence of this con game that is no game at all, given the serious consequences for social security. Prospects of quick gains allure many disadvantaged Jamaicans to their own misfortune in the long run. Muta, of course, contextualizes these developments with his debates on the reputation of police and Jamaica's anti-informer attitudes, often supported through Reggae/Dancehall music, and presents possible solutions for socially sound and sustainable crime prevention measures.

4.1. About Scamming and Its Implications

According to press reports and public opinion, this organized fraud scheme became widespread in Jamaica through the introduction of call centres. Their operators received the means at hand to start the 'scamming craze.' Many international call centres have been established in Jamaica since the 1990s, because of outsourcing telephone services from North America and Europe. Montego Bay and the surrounding parish of St James became its main base. In those call centres, employees were not only trained in customer service skills, but also in dealing with enquiries for international (mostly US-American) corporations and hence received access to lists of potential targets' telephone numbers and other data, the so-called *lead lists*. Although meanwhile such lists are sold by *brokers* who work between Jamaica and the US, it is assumed that call centre employees passed on the first lists giving the telephone scam boom a rocket launch.

Accordingly, a Jamaican scammer, who perhaps worked as an operator or at least appropriated customer service attributes, data, and call centre procedures, undertakes telephone calls with people from the lead lists and tricks them into believing that they won cash prizes, vehicles, or vacation getaways in the lottery. Sometimes, they are told that the credit commission owes them some money. To receive the prize or money, the victims – mostly senior citizens or amateur gamblers from the US – are asked to pay certain fees and taxes. They are told to transfer money via financial services such as MoneyGram and Western Union or to provide their credit card information. Scam done. If the boasting raps of many Trap-Dancehall tunes in recent history provide a reliable indicator, this seems to be hugely successful.[6]

Such large-scale Jamaican lottery scams occasionally involve dozens of self-employed contractors who, according to reports of such a case against thirty-one individuals, sometimes bilk up to more than one hundred elderly people (mostly Americans) out of sums of more than US$6 million.[7] One can easily envision the large sums of money that scammers deal with undetected on a daily basis. It is estimated that lottery scams generate US$120 million to US$1 billion revenue a year. In comparison, Jamaica's tourism industry accounts for US$2 billion per year. What Mutabaruka calls the 'scamming industry' has become a huge public affair in the US, ending in lengthy investigations by the FBI.[8]

Although this informal business has been booming since 2007, in the last few years the lottery scam ventures have entered another dimension.[9] It initiated a crime wave in Jamaica related inter alia to fierce competition that has led to several *State of Public Emergency (SOE)* declarations and an exceptionally high murder rate in rural Western parishes.[10] In 2018, SOEs were declared in several areas and parishes all over the island. Checkpoints were implemented in the entire parish of St James, causing roadblocks becoming a common sight, and turning most drivers into suspected criminals. Distribution battles over the previously mentioned lead lists led to many homicides in the Western parishes (St James, Westmoreland, and Hanover). As a valuable commodity, or key means of production for this industry, access to these data became highly contested. Rivalries, alleged treacheries, and blackmailing triggered series of manhunts between gangs, and interventions of police and even military forces. Predominant motives for murder in Jamaica have shifted from political strives and competition over drug trafficking to vendetta campaigns over lead lists and related matters. In a report published in *VICE* magazine in 2017, Kevin Watson, an investigator in Jamaica's Major Organised Crime Anti-Corruption Agency (MOCA), speaks of a deadly cycle:

> … gangs that once fought for control of the drug trade now kill each other for access to lead lists, which include names and phone numbers for would-be victims. People who handle scam money are shot for taking more than their allotted cut. Friends and family members seek revenge. Money from the scam pays for more guns and perpetuates the cycle.[11]

Muta readily refers to the government as 'the biggest scammer in Jamaica' arguing that Jamaican people have simply learned from the government 'to go above bone.'[12] Acting out his rhetorical skills, he debates the ongoing reprisal killings by reference to a well-known Jamaican proverb: *If yuh cyaan ketch Quaco, yuh ketch him shut*, meaning in that case retaliation by hurting the wanted person's relatives and friends:

> Because you know what the men do now? If dem cyaan ketch Quaco, dem ketch him shut, you know. When they cannot find the gangster, they kill the gangster's woman. When they killed the woman, the gangsters retaliate. And they hope that when the gangsters have retaliated, now they can end up and kill the gang. But the gang kills some of them. It is a vicious thing going on in Montego Bay.[13]

Such vengeful actions and reprisal killings are sadly common in violent rivalries between opposing lottery scam rings. The quest for potential victims' data and struggles over control of gang territory led to an upsurge in scamming-related homicides, making the search for anti-crime policies a high priority in Jamaica.

Before it turned into a lethal threat, the lottery scam had found some tacit complicity in impoverished urban and rural communities for its leverage in funding better housing and business opportunities.[14] Some parts of Jamaican society regarded (and perhaps still regard) the telephone scam rather a legitimate source of income than a criminal or illegal activity. Many varnish it as some sort of 'entrepreneurship for sufferers' and a redistribution of global capital as a form of reparation for colonial exploitation.[15] Economic anthropologist Jovan Scott Lewis reports on a group of Jamaican scammers who justified their scam by stating it would rectify the discrepancy between the hardship of Black Jamaicans and the material well-being of white Americans:

> There is a recognized genealogy of this exploitation's custodianship, which has changed hands over the decades with the postcolonial reorientation of British-Jamaican trade and political relations to that of Jamaica and the US. The US has become a site of engagement which not only produces notions of mobility and aspiration, but also transgression. Through the transference of that transgression's proprietorship, scammers pliantly reason that the US has acquired Great Britain's moral debts, a view which conflates race with a shift in geopolitical power and labor relations. ... In this conflation, race – and whiteness, in particular – serves as a mode of power through inequality, and thus offers a steady marker of blame across its permutations and exchanges.[16]

Lewis alludes to Jamaica's complex historical, social, and geopolitical situation. Our interviews and informal talks with many Jamaicans indicate a sentiment of victimhood, based on the experience of Black subordination from the days of enslavement and white colonial supremacy. This, in the eyes of many, legitimizes the transformation of the inherited inequality by any means. Unabated economic disparities into the age of neoliberal globalization and failed national development encourage the vindication of illegal activities in a race to get even.

In a country with a presumably corrupt administration, burdened by international debt, and a flagging economy struck by high unemployment, many people consider illegal activities such as scamming as a last resort to feed their families, break through economic and social boundaries, and become independent.[17] The practice of telephone scamming thrives within the distorted field of an island economy based on accumulated history of dependency. Driven by the desire for scarce economic capital, many scammers invest considerable time in their (self-)education in customer service matters, call centre operations, or IT skills. In sociologist Pierre Bourdieu's terms, this newly acquired cultural capital converts into symbolic capital, when material status symbols such as expensive cars, clothes, and lifestyles earn prestige through the power of recognition.[18] Within a postcolonial scope of emancipation from subjection, scamming takes on a sense of liberation. Mutabaruka illustrates this way out of poverty and unemployment in relation to often enough broken promises attached to better education:

> You have a youth, and you send him to school, and you pay money for the school so that he can get a good education. Then when he leaves school, he wants to go to university and the parents try their best to get money for the university. Because the system tells you that if you get a good education and you go to university, you are going to get a good job when you are finished. You are going to earn more money so that you can buy the necessary things to make your life comfortable in Jamaica. The parents are buying into this argument and find any means necessary to send their children to university. And the children spend many years at university and when they come out, they cannot get a job! They don't tell the children that self-reliance is the greatest science. You must not want an education for a job. You must want an education to be a better person! And if you go to university, it may result in becoming a better person so that when you leave the university, you are not afraid to go get a job and you try to create a job for yourself! ... So the youths who hoped to get a job, not knowing that the system doesn't have a job to give them, they have to start being creative in their thinking! And most of the creativity is what they call unlawful! You think that the youths who are doing the scam in Montego Bay are some idiot youths? The youths know what they are doing! And they know that it is illegal but guess what?!

> They see a way out! ... The youths cannot get no work and
> the youths go so: 'Bam!' Trying something unlawful, very
> unlawful, too! And they get through. ... The youths just use
> their intelligence and put their university knowledge to an
> unlawful way! We recognize that the law does not deal with
> justice! We see that in America, we see that here! The law is
> there to protect the system; the law doesn't protect justice![19]

This reveals that Muta neither clearly supports the *unlawful* scamming
practices nor demeans the people involved. He rather assails the
legislative and political system, which, according to him, doesn't focus
on justice for the people but on the maintenance of the status quo.
Furthermore, one can identify yet again his Rastafari approach to
self-empowerment, owed in part to the likes of Leonard Howell and
Marcus Garvey, when he postulates that 'self-reliance is the greatest
science.' In this respect, he views scamming as a possible way out of
a financial crisis leading to autonomy, without discharging the activity
from causing tremendous social ills.

In Jamaica, activities that are essential for survival are subsumed
under the commonly used term *hustling*, regardless of their formal
legality and informal economic nature. Muta depicts this situation in
the following way: 'And everybody is trying to hustle a thing. Pure
hustling is going on in Jamaica. No constructive work takes place. Many
people are hustling and making money.'[20] He implicates the absence
of formal or, what he calls, *constructive* jobs, which represent a major
reason for people's immersion in hustling, especially illegal hustling.
Dennis Chung, one of Jamaica's leading commentators on financial
and economic matters, speaks about Jamaica's *culture of hustling* on his
blog *DC Jottings*:

> ... most Jamaicans are 'doing a business' and are not 'in
> business.' What this basically means is that many of us are
> really just trying to earn money through 'hustling.' This
> is not only restricted to business startups, but it seems as
> if Jamaica has a culture of 'hustling.' So the youngsters
> who start off selling or wiping the car glass is doing it for
> a hustle. Or the politician, or public sector worker, who
> engages in corrupt practices thinks it is ok because they are
> just doing a 'hustle.' Or the university student who applies
> for a job and when you ask them what their career goal

is they say they don't know yet but just want the job as something to do and make a money. What is even more frightening is the Jamaican culture, and our governance, supports the 'hustler mentality.' … Those in authority also refuse to do anything about the situation, and we even have formal government programmes that promise job creation through mass employment. These are nothing more than programmes that give people a fish rather than teach them to fish. That is nothing more than an election promise of a 'hustle.' … Because of this hustler mentality, we have created today a huge problem of a large informal economy, numerous informal settlements, and a set of persons who cannot create any value for themselves because they have, for example, grown up learning how to sell on the streets or wipe car glasses.[21]

Chung argues that spin-offs of a hustle mentality conform with a general lack of law and order, a high crime rate, and regressive productivity and compensation, which in turn leads to the overtaxing of the few productive fields caused by dependency on IMF loans. Muta sums up these long-standing challenges of Jamaica without overdue solutions, or at least feasible counteractions, in a similar manner:

I mean, really and truly! When we see the carnage that is happening on the road, we don't blame government, you know! But I am just saying, really and truly, if the laws of the country put into effect and then you have some law and order, you would have less things to worry about! And the things that you worry about, you could alleviate those worries! But now we have problems that we cannot solve, and we have problems that we create ourselves! Because we cannot solve the problems that the politicians make us have! … And some of them don't want to listen! You have police officers who say that they don't go to certain places and rather 'make the boys kill one another!' If a man kills one another, how are you going to have a stable country?[22]

As Muta wants the government to feel much more responsible, he addresses the importance of law-abiding politicians and authorities to sustain solidarity within society. Jamaica's unstable situation, for him, almost automatically triggers a (criminal) chain reaction. For many Jamaicans, scamming is just another form of hustling and merely a characteristic trait of Jamaica's defective law and order status. It is seen by many as a form of economic self-defence, and thus celebrated in Dancehall tunes, currently in the laid-back Hip-Hop clubbing offshoot of Trap. Trap-Dancehall celebrates the trickster wit involved in telephone scams, which hardly ever led to convictions because of legal loopholes for lottery scammers until 2013. After Jamaica's anti-lottery scamming law was finally passed in March 2013, many more fraudsters have been arrested.[23] However, it seems that the bill only partly serves its purpose since the scamming *business* appears already deeply rooted and finds ways to continue thriving.

4.2.   Out of Control: The Police in Jamaica

For decades, Jamaica's police called the Jamaica Constabulary Force (JCF) has been faced with devastating records of police-involved murders on the one hand and a high homicide rate among officers on the other, according to official statistics.[24] The first aspect is linked to corruption prevalent in Jamaica's security apparatus, which coheres with a political system considered equally corrupt by many citizens and international observers alike.[25] According to an Amnesty International report in 2016, there exist credible accusations of police officers carrying out extrajudicial executions on state authorities' orders or, at least, with their complicity. Furthermore, the report states that between 2005 and 2015, more than 2,350 people were killed during police operations.[26] Although a decline of these killings has been registered in recent years through the efforts of the Independent Commission of Investigations (INDECOM), a police watchdog mechanism established in 2010, there are hardly any convictions of police officers for murder, nor hardly any prosecutions of corruption due to Jamaica's slow and ineffective justice system.[27]

The high corruption rate appears as an entrenched attribute of Jamaica's political and judicial, as well as social and economic structures.[28] Due to the profoundness of the matter, it proves difficult to effectively tackle corruption and its institutionalization. Once again, it is crucial to scrutinize the current situation within the historical framework of the island's colonial past. Structures of policing, once established by the colonial masters, are still maintained and reproduced by state officials, as political sociologist Anthony Harriott points out:

> The primary universal value associated with the police role
> in ex-colonial societies is that of order (not justice), which
> is interpreted in its concreteness as defence of the existing
> order and thus of the special interests dominant in that
> order.[29]

In a postcolonial society like Jamaica, the self-understanding of
the police reveals a colonial habitus, which is to uphold a system of
domination and to serve Jamaica's political order. The large-scale
involvement of police officers in violence and crime provides evidence
in this regard. There exists a broad consensus among citizens that all
state-run institutions are affected by corruption – a perception that
contributes to distrust of the state and to withdrawal of civil society
from crime control and other involvements in collective action.[30]
Against this obvious tendency of non-cooperation, emphasized in
many Reggae tunes, Mutabaruka frequently insists that collective
agency is necessary and demands cooperation between police and
civil society, in order to fight crime more effectively and accelerate
legal investigations.[31] However, he knows about the problems with
the so-called 'informer fi dead' culture, which corresponds to a
widespread mindset in Jamaican society, condemning 'snitches,' who
inform authorities on illegal action.[32] What is commonly justified for
minor offences, such as 'ganja hustling,' also hinders the exposure and
elucidation of many other criminal offences, including rape and even
murder:

> You have many mothers, sweethearts, wives, and girlfriends
> out there, who know that their man or their son kills and
> murders people, and they come home to them and hug
> them up tight in bed, and even wash the blood stains out
> of their shirts. A terrible thing! We understand that one
> of the reasons why the people don't want to work with
> the police is because the police has been so devious in the
> past in relationship to you when you report a man in the
> community. The same policeman goes in the community
> and tells the don: 'Sister Jane came down there and told
> me that you did this and that.' And the same woman has to
> leave the area now because they say: 'She is an informer.'
> It is not an easy thing to do! … When you see a man killing
> and raping a little girl in your community and because of
> fear you don't do anything about it, you are guilty, too!

> Because if you watch that happening and do nothing about it, you are as guilty as the man who raped and killed the little girl![33]

Whereas Muta alludes to the venal, crime-linked element within the police force as the main reason why so many people suspect authorities collude with criminals or dons of the affected communities, he nevertheless regards individuals unwilling to cooperate with the police as witnesses as equally morally guilty as murderers themselves.[34] He names Dancehall music as one reason for the Jamaican 'informer fi dead' mentality:

> All the music that the uneducated and illiterate artistes make, telling you about 'informer fi dead' and 'informer fi this' and 'informer fi that,' is because their child never got killed or raped by none of these mad people! … It is not only the incompetence of the police force, but one of the reasons why you see so many of these things happening is also due to the cultural expression that many people put on music. It influences a lot of the craziness that is going on in Jamaica![35]

These references to Muta's broadcasts once more illustrate his uncompromised stance against populism. Far from opportunist, he thus stands up against the mainstream of cultural production in his 'own field' of Reggae music. In fact, one can find many Dancehall songs painting informers in a bad light or voicing death threats against them, without distinction of the crime context. Just a few out of innumerable examples must suffice in this regard: Buju Banton's 'Informer Fi Dead' (1991), Bounty Killer's 'Spy Fi Die' (1993), I-Octane's 'Informer A Work' (2012), or the 'Informer'-collaboration of popular Dancehall artistes Vybz Kartel and Tommy Lee Sparta (2012). The song claims to represent the community, neighbourhood and so-called political garrison Gaza, which became synonymous with a group of artistes affiliated with Kartel.

Its lyrics warn informants from doing to Kartel (Mr Palmer) and Tommy Lee Sparta what Judas allegedly did to Christ or famous American mobster Salvatore Gravano ('Sammy the bull') did to fellow-Mafioso John Gotti. In Jamaica, where music (especially Dancehall) is the perceived hub of sociocultural expression, the catalyst of morality and behavioural norms, such lyrics have a lasting impact on listeners.[36] They contribute to a reign of fear, in which many crimes are not reported, thereby suggesting street justice through revenge and gang-related reprisal attacks. Many Jamaicans, especially from marginalized and poor communities, face a legal system alien and hostile to their living conditions and social status. Jaevion Nelson, a Jamaican human rights activist and development director, speaks of a complex issue. Apart from the deeply ingrained 'informer fi dead'-habitus, he regards a general attitude of officers' rudeness, biased and unequal treatment, and a limited guarantee of protection under the Witness Protection Programme as other structural issues impeding an efficient security and justice system.[37]

Other reasons for police inability to fight crimes in Jamaica may be cited in the form of over-arching party-affiliations of security forces, as Muta for instance debated with a caller from Tivoli Gardens in a *Steppin Razor* show, or lack of funding by the Ministry of National Security.[38] The latter was addressed sarcastically in the following quote directed against the formerly responsible minister for denying his officers essential radio entertaining, according to Muta:

> Mister Minister of National Security, Bobby Montague aka Sleepy, I have gotten some complaints by the police that you are giving them cars which don't have Irie FM in there. You cannot give the police a car that doesn't have Irie FM in there! They complained to me. I sped up the other day and a policeman stopped me. Before the man gave me a ticket he said: 'Muta, I don't know the kind of cars they are giving me, but the radio doesn't pick up Irie FM.' The police is asking for Irie FM in the cars! The police can't do their work properly because they don't have Irie FM in their car. You cannot send police out there without Irie FM. That is worse than sending them out without a gun.[39]

Whereas Muta ironically stresses the importance of Irie FM, he indirectly refers to lacking funding of appropriate radio equipment in police cars, implying government neglects of law enforcement. Well steeped in the Africa derived repertoire of trickster stories, Muta uses the rhetorical skills inherited from storytelling in Jamaica to bring his political and ethical messages across. Just like the popular Anansi of

Akan origin (or Anancy in Jamaica), a hero of so many folk stories, Muta's narratives signify deviance from ethical behaviour. Anansi is a spider figure with human character traits marking the juncture of good and evil, liberty and slavery, life and death, justice, and betrayal. In many narrations Anansi outwits the powerful, but eventually falls victim to his own immoral behaviour.[40] In his capacity as public spokesman for the people, Muta uses some sort of Anansi trickster play to highlight apparent failures of policing in the public interest, for instance, in the following broadcast from December 2017:

> What does the police have control over in Jamaica? It must be something that they control. They don't have control over the traffic thing. They don't have any control over the crime thing. What the hell do they have control over? ... People cross road and make the traffic block up. Taxi men around the corner make the road block up. And the police were not there. If they are there, they are just watching the thing and looking for the girl who passes by. They turn gyal watcher.[41]

Far from just being prone to 'gyal watching,' the executive is criticized for a looming political instrumentalization. Harriott, who provides a detailed account of corruption in the JCF, debates the pervasive involvement of Jamaica's elite by arguing that most anti-corruption efforts were motivated by equally corrupt motives of just getting rid of opposition party–affiliated JCF members. Proclaimed attempts of corruption control proved mostly ineffective and tended to sustain the very system introduced and defended by Jamaica's political elite. In line with Muta, Harriott suggests a structural reform which turns away from the inherited colonial management of security towards a more cooperative social management of crime control based on police-civil society exchange.[42]

Police corruption and social norms of non-cooperation vested in the anti-informer mindset contribute to the complexity of the prevalent crime crisis in Jamaica. It needs to be noted that serious crimes are also committed by those who should prevent and combat them. This asks for urgent solutions, as an important recurrent focus of Muta's rally against crime on air.

4.3. Crime Prevention: Proposals for Solution

Repeatedly, Mutabaruka plays his part in crime prevention campaigns or crime curbing initiatives. In his broadcasts, he proposes pertinent ideas to policymakers to tackle the island's crime issues. Nevertheless, he demands from the authorities the same positive attitude towards the common interest that he sees as his own responsibility:

> We must do better than that! When I say 'we' now, I am talking about 'we' and I include myself. I have the power of the microphone in front of me and I am trying my best continuously. But you must have some back-up, and the back-up is the people who you pay to look after certain things in the country. … I am trying my best to show them certain things, but all I hear is: 'Bwoy, Muta's things are too radical, Rasta!' And they know that I am saying, it can work, too, or it can be a part of the working. Because there is no 'one way' to deal with this crime situation, but there are many different aspects you can take it at! And we showed them that over many times.[43]

Let's contemplate some of the *different aspects* that Muta talks about. To achieve a lower crime rate and establish a safer social environment, he proposes concrete measures in terms of social reform, be it job creation programmes or entrepreneurship encouragement.[44] In addition, he supports crime counteraction through restrictions of dangerous weapons or even acquisition of guns in private possession by government. He also speaks out for banning violent movies from TV or, at least, rating them as *parental guidance suggested*.[45] Other suggestions include seeking advice from other countries in formerly crime- and violence-affected nations and cities:

> You need to go to some country that had some terrible civil war and find out how the people rectify. … Many countries in Africa were in a situation worse than Jamaica when it comes to bloodshed![46]

In this context, he regularly refers to Rwanda, the East African country that has ascended from genocide and a staggering civil war between the Hutu and Tutsi after 1994.[47] It is currently considered a stable African state with a viable economy, although by far more autocratic than Jamaica. The *Index Report* for the *2018 Ibrahim Index of African Governance* ranks Rwanda on position eight (out of 54) in the overall statistics of good governance and first in the subcategories Transparency & Accountability, Gender, Business Environment, and Rural Sector.[48] Furthermore, in the section *Protection against Ethnic & Religious Discrimination*, the small nation-state ranked seventeenth.[49]

Given Rwanda's history of ethnic genocide in 1994, these results show astonishing progress and support Muta's requests for political comparisons with other countries. Of course, he is aware of the entirely different political contexts of other nation-states. Nevertheless, he suggests using parts of what they are doing to stem crime as there must be something in the formula that is useful anywhere, in his view.[50] Apart from Rwanda, he sometimes refers to Columbia and its drugs and crime containment or, on a smaller scale, the city of New York with its rapid reduction of the crime rate during the 1990s.[51] 'Why is it that these ministers don't go to New York, talk to the people and find out what formula they used to make the crime rate go down so drastically?!,' Muta wonders.[52] Another potential role model for him is Norway, with its alternative penal and rehabilitation measures that include incarceration in minimum-security and open prisons such as the Bastoy Island prison.[53]

Apart from discussing possible solutions with his listeners, the 'steppin' razor' persistently requests responsibility from all parties and administrative bodies for improvement of crime prevention measures. He wants politicians to stop 'think in the box' which means that decision-makers and policymakers should learn from earlier mistakes. Taking the same wrong steps over and over again, will, according to him, never help the implementation of police operations established under pompous names such as *Operation Kingfish*.[54] Muta questions the individual expertise of certain politicians and wonders to what extent a banker such as Peter Bunting proves fit to become the Minister of National Security and Justice.[55] In fact, Jamaica encounters changes of office holders in rapid succession, involving mostly the same old faces, a course of political reform that Muta calls 'a joke business.' Thus, confronting it with words like these: 'Because you change the man, you do not change the thinking. You don't get the solution by changing the man. They need a strategy!'[56]

A sound strategy seems indeed of highest priority to tackle the current situation of largely uncontrolled arms exports into the Caribbean. Muta pleads for a transnational solution of the unchecked import and distribution of guns in the region. Given that neither guns nor ammunitions are produced in Jamaica, he also suspects that the shipment of guns involves the authorities. Although Muta warns against conspiracy theories and regards them with his unabated scepticism, he assumes a real conspiracy behind American gun shipments to Jamaica.[57] He speaks of a shady triangle trade between the US as the shipper, Haiti as the branch, and Jamaica as the receiver.[58] Muta condemns these irresponsible greed behind trading arms from the US to Caribbean countries and charges obvious double standards in crime prevention:

> Something doesn't taste good. Trinidad's biggest crime problem is guns. Little St Kitts, you know! They have to call out the soldiers in the streets because the crime rate jumped up. Barbados has a big crime rate! … I really want to figure out how is it that so many countries in the Caribbean have an escalation of gun activity!? … The US stationed FBI down here because they know that they better do something about the scamming as it is affecting their citizens. They are looking out for their citizens! But the proliferation of guns, which the scammers use and buy, is coming from America. The US is not interested in that! They are interested in their own family! We must be interested in our own family, too, you understand!?[59]

In this context, he angrily appeals to Jamaican politicians as well as the Caribbean Community CARICOM, a regional organization of fifteen Caribbean nation-states with economic, social, and cultural aims, challenging the elites to call officials in the US for better prevention measures of arms exports.[60] Yet Jamaica's as well as CARICOM's decision-makers rather gear to please the US and don't dare address the gun trade issue with government officials. In turn, public statements in the US tend to deny participation in the triangle trade, blaming others for the upsurge.[61] For Muta, this clearly typifies an asymmetrical relationship, namely the hegemony of (self-designated) *First World Countries* over so-called *Third World Countries*.[62]

But Muta does not stop there. He does not seek cheap applause for populist accusations of the rich and powerful. Rather, a violent mindset held by some Jamaicans comes into scrutiny as well. According to Muta, what he conceives as 'ghetto mentality' turns into self-fulfilling prophecy conditioned by 'mental slavery.' 'If a person's mind is not intact, then viciousness and criminality will proceed,' he discloses in an episode from May 2016.[63] Therefore, he puts the blame not merely on poverty and structural discrimination but also on a lack of discipline and morality in the ghetto. Critique in Muta's reflections on and from the 'cutting edge' hardly ever comes without self-critique. This may be seen as one of those strengths that turned both weekly shows into long-lasting success stories. Whilst reflecting on the reasons for Jamaica's criminal environment, he touches upon the paradox that although Jamaica is economically more advanced, its crime rate is much higher than Cuba's and Haiti's, the two neighbouring islands.[64] He names these countries to show that crime doesn't necessarily coincide with a country's rate of poverty. Therefore, social rehabilitation in his eyes needs to take the form of mental transformation:

> You have certain ghettos that can be transformed even though they are ghettos. I remember Black Rose Corner. The place looked well, and it was ghetto! So it's not like that you have to move out of a ghetto to make the thing don't look like a ghetto. Of most people who live in a ghetto, where they claim that this is a ghetto, it is their mind that is in the ghetto! ... People's mind live in the ghetto so much, so that their environment around them has transformed! But yet you want to clean up around your environment! Because it works both ways: if your environment looks a certain way, then it affects your mind, too![65]

Preventing his analyses to turn into monologues, Muta debates crime factors and appropriate prevention measures live on air with call-in interviewees such as Jamaican anthropologist Herbert Gayle or gender researcher Natasha Mortley. Gayle, who believes there is a direct connection between the poorest people's level of education and a country's degree of violence, calls for more leadership figures in the communities to build up small enterprises.[66] In line with this reasoning, Muta constantly advocates entrepreneurship, quotes business ideas for small enterprises and tries to motivate his audience to find a 'loophole' in the system for constructive job development. Natasha Mortley discusses in one of his shows the findings of the pilot study *Males, Crime and Community in Jamaica*, which was conducted by the University of the West Indies.[67] According to her, the study revealed that Jamaican men satisfy their need for respect mainly with three factors, namely guns, money, and politics within overall schemes of masculinity as dependent on protecting, providing, and boasting.[68] Muta partially agrees with Mortley and the study's results, as he sarcastically weighs in on sexist ideas of masculine identity prone to violence among Jamaica's male youth:

> When you have a gun and money now, it's like you have power. … The youths don't want any job! They have a job already; they have a big gun! What their penis cannot do, their gun will do it. Because that is the power now that they have. The gun is like a phallic symbol. It compensates for the powers where they lose out on girls.[69]

The gun induces symbolic capital by fear. Particularly Dancehall offers many examples for the submissive name-dropping of famous *gunmen*. This works as power by recognition and unveils gestures of subordination. Thus, armed men substitute their lack of social capital, status, and sincere respect through a martial code. In other words, they put lots of effort in showing off 'the toughest,' which eventually generates another form of prestige. Especially in crime-ridden areas of Jamaica, where it is hard to agglomerate economic capital through honestly earned remuneration, due to a lack of formal cultural and social capital among male teenagers belonging to the deprived segment of society, the choice of a criminal path of life seems rewarding. Muta also sees a nexus between the common Jamaican notion of masculinity and the influence of Dancehall music. He addresses the negative influence of gun- and violence-glorifying lyrics many Dancehall artistes present, whom he even calls by name: 'Alkaline and Popcaan! These artistes feed them the more madness in their head!'[70] Concerning this matter, criticism from Jamaican sociologist Leroy Dixon emerged about Popcaan's explicit lyrics in his song 'El Chapo' (2017).[71] In the song, whose title alludes to the infamous Mexican drug lord and most likely the Netflix series, Popcaan delves into cinematographic violent fantasies that no trigger warning would easily cover.

Popcaan identifies himself as a 'badman,' according to Dancehall critic Donna Hope.[72] The homage to El Chapo, who it is said has killed more than two thousand people, glorifies himself shooting guns.[73] Like the acclaimed role model, he refers to military weapons, such as MAK 90, M1 rifle, mini 'K and Intratec, in an almost erotic, yet certainly erratic manner. In the chorus, he equals himself as El Chapo, an *evil head* and *killy killy*, the Jamaican Patois paraphrase for murderer. Whereas so-called gun lyrics (in accordance with the image of a badman) were already well-liked in Jamaica's musical scenery in the late 1980s and early 1990s, namely by such artistes as the in/famous Ninjaman, they obviously have become even more popular since the mid-2000s.[74] Compared to Ninjaman, the Anansi play with badness has arguably evolved into a less metaphorical threat with violence nowadays.

With his broadcasts, Muta critically reflects on the idealization and legitimation of violence, particularly in Dancehall music and on the gun-associated socialization of the genre's followers. He infers that artistic production may contribute to a violent *gun is power*-habitus and thus to Jamaica's crime issue.[75] In this context, he also directly appeals to the Dancehall artistes to come to grips with their responsibility as entertainers, given their effectual status as role models, wanted or not:

> Maybe not the music creates the crime, but it helps to propel it! So when an artiste says that he only reflects the society, sometimes he creates what is going on in the society, too. Yes! I am an artiste, too. And I saw the effect of it internationally when I went out there. I went to certain countries in Africa, and some ministers in the governments told me that they used to listen to me when they were studying in Europe. That is why they came back to Africa! Because they heard me saying 'it no good fi stay inna whiteman country too long!' The music infiltrates your mind and your soul, and makes you react to it![76]

Summing up, Mutabaruka proposes several ideas on crime prevention. He pleads for political advice from abroad and asks Jamaica's political elite to establish effective police operations and interventions, to employ competent ministers for suitable assignments, and to immediately combat America's arms trade. He furthermore talks about Jamaica's ghetto mentality and masculine (gun-associated) identity, two social aspects that contribute to the crime issue and should inevitably be transformed. That's what makes the *Cutting Edge* and *Steppin Razor* programmes unique. When Muta challenges Jamaican social norms and widespread beliefs or doubts ominous events (e.g., the gun shipments from the US), he encourages (Black) people to look behind the facade and start asking critical questions. In an interview with the co-authors, he acknowledged his strategy of sincere scepticism:

> I think for myself! Critical thinking is the business of understanding something that you doubted. When you want to understand something that you doubt, you start to examine it more. Because doubt is the first step towards knowing. Through doubt you are going to examine the thing.[77]

Especially for those mostly young male, 'impulsive and undisciplined' sectors of Jamaican society, Muta's radio shows function as public awareness campaigns that encourage to scrutinize apparent reality of soaring crime waves. In this way, the Rastafari thinker encourages people to help themselves and embrace a different consciousness and worldview, quite similar to Marcus Garvey's goals of economic and cultural self-reliance outlined in so many issues of his weekly newspaper *Negro World*.[78]

NOTES

1.   BBC (2006).
2.   Cf. Amnesty International (2016, 9) and UNODC (2019).
3.   Cf. Bureau for International Narcotics and Law Enforcement Affairs (2019, 195ff).
4.   Lewis (2018, 1030).
5.   Cf. Eldemire (2018).
6.   Cf. Ibid. and Lewis (2018, 1029-1040). During a *Steppin Razor* show,

Muta plays an audio tape of a recorded telephone fraud, cf. SR 8 (2015). Thus, his listeners get an inside perspective and a basis for further observation.

7.   Cf. *Seattle Times* (2019).
8.   SR 7 (2015). Also cf. Hamilton (2017).
9.   Cf. Lewis (2018, 1031).
10. In 2017, there were 341 homicides in the parish of St James, the highest number amongst all parishes. The murder rate revealed that there were 183 murders per one hundred thousand people in St James. Cf. Dig Jamaica (2019).
11. Hamilton (2017).
12. SR 1 (2014); SR 28 (2016).
13. SR 47 (2017). English translation: *If you can't catch Quaco, you catch his shirt.* It is said that Quaco was a rebellious slave in Jamaica and the British soldiers tried to shoot him after he had managed to escape to the Cunha Cunha Pass. However, they only found the remains of his shirt hanging from the plants. Cf. SR 27 (2016).
14. Cf. Hamilton (2017).
15. Many Dancehall artistes, most notably the incarcerated Vybz Kartel, have thematized scamming and promoted it as reparation in their lyrics. Cf. Vybz Kartel/Gaza Slim (2012).
16. Lewis (2018, 1033).
17. Cf. Lewis (2018, 1033f, 1045f).
18. Cf. Bourdieu (1990, 112–21).
19. SR 1 (2014).
20. SR 50 (2017).
21. Chung (2017).
22. SR 31 (2016).
23. Cf. Davidson (2015) and Law Reform (Fraudulent Transactions) (Special Provisions) (2014).
24. It should be noted, however, that the latter is considerably lower than the first. For comparative statistics concerning the year 2015, cf. UNODC (2019, 73–74).
25. See for instance the *Waiting in Vain*-report by Amnesty International (2016).
26. Cf. Amnesty International (2016, 13).
27. Cf. Amnesty International (2016, 11, 40–43); Bureau for International Narcotics and Law Enforcement Affairs (2019, 197).
28. In the course of the *Corruption Perceptions Index 2018*, which measures the perceived levels of public sector corruption, Jamaica scored 44 on a scale of zero (highly corrupt) to 100 (very clean). Cf. Transparency International (2019, 1f).
29. Harriott (2000, xxii).
30. Cf. Waller et al. (2007, 25).
31. Cf. SR 17 (2015) and SR 18 (2016).
32. In *Crime and Punishment Around the World*, Glendene Lemard (2010, 208)

provides the following definition of that term:

> … Jamaica has a cultural idea of 'informer fi dead,' which means that any person known to give information to the authorities with respect to a crime should die. This phenomenon is prevalent in urban Jamaica and has been reinforced by instances in which witnesses have been killed before being able to offer testimony in a case.

33. SR 18 (2016).

34. A prime example of such an underground cooperation between state and non-state actors was the JLP-affiliated relationship between Tivoli-based don Dudus Coke and former prime minister Bruce Golding. See also Hawthorne (2018, 109–114).

35. SR 18 (2016). Note: Mutabaruka's pungent comment on the illiteracy of certain artistes must be understood allegorically as it merely indicates his negative stance toward certain contents shared by Dancehall artistes.

36. Cf. Cooper (2004) and Hope (2006).

37. Cf. Nelson (2015).

38. Cf. SR 31 (2016).

39. SR 47 (2017).

40. Such trickster figures as Anansi in Akan (or Anancy in Jamaica) belong to forms of expression of Akan ethics and intend to exemplify social misconduct in Jamaica just as they had done in the Akan kingdoms (of Ghana today). They are often told to children as a means of moral education, cf. Bennett (1979).

41. SR 49 (2017).

42. Cf. Harriott (2000, xviii, 47–71).

43. SR 39 (2017).

44. Cf. SR 1 (2014).

45. Cf. SR 28 (2016).

46. SR 32 (2016).

47. Cf. SR 24 (2016) and SR 46 (2017).

48. 'The Ibrahim Index of African Governance (IIAG) is an annually published index that provides a statistical measure of governance performance in 54 African countries. Governance is defined by the Mo Ibrahim Foundation as the provision of the political, social, and economic public goods and services that every citizen has the right to expect from their state, and that a state has the responsibility to deliver to its citizens. This definition is focused on outputs and outcomes of policy. The IIAG governance framework comprises four categories: *Safety & Rule of Law, Participation & Human Rights, Sustainable Economic Opportunity and Human Development.* These categories are made up of 14 subcategories, consisting of 102 indicators. The 2018 IIAG is calculated using data from 35 independent African and global institutions.' Mo Ibrahim Foundation (2018, 137)

49. Cf. Mo Ibrahim Foundation (2018, 16, 110).

50. Cf. SR 24 (2016) and SR 43 (2017).
51. Cf. SR 3 (2014); SR 9 (2015); SR 24 (2016).
52. SR 9 (2015).
53. Cf. SR 24 (2016) and SR 32 (2016). For more information on *Prison Island* cf. Shammas (2015).
54. Cf. Leslie (2010: 49f).
55. Cf. SR 43 (2017).
56. Ibid.
57. Cf. SR 41 (2017). In a broadcast from January 2016, he debates with a call-in candidate, SR 18 (2016): 'You see the conspiracy thing, it looks like Black people are more concerned about conspiracies than really solving their own situation. I don't say that conspiracy cannot be true, you know, but the amount of conspiracies I see Black people are holding on to over the years, I must say: 'But wait, why we keep developing conspiracies?' Every time something is happening, we say it is a conspiracy against Black people. When, really and truly, some of the things are caused by ourselves, too!'
58. Cf. SR 23 (2016).
59. SR 41 (2017).
60. Cf. Ibid.
61. Although the US are the major gun and ammunition importers for the two Caribbean countries, the US Department of State speaks of a *guns for marijuana trade* that, allegedly, only happens between Haiti and Jamaica. See also Bureau for International Narcotics and Law Enforcement Affairs (2019, 196f).
62. Cf. SR 18 (2016). Note: Although these contrasting designations may not be up to date anymore, they help to describe the gulf between rich/powerful and poor/powerless countries, cf. Taylor (2011). Mutabaruka emphasizes this fact by using them in his narratives.
63. SR 23 (2016).
64. Cf. SR 32 (2016).
65. SR 24 (2016).
66. Cf. SR 39 (2017).
67. Cf. Wilson-Harris (2017).
68. Cf. SR 45 (2017).
69. SR 49 (2017).
70. Ibid.
71. Cf. Dixon (2019).
72. Cf. Hope (2006: 90f).
73. Cf. CNN (2022).
74. Cf. Doumerc (2003, 86). For instance, in December 2009 the lyrical feud between Dancehall protégés Vybz Kartel and Mavado (also known as the Gully vs Gaza-conflict) led the leading politicians at that time to summon an official meeting with both artistes appearing in public in order to eliminate their hostility and lyrical warfare, which had

resulted in innumerable conflicts and even killings between particular (mostly young male) fans in the months prior. Interestingly, it is said that the conflict was presumably political due to Gaza's association with the PNP (representing Portmore) and Gully's association with the JLP (representing Cassava Piece). For further information, cf. Dreisinger (2010).

75. Mutabaruka's views on Dancehall are presented at large in chapter 5.2.

76. SR 35 (2017). Here, Muta responds to Vybz Kartel's statement featured in his song 'Mr. Broadcast Commission (Anuh My Music)' (2013): 'My music is a reflection of the broader society. Without a violent society, we wouldn't have violent music. Art is an expression of life.'

77. Interview 1 (2018).

78. Cf. Phillips Fein (1964, 448).

'EVERYTHING WE DO, DOESN'T REFLECT US AS A PEOPLE'
On Jamaica's Society

The only thing that can keep the people comfortable is the little music that is being played about the place. The little music keeps the people sane! Whether it is nasty music or not. But you can see how the people react to this music!

Mutabaruka: *Steppin Razor*, December 4 (2014)

When Europeans go to an African land, they come with their Bible and their gun and teach you how to pray. And the story goes that after we closed our eyes and prayed, when we open the eyes, they have our land and we have the Bible.

Mutabaruka: *Steppin Razor*, November 23 (2017)

This chapter explores Mutabaruka's perception of Jamaican society and its manifold identities through his narratives in the *Cutting Edge* and *Steppin Razor* programme. Referring to his Afrocentric perspective, he concurrently employs subversive (self-)questioning, sometimes ascending to acrimonious verbal exchanges with imagined and real adversaries, including his callers and/or studio guests. His main target comes in cultural biases and an alleged narrow-mindedness of various actors in public life. Listening to his broadcasts, one is forced to assume that Muta likes to turn (almost) everything upside down regarding social order or cultural and religious norms in Jamaica. Nothing appears safe or, much less, sacrosanct, within his reach. Not even views and conceptions held in his 'own' Rastafari community, much less his favourite targets: politicians, 'the powerful,' and state executives. Often in real or fictional discourse with his listeners, he airs his positions and negotiates them. Let's zoom in on some of his viewpoints in the subsequent sub-headings.

5.1. A Class Habitus: The Jamaican (Social) Logic

In recent centuries, Jamaica has been a 'melting pot of cultures and ethnicities,' especially shaped by the influx of enslaved labour from Africa and indentured labour from countries such as Scotland, Germany, India, and China.[1] Although Muta agrees that European and Asian influences have been part of Jamaica's demographic history and have contributed to a Jamaican identity in some way, he considers Jamaican culture predominantly African, African-Caribbean, or rather Black. In this context, he regularly outlines a class habitus that he associates with the deprived section of Jamaica's Black population. Muta's narratives engage with Jamaica's intrinsic colour-class stratification and social segmentation. Let us briefly consider the sociological notion of class and group habitus, according to Pierre Bourdieu:

> Since the history of the individual is never anything other than a certain specification of the collective history of his group or class, *each individual system of dispositions* may be seen as a *structural variant* of all the other group or class habitus, expressing the difference between trajectories and positions inside or outside the class.[2]

Therefore, all coexisting variations of group or class habitus are nevertheless shaped by the same historic experience. A specific class/group habitus – in this case the habitus of Jamaica's Black disadvantaged social sector – is but one expression of many variations relative to different experiences by individuals who belong to a respective collective. In the *Steppin Razor* broadcast, Mutabaruka pays attention to a particular class habitus and offers constructive criticism, when appropriate, to contribute to a transformation of this habitus into one characterized by an African-centred consciousness. The transformation of a colonial state of mind into a liberated reclaim of the stolen African identity is his clear aim. So far, the habitus of many Jamaicans has strongly been shaped by postcolonial and other detrimental influences of cultural imperialism, which are avidly addressed by Muta during a so-called *Cutting Edge University* section in his broadcast:

> Do we let people take advantage of us all the while? Especially the Arabs and the Europeans?! The mark is so indelible in our consciousness, so we don't even realize that we are playing out a designed and orchestrated system. A system that is designed to make us feel down and out, and to make us feel as we don't have no self-worth and no value. Many people don't want to recognize and admit that a lot of the things which are taking place right now, whether in Africa or anywhere African people find themselves, can be traced back to early events in history. And the labour, the blood, sweat and tears of our people allowed other people to rise up and legitimize their cruelty and wickedness to the point now, where we seem to be so blissfully ignorant that we just accept what is taking place as reality. African people live in an illusion. And that illusion is created by their lack of information and understanding of how cultures diverted us from our consciousness and awareness of ourselves. We lost that integrity that was able to carry us to this point. We survived the transatlantic slave trade, the Arab invasion of Africa, all the diseases and the drought, and their crucifixion. We have to wake up. We cannot live the reality of a next man. We can't define things according to the logics of the invaders and enslavers. We must return to our ancestor's legacy and what we are able to create right now for ourselves.[3]

This resembles Paul Gilroy's reminder 'that there are limits to what we can blame on the leviathan of white supremacy ... (and) that we must pay attention to both inside and outside aspects of our experiences of subordination if we are to comprehend it properly.'[4] Especially in broadcasts shortly before culturally biased Christmas and other Christian holidays, Muta brings up crucial issues, for example, when he discusses consumerism that eventually causes pain for the greater part of Jamaica's society:

> Some people don't have the money to spend, but they spend it anyway. ... This is how Black people run their thing. They buy what they want and beg for what they need. It cannot work that way. Because when January and February come, your needs are not going to be fulfilled. Then you are going to cuss, and behave bad and lick your

> child like it is your child's fault. You are going to cuss your
> man because he never did this and never did that. And you
> took the money to buy fingernails because you went to a
> party, and you had to look the best.[5]

This quote refers to a common habitus amongst deprived Jamaicans
in over-consumption of status symbols. It refers to spending the little
money they have on their appearance. In this excerpt, he addresses
females for investing in artificial fingernails, hair extensions or wigs,
and chic dresses:

> Black people have no money, but when Christmas comes
> you see the false eyelash, the false bottom, the false breast,
> the false this, the false that. All the things they never need,
> they buy it at this time of the year. And the things they need
> for next year, they cannot get it.[6]

In this regard, the radio host cites Martin Luther King Jr.: 'Black
people buy what they want and beg for what they need.'[7] The famous
Baptist minister and leader of the nonviolent American civil rights
movement in the 1950s and 1960s once gave the following statement
analysing the financial situation of Black people, using the then current
terminology:

> … Negroes too often buy what they want and beg for
> what they need. Negroes must learn to practice systematic
> saving. They must also pool their economic resources
> through various cooperative enterprises. Such agencies as
> credit unions, savings and loan associations, and finance
> companies are needed in every Negro community. All
> of these are things that would serve to lift the economic
> level of the Negro which would in turn give him greater
> purchasing power.[8]

Muta regularly refers to Martin Luther King and contextualizes
his speeches and sermons, thereby uncovering similar practices
among Jamaican people in the present. Agreeing with the civil rights
activist, Muta emphasizes the need for financial responsibility, prudent
investment, and economic self-reliance – all matters of paramount
importance for undermining the common economic plight of many
Jamaicans. The Rastafari presenter has always been aware of the
importance of economic self-empowerment and refers to his own

creativity as a source of economic capital, from his poems to talk shows and tours as entertainer or performing as master of ceremonies.[9] On this point, he urges his listeners not to squander money but to focus on self-reliant and conscientious concepts. In fact, Muta's educational streak may be identified as a *Black salvation*-impetus, which prompts him to be a self-help advocate for Black people and their financial well-being.

Muta prefers to speak about what he regards as *Black people mentality* in group consumption, whether appropriated from Hip-Hop video clips or other media promoting capitalist stereotypes of prosperity. During an internal discussion with his radio team, in which his young colleagues favoured living in concrete houses over wooden board houses, he casts the following bold statement:

> Jamaican people feel that when they live in a board house and then build a concrete house, they are moving up. This is foolishness! I have a board house in Treasure Beach, and it is like a landmark in Jamaica! The most unique houses that I have seen when I travelled were board houses. In Jamaica people feel that a board house means you are suffering, or you are poor. That's why many Jamaicans 'concrete up themselves.' I could never live in a concrete house where there is just pure concrete when I turn around. ... Black people have a mentality about wood! They feel that a wooden house means sufferation.[10]

This quote challenges common attitudes of some of Muta's fellow Jamaicans allegedly rooted in (post-)colonial prejudice. As so often he contrasts these habitualized norms with his own experiences. In his critical discourse on class habitus, Muta touches upon a wide range of subjects. One should recognize that even food and eating habits are frequent topics in his radio show. For instance, it is his heartfelt wish to introduce his listeners to alternative ideas on food consumption and production, as he promotes his vegan (or *ital*) lifestyle, 'duns' the government to protect Jamaica from imports of plastic rice and curious onions, and rails against American fast-food chains such as Kentucky Fried Chicken.[11]

In connection to this, he also addresses changes in farming, suggesting that young people have given up the hard work of being involved in agriculture, particularly in Jamaica's subsistence areas in the mountainous interior: 'They don't want dirty hands. They prefer to type or press cell phone rather than take up a machete or a plough to plough some things.'[12]

The lack of interest in farming illustrates not only a Jamaican phenomenon but a global one. Muta's standpoint, however, correlates with the Rastafari concept of self-reliance: 'We are the 99 per cent, and they (the government; authors' note) are the 1 per cent, but they rule everything. It's really a country where the minority feeds you. The majority is supposed to feed itself!'[13] Muta experienced agricultural work when he lived in Johns Hall, St James.[14] Given that this was part of his socialization and thus shaped his habitus, it has contributed to his vindication of self-reliant food provision.

He often thematizes certain practices of Jamaicans that he considers either contradictory, imprudent, or merely displaying the deeply rooted 'indiscipline' amongst society at large, when collective security and the common good come to the fore. The prevalent anti-law and order mentality is what he associates with the 'Third World mind.'[15] He shifts responsibilities for anti-social attitudes to the elite's involvement in corruption and criminality, thus setting the wrong example for less privileged people. For instance, Muta alludes to the driving behaviour of aggressive motorists or to street hawkers who occupy Jamaica's sidewalks with their products so that people need to walk on the street.[16] These may seem to be banal topics at first, but Muta warns convincingly: 'We have a condition where we need to come out of it, you know. Because you cannot have good governance (and) you cannot have a stable society with people who don't respect order.'[17] Nevertheless, Jamaican society is not only shaped by what Muta considers a 'Third World mind,' but peer-group pressure for conformity, that according to his social analysis, conditions certain practices as well:

> I never knew that so many people in Jamaica bleach until the other day when I walked through the plaza and saw the fireworks people (women who sell fireworks; authors' note). A pure bleach out! Right now, they don't bleach because they are afraid of their Black, (but) just through they live in

> a little cave there where everybody is doing it, so they also
> do it. It's like everybody is wearing tear up jeans (ripped
> jeans; authors' note) now, so everybody puts on tear up
> jeans. Nobody wants to be unique; nobody wants to say
> that they are different. It's like an army, they dress in a
> uniform. It's something about a thinking.[18]

Fashion and appearance, coined 'style and pattern' in Dancehall
lingua, forms an important part of a shared Dancehall habitus,
designed by the informal rules of conformity. Peer pressure embodies
behavioural and cognitive structures into the dominant yet dynamic
habitus in the field of Dancehall. What may be referred to as the
Dancehall habitus is, of course, open to permanent creative (re)invention
and adoptions to outside influences, for instance, the field of Hip-Hop
culture or the film industry, particularly gang, drug cartel, or mobster
and Yakuza movies. Hence, the obvious imports of set pieces, such as
references to 'El Chapo' (see Popcaan's lyrics quoted in chapter 4) or
various Yakuza and Ninja symbols in artistes appearances and song
contents, are a part of this habitus. Due to the overarching influence
of Dancehall on Jamaica's Black disadvantaged class – the so-called
'ghetto youths' – these clichéd absorptions enter everyday practices.
Cultural anthropologist Norman Stolzoff writes: 'Styles of clothing,
haircuts, and jewelry worn to dancehall sessions have now become daily
garb. These fashion statements are a source of ongoing controversy,
and they have come to signify a subordinate and oppositional position
within Jamaica's race-class hierarchy.'[19]

Donna Hope, one of the most prolific cultural critics of Dancehall,
deals with these contentious issues encompassing the sexual politics
of Reggae music (including Dancehall) in more detail, employing a
specific gender and class perspective. In her influential book *Inna Di
Dancehall*, Hope emphasizes the convergent analogy of the Dancehall
and (Black) lower class habitus:

> Dancehall music and culture, as the most contemporary
> manifestation of what is deemed Jamaican 'low culture,'
> actively creates and re-creates symbolic manifestations of
> the tensions that operate in society. The play across the
> field of popular culture, where the dancehall, as inner-city
> and lower-working-class culture, works to both produce

and reproduce varied and competing forms of personhood
in Jamaica. …, the male-dominated dancehall landscape
represented a development in the petty commodity
sector aggressively created by poor blacks. The dancehall
encompassed the thrust for economic sustenance on behalf
of many dispossessed Jamaicans; the creation of a voice for
the voiceless; and a bid for survival and escape from the
poverty-stricken lifestyles of the inner cities of Kingston
and St Andrew.[20]

Being the antipole to *high culture* and the genuine articulation of
downtown people, as described by Donna Hope, Dancehall culture and
its implications cohere with insubordinate attitudes against formally
dominant forces in society and thus have immense potential for
subversion.[21] Dancehall as culture and counterculture has managed
to achieve informal dominance among the masses, equalling or
perhaps even exceeding political influence. As a cultural and social
phenomenon, Jamaica's Dancehall culture has successfully globalized
almost around the world, it has created a *Black space* on the island and
multiple and diverse expressive fields intricately respondent to this
Jamaican invention globally.

Muta's narratives concerning Jamaica's class habitus should be
considered in relation to this particular field as well, simply because
of its dominant influence in everyday life. Interestingly, as illustrated
under the next sub-heading the radio host proves by no means timid
about daring its popular heroes. Although an advocate of the Black
lower class and a dissident to mainstream ideas, he does not easily
accept certain manifestations of Dancehall and criticizes some of
these harshly. Of course, he does not deprecate this entire genre of
Reggae, evidenced by recorded jingles for his *Cutting Edge* programme
spoken by the likes of Bounty Killer, but upholds values first ventilated
by *Foundation Reggae*. Shaped by Rastafari philosophy and culture,
particularly within the Nyahbinghi House, Muta critically reflects
upon detrimental Dancehall values, which pose challenges to his own
habitus, rooted in Black (revolutionary) consciousness.

5.2. The Music of the People: Reggae vs Dancehall?

Music may be considered Jamaica's *heartbeat*, particularly Reggae, its gift to the world and its offspring, Dancehall Reggae.[22] Of course, many 'foreign' genres such as Hip-Hop, Gospel, Soul, or Reggaeton are also very popular and were complementarily influencing and influenced by Reggae.[23] In Jamaica, music is by far not restricted to formal settings such as *stage shows*, street and club parties (so-called *dances*). It rather accompanies the entire course of the day, from bus rides to lunch and dinner gatherings or Sunday's church meetings; it appears adequate to locate it at the centre of people's cultural expressions. Reggae and Dancehall have shaped a prevalent Jamaican identity relating to fashion, dance, symbolic and verbal articulation, mindset, lifestyle, literature, world views, and even food.

The culture, much more than a mere musical genre, lingers at the core of a collective habitus. Mutabaruka regularly refers to the importance Reggae music has had for the constitution of diverse cultural expressions in Jamaica and globally. However, this does not keep him from harshly criticizing certain Dancehall outputs, when and where necessary. In this context, the tone of Muta's statements occasionally turn highly emotional. Whereas he regards Reggae as the 'music of liberation and hope,' he associates some Dancehall practices with materialism, explicit language, gun glorification, and disrespectfulness.[24] His antipathy against the decay of some artistic productions make him suspect another conspiracy, in the form of capitalist corruption:

> Is it a conspiracy? Was it planned and designed that a country that gave the world a music of liberation and hope, a music that connects the Africans with their Africanness, has to see what the music has become today? The materialism, bling, sexually explicit language, gun, disrespect, and culture that comes with it. What went wrong in Jamaica? We have to ask that question, you know![25]

To no small part, the Dancehall genre appears dedicated to gun lyrics and gangsterism. In celebration of vanity, 'bling,' and materialistic values, the genre's idiom and its inherent culture (fashion, appearance, dance styles, etc.) feature a so-called *slackness* that is inclined towards sexual explicitness and vulgarity.[26] Often considered by (mostly foreign) journalists and critics to be heteronormative, toxic masculinist, homophobic, and misogynist, slackness and gun lyrics receive great popularity in the Dancehall field.[27] Emerging from Rastafari-inspired DeeJays of the 1960s–1980s, Dancehall called *Raggamuffin* style in the late 1980s went through a paradigmatic shift towards secular themes, in the form of violence and sexuality. This, of course, corresponds with political and cultural shifts in Jamaican society. In his critically acclaimed book *Wake the Town and Tell the People: Dancehall Culture in Jamaica*, Stolzoff designates an interplay of several factors that contributed to the continuous rise of Dancehall music in popularity, namely:

- the country's political shift from Michael Manley's laudation of democratic socialism with an African-Jamaican flavour to Edward Seaga's neoliberal (capitalistic) US-oriented agenda in 1980

- the ideological and cultural shift from an internationally oriented music market to a domestically oriented one in the aftermath of Bob Marley's demise in 1981

- the moral shift from Afrocentric values and the *brotherly love* and *unity* as promoted by Rastafari and socialism during the 1970s to the embracement of consumer capitalism and the celebration of the *local* reality, as expressed in the Patois vernacular and through the celebration of sexuality and gangsterism in the 1980s.[28]

Stolzoff's analysis partially responds to Muta's question cited above and provides an explanation for the musical and cultural transformation in Jamaica, from Rastafari-influenced *Roots Reggae* towards the sexually explicit and violence-glorifying Dancehall.[29]

The author points to some obvious aspects of the entire picture, which certainly is far more complex:

> Through the idiom of dancehall music and in the social context of dancehalls, the lower classes created a response to changing political-economic realities. For instance, the lower classes were agents in choosing to elect Seaga and to embrace consumer capitalism, and the dancehall was a primary vehicle for articulating these views. ... Another

event leading to the rise of the dancehall style was the death of Bob Marley in 1981 at the age of thirty-six. As a result, the black lower class lost its most visible and powerful voice. In the wake of Marley's passing from cancer at the prime of his career, the otherworldly millenarian message of the Rastafari was no longer as compelling as the ethic of instant gratification. ..., the dancehall itself became a symbol of the division between uptown and downtown, between a music that was increasingly oriented to an international market (roots reggae) and one that spoke to the local sensibilities of a younger generation of dancehall fans.[30]

Correspondences between artistic fields such as musical genres and the global stage of power and economic as well as symbolic means of domination are not easily grasped by social science. As a practitioner in the same field of Reggae, Muta does not hide his depressed sentiments about recent developments of Dancehall. 'It is not a soul music, decadence takes over,' as he laments in a *Cutting Edge* episode from 2017.[31] His claims of a conspiracy may not necessarily be taken verbally, but rather as provocative questioning for his younger contemporaries and fellow artistes to review their renunciation of spiritual and revolutionary cultural production. He further critiques an adoption of dominant values of violence and capitalism as a presumed co-optation derived from 'foreign,' i.e., external interests:

It's like they found out that we get presumptuous and use Reggae music to really heal the minds of the oppressed, and then all of a sudden, we just see this thing coming in they called Dancehall culture. Maybe the rise of that culture is a conspiracy against the rise of militancy and really holistic temperament that the Reggae music gave us.[32]

Muta uses the rhetorical strategy of juxtaposition: on the one (positive) side, he refers to Roots Reggae with its conscious and uplifting message about spiritual redemption and socio-political protest, on the other (negative) side to (certain expressions of) Dancehall prone to what he considers 'immoral and decadent gun- and slackness-lyricism.' Yet it is Dancehall that represents Jamaican popular culture and mainstream, as Muta is very much aware of when he refers to crime and gun issues in Jamaica: 'Apparently the people are listening to the more negative message. It has more influence over here because of the dramatic situation we experience in Jamaica.'[33]

From many talks and discussions in *Cutting Edge* and *Steppin Razor* it appears evident that Muta doesn't treat the subject lightly and expresses his anger at Dancehall culture, wherever detrimental to the common good of society. He criticizes certain practices of actors in the field of Dancehall, including the sexist imagery and (self-) presentation of women on album covers and in the actual Dancehall arena. He criticizes vulgar dress codes at dances, dance styles such as the ominous *daggering* – 'staging' sexual intercourse in public – or the obscene presentation of the female body in video clips: 'When you look at the videos! …Our young African sisters, they wine and twist around and go around, and men cock them up in the air and stab them… Man, how did Jamaica end up here?'[34] Or in another broadcast: 'I am telling you! If I see one more bottom on TV to rhaatid, I am going to mash it up. Too many bottoms; I cannot take it!'[35]

Dancehall sessions and parties are competitive sites of distinction.[36] The omnipresent judgement of taste determines dress codes, or rather, subtle pressures to undress (oneself), particularly for women, as Muta relentlessly reflects on air. He is one of the few social critics presenting an antidote to the 'dressed to impress' informal rule, apart from conservative voices in media, such as some columnists of the *Gleaner* newspaper. His frame of reference is distinctly different from colonial puritanism, sometimes implicitly revoked in mainstream media. Being aware of the Dancehall arena as a battlefield for the accumulation of symbolic capital through recognition and respect by others, Muta deconstructs superficial 'embodiments of coolness,' described by Stolzoff in this way:

> The primary fashion designs for the divas are variations on the X-rated theme. … Most men enjoy the divas' provocative dressing and their open embodiment of sexuality, as evidenced by the hundreds of songs produced each year dedicated to these women. … Unlike the divas, the dons and the rude boys tend to cover their bodies from neck to ankle in dancehall-styled suits. They embody coolness, commanding respect from those they encounter.[37]

Within such an arena or battlefield of accomplished differences, referred to as *war zone* by Stanley Niaah, ascriptions and denominations such as *diva, don,* and *rude boy* imply certain codes of behaviour, e.g., a masculine, rude appearance, or the 'Go go'-dance style of Dancehall queens.[38] Mutabaruka, in his sarcastic usage of Patois, undresses many fashions and dancing styles for their sexist content. In relation to the daggering dancing style, he does not spare this rudeness from equal terms:

> When they go to a dance, the denim shorts itch up in their crotches and they want it that way, too! They have on the longest fingernails, the shiniest shoes, and their false hair! And when you see what they are doing. They simulate sex! You see men jumping on the women and behaving like dogs! Where did we get this culture from? And as a matter of fact, too, the man turns the woman around backwards, you know. I question myself: 'Wait, are these two human beings?' Because I just see the puppies at my yard behaving like that. My puppies are discreet. If they have sex in my presence, they just mask it. But, these people do it in front of light! All the light shines down on the man, and the woman's crotches point up in the video.[39]

It must be hard to find a Jamaican, regardless of social background, who will not be made to laugh by this narrative. Muta makes the dancers look foolish as he compares their way of dancing with the sexual intercourse of his puppies. In the 2000s, the daggering style (or dance performance of coitus-like postures and pelvic grinding moves) had just become popular through much celebrated Dancehall tunes like Mr Vegas's 'Daggering' (2008), RDX's 'Daggering' (2008), and Aidonia's 'Flying Dagger, aka 100 Stab' (2008). In the chorus of his song, Mr. Vegas for instance praises daggering as the girls' choice, from a male perspective obviously. Artistes never get away with such counterfactual posturing in Muta's radio talks.

Although music associated with daggering has been banned from Jamaican radio and television since, the release of topic-related songs and the performance of daggering is still commonly practised in the (underground) Dancehall arena.[40] Muta thinks that the Dancehall culture doesn't help the healing of its patrons, traumatized by poverty and lack of opportunities, but rather represents the expression of the traumatized:

> In their soul, they are perplexed. Jamaican people seem to be so traumatized and because of that they go to certain places to heal themselves. But, really and truly, it is not healing them because that terribleness follows them into the Dancehall, and it gets crazy in the Dancehall![41]

Thus, he questions the origin of such a dance culture and disagrees with references grounding the sexual explicitness in a presumed African heritage, a suggestion some researchers have made.[42] For Muta, such explanations only give a wrong impression of the matter and a biased picture of Africa, as 'there is no claim that men stand behind women and jump on them at a dance in Africa.'[43] On this comparative level, there seem to be indeed more differences than commonalities between (West-)African fertility rites and the dance hypes owed to an escalating competition in taboo-breaking.

In spite of all his critique, one must emphasize that Muta doesn't oppose Dancehall music or *riddim* per se, but the explicit lyrics which are commonly voiced on these riddims and 'the culture that identifies the music itself.'[44] In his radio shows, he often plays tunes that are classified as Dancehall (concerning the instrumental's beat or style) but contain positive and life-affirming lyrics such as in the song 'Simple Blessings' by Tarrus Riley and Konshens (2017). It's praise of simple blessing, such as quality family time, sharing and caring, good friends, good food and so forth provide a Dancehall antithesis to highly ambivalent treatises on sex and violence.

Simplicity celebrated in these lyrics conforms with a long-standing Rastafari concept. Therefore, he helps his audience to make decisive distinctions by exemplification. Although Mutabaruka complains about the decadence of many of today's Reggae and Dancehall producers and singers, inter alia bemoaning off-key singing and the common abandonment of live instruments in favour of overused digital templates, he understands and acknowledges innovation.[45] Against certain conservative attitudes in international Reggae circles, with an exclusive preference for Roots Reggae, he underlines the need of constant revisions. In a beautifully grafted argument, he rebukes any freezing in time, as the hype of today inevitably becomes a thing of the past tomorrow:

> You have some people being stocked in the 1970s! I love '70s, you know! But Reggae has evolved, and younger people now say certain things. You have to listen what they are saying! You cannot just cross it off. You want them remember history, but you don't want to recognize what is going to be history? Because the music of today will be history tomorrow! You understand!?[46]

On the one hand, as depicted above, the progressive Rasta voice on air admonishes people who only listen to old school Reggae from the 1970s. On the other hand, he reprimands Jamaica's younger generation in parallel, admonishing their limited musical scope, when only listening to 'things for their age.'[47] With his broad range of musical knowledge from Algerian Rai to Indian Bhangra, various African musical styles, including the Techno-style versions of South African Kwaito music, he even less sympathizes with the almost total neglect of Reggae's preceding genres, such as Ska and Rocksteady in contemporary Jamaica. Muta directly addresses the younger disc jockeys from Irie FM in this regard:

> How can you work on a radio station that is dealing with Jamaican music in all its genres, and the only thing you know about is the music which prevails in your time? It's madness! … White people take the music and play the music to a level! The Africans take the music in the side of Africa and play it! The Japanese take the music and play it on a level! So they know about Rocksteady and Reggae, and they still listen to Ska. … How is it possible that you have a Reggae radio station and the youths who are there on the radio station open up their eye wide when you ask them about John Holt!?[48]

Knowing about the thought-provoking comparison between global appreciation of all musical styles of Jamaican origin and a lack of knowledge among the island's own younger generations, Muta demands more respect for the founding fathers and mothers in Dub, Rocksteady, Ska, and other earlier genres in his programmes.[49] By mentioning Austria's Rise & Shine Festival (a Dub festival, in which Muta shared a panel on his African experiences with Werner Zips in

2016) as well as the plurality of Ska bands in North America during a broadcast episode, he vividly points out the global spreading of Jamaican music, spawning a great variety of local adaptions. This may be viewed as the outcome of what Carolyn Cooper calls the *glocalization of Reggae* on a global level.[50]

What may perhaps be increasingly viewed as cultural appropriation, following international trends to call for cultural purity, is also a consequence of the active dissemination of Reggae by Jamaican artistes travelling to all corners of the earth and even settling in remote places such as Japan or India, educating local youths in Jamaican lingua, styles, and musical expressions. Muta's extensive experiences in foreign countries from Africa to Asia, Europe, and the Americas instigated his awareness of music history blind spots among younger Jamaicans: 'It hurts me when I see white people talking about the music, and I ask myself: How come Jamaican youths don't know about the music like them?!'[51] In this context, he suggests qualified education in Jamaican musical history for upcoming radio operators and commends thorough engagements with all possible sources on the music, be it books, oral testimony, or the Internet. Furthermore, he promotes what he calls a *South-South connection* between Jamaica's and Africa's Reggae and Dancehall acts. Instead of an orientation towards the North American music market, he feels confident that such a connection could prove fertile due to the attention African artistes receive nowadays, not just within the Afrobeats hype:

> We need to direct our attention to a South-South thing where we connect with Africa! Because right now the youths in Africa appreciate the music, you know! They love the music! And right now, there are more and more festivals happening in Africa! … At this time, we understand how important it is to return to what we call 'Sankofa'! To our things, our Africanness! Food, clothes, and music. We need to revisit it in a very serious way![52]

Sankofa, a West African emblem or, more precisely, an Adinkra symbol of the Akan people, is not merely a film, in which Mutabaruka starred as one of its main characters, the rebel slave Shango. Its metaphorical meaning is to learn from one's past, symbolized by a bird picking the best from the past to work in the present for a better future.[53] Reporting on his visit to Zion Radio, a local station in Côte d'Ivoire, Muta exemplifies the meaning behind this symbolism (in a broadcast on Irie FM in April 2016):

> When you leave Jamaica and go out in the world, you see the positive influence of Reggae music and Rastafari on the world. … It is not the music that is being played right now in the popular culture of Jamaica which does that. What we see is a reversal! And we don't fight against Dancehall music because the Ivorians told me that when they listen to the Dancehall music coming from Jamaica, all they do is using the riddim and putting their kinda lyrics to it. The brethren told me that there is no way they could talk certain things on a record like what they hear the Jamaicans talk on the record to degrade women in their country. … Zion Radio started to promote specifically Reggae music and Rastafari culture in the Ivory coast. Zion Radio is like a little child to Irie FM, using Reggae music as its main musical genre to promote the radio station. … This will help to facilitate a wider and more appreciative expansion of what the Africans doing in relationship to the Reggae music and what we have to offer now outside of the bling and the wing and the thing. The promoters are seeking to bring the youths into a certain clarity. And they have the feeling that the clarity can come through Reggae music and Rastafari. … Maybe if we follow that part, we can save some of our children.[54]

By critical comparison again, Muta reminds Jamaican artistes and their fans alike to reconsider problematic contents. If African artistes can use the music for positive, progressive messages, then why should the originators of the genre in Jamaica not do better in respecting their own heritage. For Muta, Jamaican entertainers should borrow the insightful way of Sankofa as a foundation or cornerstone for advancements. Reggae's lyrical treasure addresses ideas of resistance and emancipation, which Muta perceives as the genre's very essence and the reason for its major global breakthrough, beyond the original aim of the Black Liberation struggle. When he speaks about Reggae's values, not only for Jamaica but on a universal level, it becomes clear that he misses the spiritual, Afrocentric, and Black consciousness-expanding component in Dancehall music and culture:

Jamaica is almost like a beacon of hope and salvation for many Caribbean people because our music has led the way. Our music in terms of militancy and hope for African people in this part of the world, and for many people who are suppressed all over the world. Our music has created that level of thinking and consciousness. ... Jamaica is like that candle on top of the dark mountain. Sometimes a candle on a dark mountain shines brighter than thousands of candles. You don't see it? ... We owe the years of struggle to make Jamaica be a light out there for the oppressed through songs, poetry, and action. Our voices have been heard and known for liberating people from their oppression. When the Berlin wall came down, they were singing Bob Marley songs. When I toured in Zimbabwe and South Africa, it is our poetry and our songs which strengthened the people in their time of depression.[55]

Muta's sometimes quite emotional rebukes of some artistes and some artistic production should not lead to any form of dismissal of Dancehall as such. Seen in context with his positive evaluation of the creativity, original Africanness, and potential force of transformation, his questioning does not support negative clichés about Jamaican popular culture. Beyond doubt, Dancehall as a genre has tremendously contributed to class struggles over power and space in a postcolonial context. Through legions of conscious artistes from the great U-Roy to Brigadier Jerry or Tony Rebel, Dancehall has a heritage of burning social commentary akin to Rastafari philosophy. The genre plays an ongoing role for the re-negotiation of socio-political imbalances. Therefore, Dancehall still provides a manifold space of permeability between the marginalized mass(iv)es and the elite within Jamaica. Scholar Sonjah Stanley Niaah reminds us of the continuity of such performance spaces since the days of slavery:

Whether on ship decks, in school rooms or shrubs, or on the streets, the enslaved and, later, the freed Africans or peasantry settling across the island of Jamaica, and especially in Kingston, occupied marginal lanes, river banks and gully (ravine) banks, not only for housing and subsistence, but for performance as well. Articulation of the self in these spaces was, and continues to be, potent, as their marginalization is at once their power. ... Among the antecedents of contemporary dancehall are, for instance, both the slave ship dance (or limbo) and the plantation dances ....[56]

However, from a Rastafari perspective, held by Mutabaruka, the contemporary Dancehall ethos has its downsides in the sexualized, sexist, violent, materialistic, and extrinsic values and practices. Muta engages in this complex field with an oppositional fervour, whenever he deems it necessary. This sympathetic, but at times ferocious engagement goes back to the 1980s, when he publicly took on the Shaka Zulu lyrics of Major Mackerel in the song 'Pretty Looks Done' (1987), condemned as demeaning one of the greatest African leaders in history and unconsciously reproducing racialist stereotypes. He questions certain forms of symbolic capital rooted in experiences deemed 'foreign' to an African cultural and experiential framework. Similar sentiments have been given voice by several Roots Reggae artistes feeling betrayed by their Dancehall heirs.

5.3. European Remnants: Christmas, Church, and State

This section outlines Mutabaruka's treatments of Jamaica's religious structures and his recommendations for the revitalization and recapturing of African values. Inasmuch those traditions are still remembered and kept alive in contemporary Jamaican cultures, he calls for their conservation, which, of course, does not preclude adaptations to current needs and interests. Christianity in Jamaica remains ambivalently linked to the history of slavery and the missionary activities under colonial rule. Conversion from African religions and practices was sold to the enslaved by raising hopes for a figurative 'conversion' of 'their 'ownership' to God rather than their earthly masters.'[57] Many enslaved Africans started to embrace Christian beliefs under this prospect of physical liberation, transmitted by white European (since the middle of the eighteenth century) or Black American missionaries after abolition (mostly Baptist preachers).[58] With time, Christian ideals were transformed into an anti-slavery stance, based on spiritual conceptions drawn from African experiences. Apart from Baptist denominations constantly growing in strength, the so-called Myal religion had numerous followers and persisted in different forms now known as Revival.[59] The field of multiple religions of Western and African origin thus mirrors the colonial past of (violent) intercultural exchange. Allegedly, Jamaica has the most churches per square mile of any country worldwide, a view shared by Mutabaruka in a personal interview:

> Jamaica has the most churches per square miles, more than any other country! … If you walk from here (referring to his house in St Andrew; authors' note) to Kingston, you will find more than twenty-five churches. Because you have people who keep church in their yard. They put up a tent. If there is no church, they are going to make a church there![60]

As there are indeed hardly any reliable statistics for all these unofficial private churches, the abundance of places of worship with perhaps just a handful of believers illustrates the informal formations of churchlike congregations. Whereas the small nation-state has impressive churches mostly built during the colonial era, many Jamaicans celebrate mass in simple tents or concrete houses, often without roof and much furniture. The convergence of that many places of worship and the incompatible crime rate quite often becomes the object for Muta's rhetorical *Cutting Edge*. For the 'verbal swordsman,' this incongruousness between religions preaching godly love and the plague of violent hate crimes are gloomy indications for hypocrisy.[61]

Frequently, he reminds his listeners of the upsetting history that Christianity – which he calls a 'bloody religion' – and its propagators manifested.[62] In particular, he refers to the enslavement of Black people 'in the name of Jesus Christ and the Pope of Rome.'[63] Since his childhood, Muta was exposed to the violent European history of wars and conflicts by his mother, who took him regularly to movies, thereby establishing his global (historical) vision. Retrospectively, he is aware of the tremendous impact the movies (and also books) had on his African-centred belief developing in contrast to the European (colonial) values surrounding him (as he also emphasized in chapter 1 of this book):

> Since we are Rasta and we search and articulate, it made sense how we could understand European history and how

> we could see what Europe did to other places, including
> themselves! We must now look through our own spectacles
> to understand ourselves, like Marcus Garvey said: 'The
> white man and Chinese man see God through their own
> spectacles. We must see God through our own spectacles,
> the God of Ethiopia.'[64]

This juxtaposition of knowledge acquired at school on European history with his mother's unpolished stories and impressions from cinema films dealing with European history is key in this regard for an understanding of his explicit condemnations of European colonialism and religious conversion walking in tandem. Confrontation with written and audio-visual sources on European imperialisms of different national origin formed his keen understanding of European nations' misanthropic self-interests in stark contrast to the idealized versions learnt through formal education and preached in (some) churches. This enabled him much later to scrutinize and challenge specific European religious and political ideas and ideals. 'You have to understand European history in order to understand African history,' he argues and hence debunks the oppressive European efforts used to enforce European values and Christian denominations among formerly enslaved Africans in Jamaica.[65] In expressing his contempt, he does not distinguish much between the past and the present. Strongly inspired by Marcus Garvey's suppositions about a Black God, Muta evokes the European origins of Jamaica's prevailing Christian traditions. Especially when it comes to celebrating Christmas, the radio host literally *burns fire* upon this European remnant and all its related 'social ills':

> Most of the holidays that we have were given to us by
> Europeans. Look at Boxing Day. Boxing Day was a day after
> the day of Christmas when the aristocrats in England and
> Europe boxed what was left and gave it to the servants and
> helpers. They call it Boxing Day. Why the hell do we have
> Boxing Day as a holiday? ... Why do we have to celebrate
> everything that Europeans have given us and legitimized
> in our consciousness? The two major holidays of the year
> are Christian holidays given to us by Europeans. There is
> nowhere in the Bible that tells you to celebrate Easter and
> Christmas. Nowhere! ... Europeans came, gave us Easter,
> and let us have a rabbit that lays egg; Santa Clause, the

obese white guy who only deals with children. When he cannot find the children, he stays at the North Pole with some little, short man. He is not to be trusted. And you have people walking around with Santa Clause hat on their heads and dress up in red and white for Christmas. They don't have anything to do with Jesus! Santa Clause is more important to Christians at Christmas or to Jamaicans in general, and even to the Western world. Santa Clause takes presidency over Jesus during Christmas. You don't see nothing wrong with that? That we don't have any snow, and we are dreaming of white Christmas and putting white spray on the glass like we wanted it frosted. And we put up a tree in the house. Why the hell do we put up a tree in the house? What does the tree in the house have to do with Jesus? Jeremiah in the Bible tells you: 'Don't cut down the trees in the forest and put it in the house and put gold and silver on it.' For those who believe in the Bible.[66]

The reference to Jeremiah shows that Muta diligently knows the Bible and can cite particular passages 'on the spot,' to expose the contradiction between certain Christian views and practices (e.g., the Christmas tree). Muta's daughter Ishiwawa remembers her father reading the Bible diligently during her childhood days. She stresses that his knowledge about the Bible makes him an unpleasant discussant for many Christians:

Some of the common Christians they may not really fully grasp his religious ideologies because they are not as well-read as him. So when he is arguing a point, they cannot really match the point because they don't have read extensively as him.[67]

Being obsessed with reading, Muta truly epitomizes his guiding principle: 'the more information is the more inspiration.'[68]

Muta regards Christmas predominantly as a business venture dedicated to the accumulation of economic capital among the rich, especially for traders of Chinese and Indian family origin in control of most consumer markets in Jamaica. Occasionally he considers those post-abolition immigrants as trailblazers in ruining authentic Jamaican craftsmanship. With more than a hint of sarcasm, he attacks them for importing faked Jamaican craft: 'It comes from TaiOne (meaning Taiwan in a pun derived from the song *African* by Peter Tosh

(1977a); authors' note), TaiTwo, and TaiThree. Made in China, made in Ankara, and those things.'[69]

Against this backdrop, Muta criticizes free-market capitalism. He identifies the *Chiney man* as the biggest profiteer from Christmas season. Local street hawkers notably buy products from the Chinese wholesale dealers to sell them by retail for marginal profits. His radio talks thereby refer to marginalized Jamaican voices bemoaning their precarious situation, due to small-scale market disadvantages. He demands a fair share in Christmas business for them.[70] Nonetheless, he exposes capitalism as the rule of the world economy game and background for the institution of Christmas in Jamaica: 'Most Jamaicans don't celebrate Christmas; they celebrate the almighty dollar. They just want to see how much money they can make. From the Chiney man, the Indian man, the Black man. All of them.'[71]

According to Muta the original intent of Christmas has dwindled away under capitalist conditions. Adding insult to the injury that Christmas has never been based on facts, given that Jesus' date of birth is unknown.[72] He boldly postulates: 'There was never a man named Jesus Christ born on 25th of December. Christmas has nothing to do with a man who was born two thousand years ago. Nothing at all! It is a European construct, but everybody gets caught in it!'[73]

Muta redefines intellectual insubordination by negating European values and recommending an African-centred perspective instead. His resistance is also evident in the debate on Jamaica's (political) mainstream perception of the country's holidays and commemorative events. Whereas Jamaica, under the direction of the Ministry of Culture, has annually celebrated the so-called *Reggae Month* in February to 'highlight and celebrate the impact of the musical genre on the country's social, cultural and economic development' since 2008, an official island-wide *Black History Month* funded by the government was somewhat flawed in recent years.[74] Overlapping with Reggae Month, Black History Month was once a month-long celebration of the achievements of Jamaica's African-Caribbean population. Its demise, under the presumption that it was a Black American import, comes under the scrutiny of Muta's postcolonial vision, putting his voice to the wounds of mental slavery:

365 days a year we celebrate white history. And you don't believe me? Look at the women down the road! Look at the men down the road, in the stores! Listen to the politicians! Look in the Parliament if you don't see white history in there. Look in the church if you don't see white history in there. Check your thoughts and think seriously! Your consciousness! You don't see that it is a white history you are celebrating?! Most of the year, we celebrate white history. And we just say one month (referring to the Black History Month; authors' note) and people say: 'This is an American thing.' Halloween ain't an American thing? And Thanksgiving? You don't see nothing wrong with these things? That everything we do, doesn't reflect us as a people. Then we have leaders, who guide us into the same reflection of white people. The politicians and the church people don't think any different. They just push the food a little further, continuously. The politician promises you prosperity when you are alive; the preacher promises you prosperity when you are dead. Everybody promises Black people things, and nobody comes out with the real thing.'[75]

This falls in line with Mutabaruka's more general debates on the intermingling of politics and religion in Jamaica. He treats the lack of a clear (legal and political) line of distinction between church and state to a long anachronistic 'European idea' before so-called Enlightenment at the end of the eighteenth century, and confronts Jamaican policymakers with the unresolved ecclesiastical embeddedness of (many) Jamaican schools:

The church is not supposed to be intertwined with the state! Because the law of the land overwrites what the church is saying! If a man does something in the church, and even though he might repent, the law of the land says: 'Watch yah, you have to go to a court to get trial, and either you go to prison or you get hanged or something.' The church cannot decide who must go to prison and who mustn't go to prison! It is up to the state to decide that! Even though the church has its certain rules and regulations, it cannot decide on a statical (state-run; authors' note) point, as it also relates to the child in the school! ... Statical people run the state, church people run the church! Because if the church and the state are going to be one, you are going to have something named theocracy, which is a problem! Theocracy is when they say, 'God rules.' So it is a

government where God rules. The only problem with this
is that God is not going to decide who must die and who
mustn't die. It is a group of man sitting down in the name of
the church and decide that! … And right now, what we find
in Jamaica is that they don't want to accept certain people
at school, because most of the schools are connected to a
church! … So we are calling upon the state to recognize
the rights of a Jamaican student! … School is supposed to
educate you, not to brainwash you into a doctrine that is
imposed on people and has enslaved them for five hundred
years and more. Because that is what it is doing. And the
custodians of this indoctrination are the same slaves. White
people don't have to be here again since slavery, you know.
They just get some Black people, inculcate them with their
Anglican, Roman Catholic, or whatsoever religion, put it in
their heads and then just send them out there in the state.
So you find that, what they say is a religious education, is
only Christianity.[76]

To fully appreciate the sarcasm, one must bear in mind that many
Rasta Houses stand for an African theocracy under the leadership
of H.I.M. Emperor Haile Selassie I. The Rastafari radio anchorman therefore puts the argument upside down, claiming that it is
really the modern state, failing its democratic constitution by 'mixing
up' theology and education in church-run schools. At one sweep,
he differentiates between the duties and responsibilities of religious
and political leaders, whom he reproaches with their tacit embrace
of theocratic reign. He argues for a clear-cut separation of church
and state from the individual perspective of Jamaican adolescents,
experiencing mixed-up education. Again, his poignant comments
on the Jamaican government's theocratic mindset will make a lot of
listeners 'skin teeth' (or *laugh* in a Patois expression):

People stand up in Parliament talking about Jesus and
the Bible?! They want to put theocracy on us, you know!
Because anytime they cannot solve something, they start
to turn to Jesus. They don't want to turn to Jesus, when
everything is nice with them and it doesn't go bad, you
know. … It's an indictment on how they see state and
church. Church and state mustn't mix! … Anytime you
hear people start suggesting that, it is because they don't
have a solution for the thing. And when they say it, it

doesn't find any solution. Because within the human beings the solutions on human problems exist. You cannot go outside of the human consciousness to find a solution that man creates! Man must find solutions in himself! All the divinity that you are looking for, must be found in the humanity. That is where divinity lies. When you find your humanity, you find divinity! There is no divinity outside of man or woman, because it is consciousness you are working with. Consciousness rose from human beings. Intelligence and understanding are based upon the environment where the human being lives in. And if he cannot control the environment where he lives in, the environment is going to turn against him, as we see in Jamaica![77]

Muta's contemplations on divinity in humans to find remedy for challenges and issues are shaped by his Nyahbinghi experience, according to which Haile Selassie I. is a living God, represented in all his followers. This goes hand in hand with rejections of supernatural belief in a supreme being outside of humans. Thus, for Muta, Haile Selassie is not a supernatural God but is manifested in the human being or, in Rasta philosophy, the so-called *I-and-I* spirituality.[78] His anti-supernatural stance furthermore leads him to consider himself as the biblical 'doubting' Thomas, who, so the story goes, was Jesus' distrustful disciple. In a debate about Christian preachers who offer miracle-evoking meetings in Jamaica, Muta identifies with this notorious sceptic:

I, Mutabaruka, and I will sign a paper to it, am willing to cut off my locks and go to church, if one of those people can help a man, who has one foot, to grow back his foot with a miracle from God or Jesus! Because I am a Thomas, you know. I am worse than Thomas, too.'[79]

The biblical saga indicates that after Jesus Christ's resurrection, Thomas met Jesus and was doubtful about the authenticity of his former leader until Jesus proved him wrong by showing him the nail-holes in his hands. 'Thomas became one of the most devoted disciples because he never just believed, he wanted to know,' Muta explains further.[80]

In another thought-provoking episode, the radio presenter utters a carefully considered criticism of the Christian vestiges in society and the political elite. Due to his presumably 'anti-Christian stance,' he reaps a lot of criticism from some sections of society opposed to Rastafari philosophy. Sometimes even live callers during broadcasts articulate their repudiation, though not often, to the extent of referring to him as 'Satan incarnate.'[81] Muta appears almost motivated by such rejections and generally takes criticism light-heartedly. Listening to a substantial number of his talks, one gets the impression that he constantly tries to craft even more controversial narratives, attempting to self-fulfil the prophecy of the 'steppin' razor.' Authenticity, genuineness, and a good dose of radicalism make the recipe of his programmes:

> We try to heal the people with certain meditation and certain thinking. We try to really communicate to the people in the best way I can communicate with them. Because we don't come with any degree for journalism and any degree for that. We just come as we, and so we are speaking to you. Who doesn't like it, bite it! So it goes. And we see that the communication is real, and people gravitate towards the communication, whether uptown, downtown, or middle way. Some people don't like how I say the things; some people prefer I say it the other way. But we cannot do it the other way, as we stay so.[82]

This section of the book outlined that Muta promotes a self-determined conception of religion and spirituality, apart from heteronomous practices dictated by (post)colonial actors, but rather influenced by African experience and memory. As mentioned earlier, he declined our proposal for a book title such as 'Rastafari Verbal Swordsman,' making it apparent that he does not conceive of any of his programmes as some sort of religious proselytizing. However, he understands that everyone, at least in Jamaica, knows that he is Rastafari from head to toe. But he declines to speak for Rastafari, by always insisting to reason as Mutabaruka, once and for all. Which is reason enough to take a closer look on his representation of Rastafari on air.

NOTES

1. Henriques (2011, x).
2. Bourdieu (2013, 86).
3. CE 13 (2017).
4. Gilroy (1993, 10f).
5. SR 48 (2017).
6. SR 47 (2017).
7. Ibid. and SR 48 (2017).
8. King cited by Carson et al. (2000, 374).
9. Cf. Interview 1 (2018).
10. SR 27 (2016).
11. Cf. SR 16 (2015); SR 18 (2016); SR 31 (2016); SR 32 (2016). Self-destructive eating habits facilitated by global food chains were also one of the main subjects of Muta's various talks as guest lecturer in anthropology courses at 'our' University of Vienna (for instance on December 12 and 13, 2011).
12. SR 30 (2016).
13. Ibid.
14. Cf. chapter 1.5.
15. Cf. CE 12 (2017) and SR 17 (2015).
16. Cf. SR 49 (2017).
17. SR 21 (2016).
18. SR 50 (2017).
19. Stolzoff (2000, 2).
20. Hope (2006, 9f).
21. Cf. Hope (2006, 18f.). It is important to note in this regard that there are also Dancehall supporters from the *uptown* area, representing Jamaica's middle and upper class. However, the majority of supporters are from the underprivileged sector of society.
22. Given that Muta differentiates between Dancehall and Reggae, we stick to his distinction, which also corresponds to Moskowitz (2006). However, this should not be seen as a strict juxtaposition, as even the originators of Reggae consciously upheld the Dancehall as its most lively expression. Bunny Wailer may be referred to in this regard, who even in his seventies always included a Dancehall section of the early Wailing Wailers classics in his show, cf. Zips (2021).
23. In fact, music may be seen as the bridge(s) connecting the three authors of this volume. When Mutabaruka hit the international arena with his *Check It!* album (1983a), Werner Zips, then anthropology student, was instantly excited about Muta's revolutionary poetry, later on teaching on this subject, and working with Muta on various projects, such as the film on his 'triumphant return' to Africa, namely Ghana, for Panafest 1997. Sebastian Schwager, an ardent Reggae-lover and musician himself became motivated to study anthropology and eventually decided to turn

his interest into a master's thesis under supervision of Werner Zips. For more information on Schwager's music, visit his website: https://linktr. ee/sabolious and https://www.anaves-music.com/.

24.   SR 22 (2016).
25.   Ibid.
26.   Cf. Stolzoff (2000, 104–106).
27.   Cf. Cooper (2004, 73f) and Stolzoff (2000, xxi, 100).
28.   Cf. Stolzoff (2000, 99–104).
29.   See also Hope (2006, 1–24) and Wynands (2000, 162–74).
30.   Stolzoff (2000, 100ff).
31.   CE 12 (2017).
32.   SR 23 (2016).
33.   SR 49 (2017). See also Stanley Niaah (2010, 16).
34.   CE 12 (2017).
35.   SR 29 (2016).
36.   We use the notion of distinction as coined by Pierre Bourdieu in *Distinction: A Social Critique of the Judgement of Taste* (2010). Its German title 'Die feinen Unterschiede,' which may be translated into 'accomplished differences,' appears even more telling.
37.   Stolzoff (2000, 206f).
38.   Cf. Stanley Niaah (2010, 3); see also Zips (2008, 233).
39.   SR 18 (2016). Note: When Muta speaks about *in front of light* or *in the video* he broaches the common practice of videographers capturing the party on film and spotlighting certain dancers in the searchlight, see also Stolzoff (2000, 206).
40.   Cf. Katz (2009).
41.   SR 18 (2016).
42.   Sonjah Stanley Niaah (2010, 121f) outlines the connection with African dance patterns and their sexually charged movements, relying on earlier accounts of Carolyn Cooper (1993, 11; 2004).
43.   SR 24 (2016).
44.   SR 23 (2016). Cf. also CE 12 (2017).
45.   Cf. SR 35 (2017).
46.   SR 17 (2015).
47.   SR 28 (2016).
48.   Ibid.
49.   Cf. Ibid.
50.   Cf. Cooper (2012, 3) and SR 28 (2016). For more information about the festival in Austria: http://www.riseandshine.at/.
51.   SR 28 (2016). In this respect, see for instance the book *Everything but the Burden* edited by Greg Tate (2003), in which different authors write about the appropriation of the Black American Hip-Hop culture by white people.
52.   SR 28 (2016).

53. Cf. Kuwornu-Adjaottor/Appiah/Nartey (2016, 26).

54. SR 22 (2016). Note: From time to time, Muta visited Zion Radio, a radio station in Abidjan (Ivory Coast), and broadcast his two programmes *Cutting Edge* and *Steppin Razor* from there.

55. SR 47 (2017).

56. Stanley Niaah (2010, 18).

57. Gordon (1998, viii).

58. Cf. Chevannes (1994, 18) and Gordon (1998, viii).

59. Cf. Chevannes (1994, 17–22).

60. Interview 1 (2018).

61. Cf. SR 10 (2015).

62. SR 17 (2015).

63. SR 15 (2015).

64. Interview 1 (2018).

65. Ibid.

66. SR 50 (2017).

67. Interview 4 (2018).

68. SR 38 (2017).

69. SR 47 (2017).

70. Cf. SR 50 (2017).

71. SR 50 (2017).

72. For instance, Doggett (2006, 579) debates: 'Although scholars generally believe that Christ was born some years before A.D. 1, the historical evidence is too sketchy to allow a definitive dating.'

73. SR 4 (2014).

74. Jamaica Information Service (2015).

75. SR 50 (2017).

76. SR 15 (2015).

77. SR 40 (2017). As a matter of fact, from former prime minister Portia Simpson-Miller to former Minister of National Security Peter Bunting, to current prime minister Andrew Holness, many Jamaican parliamentarians spoke about a *divine intervention* that would help to face Jamaica's issues such as crime. That's why Muta quizzically names Peter Bunting 'Mr. Bunting the Divine' and Andrew Holness 'St Andrew the Holy One' or 'St Andrew of Holiness.' Cf. SR 31 (2016); SR 39 (2017); SR 41 (2017).

78. Cf. Mutabaruka (2006a, 30f).

79. SR 10 (2015).

80. Ibid.

81. Cf. CE 6 (2015) and SR 10 (2015).

82. SR 50 (2017).

CHAPTER 6

'NO LIKKLE CULT'
On Rastafari and Africanness

It were Rastafari who were shouting for reparation! So
they are not some lazy people sitting back and just smoking
ganja! Even though that is the expression that was there
and is still there.

Mutabaruka: *Steppin Razor*, March 17 (2016)

We don't stop Black History month on none of the
programmes, you know. Every month! So anytime you hear
we are going in certain things, it's because we are conscious
of what we really want to bring across to the people as
it relates to their African-centred perspective and their
Africanness.

Mutabaruka: *Steppin Razor*, March 2 (2017)

Rastafari to Mutabaruka represents no learned knowledge, as he
repeatedly declares.[1] For him, the experience of Rastafari in 'first time'
– meaning the roots of the philosophy and culture – derived from a vision
of full emancipation within Black Power consciousness. Therefore,
neither the Bible, nor the two autobiographic volumes written by
H.I.M. Emperor Haile Selassie I. during and after the Second World
War, nor the 624-page strong collection of speeches, published in
Addis Ababa under the title *Important Utterances of H.I.M. Emperor Haile
Selassie I*, were authoritative textbooks for the spread of the philosophy,
as he emphasizes: 'No autobiography and no selected speeches of
Haile Selassie guided Rastafari! Rastafari had a conversation because
Rastafari knew of Haile Selassie as a revolutionary and liberating
force.'[2] Muta's statement in a fairly hot-tempered reasoning with a

caller about the origins of Rastafari hints at his personal conception or vision, which emphasizes an Afrocentric spirituality of liberation and a certain *livity* that goes along with it, instead of religious or Bible-related written sources and Haile Selassie's own publications. The following chapters present and discuss some of Muta's perspectives on Rastafari as transmitted live on the radio, secondly, his activism relating to claims for *reparation* in the case of the violent Coral Gardens incident and, thirdly, his notion of decolonization, which coheres with his understanding and public manifestation of *Africanness*.

6.1. The Roots of the *Original* Rastaman

The radio host's reasonings relate, but do not entirely coincide with defining tenets of other Rastafari organizations (or *Houses*) such as the Bobo Shantis or the Twelve Tribes of Israel. In this regard, one should not search for internal divisions, contradictions, or even rivalries. The openness of Rastafari reasoning – as opposed to the development of closed doctrines – is a defining element of the dynamism and inclusiveness of this philosophical tradition, according to Muta:

> There is a unity in Rasta that is not uniformity. People believe that to be unified you have to be uniformed. Like you are in an army. I put it into people that Rasta is very unified, but really we are not uniformed. I am not seeing uniformity as a prerequisite for unity. That is what the sociologists are searching for. They are searching for a uniformity in the reasoning and the behaviour of Rastafari; a uniformity that is not there and you will never see, because it is an evolution that is taking place. It is not a stock thing.'[3]

As he already described in his autobiographical notes (see chapter 1), Muta was once attracted to the Twelve Tribes of Israel organization, based in Hope Road/Kingston, not too far from the original Tuff Gong studio (now the Bob Marley Museum). He later turned away from the Twelve Tribes due to their strong reliance on the Bible, even though it was deconstructed and reinterpreted through African or Black experiences. According to his own words from a personal interview, the ecclesiastically structured and religious character of this large Rastafari House, which has been also base for many great Reggae artistes such as Bob Marley or Dennis Brown, did not correspond with his broad African re-orientation and wish for a radically different *livity*, or way of life:

> The idea of Twelve Tribes was kinda fascinating: a very structured and organized group of Rastafari; a lot of intellectual uptown youths, who could articulate Rasta on another level. Because, really and truly, many Rasta, if you talk to them, they cannot really articulate why they are Rasta! The Twelve Tribes were structuring it. And coming from school, you want to see that. But then after you have started to dig deep, you realize that it's not the structure that matters, but it is the experience. It wasn't allowing you to experience what Rastafari is in its essence. Rastafari is a way of life, it is a *livity*, you know! And it is not a *livity* as it relates to the dogmas and religious ideas of Christianity. It goes outside and beyond Christianity. It is like an ancient person living in the present! ... So the Nyahbinghi weren't structured. But they were defining what I wanted to see in Rasta: the experience! The experience of living in the bush, using woodfire instead of electric stove, planting trees and vegetables and eat them. The idea of doing things that you wouldn't normally do! The Twelve Tribes person studies and reads the Bible. That is studying Rasta in order to come to a conclusion about Rasta. The *livity* of Rasta is beyond religion, beyond studying the history of Ethiopia and beyond just saying 'the King of Kings, the Lord of Lords, the Conquering Lion of Judah, Emperor Selassie the First.' It is a *livity!* ... It was Rastafari that makes me know how to chop coconut without making the water spill! And it was Rasta that makes me know that you have three eyes in the coconut. One of them is soft, so you can dig it and drink the water out of it. These are just some simple little things, but it is *livity!* That is really what grabbed me! It moves beyond just God.[4]

Accordingly, the Nyahbinghi House and many of its members, particularly some of its elders such as Bongo Hugh (or Bongo Hu-I), appealed to his own vision. This regionally well-known *bushdoctor* practised his holistic approach in a medical office close to the Desnoes and Geddes factory near Montego Bay and was something like an unofficial centre of knowledge for Rastafari *livity*. Additionally, he opened up a cultural centre near Cambridge in the parish of St James, which represented perhaps the first temple of contemporary Rastafari art in Jamaica. Under the full name *Rastafari King Selassie I Divine Nyahbinghi Theocracy Contact Centre* it organized contact tours for tourists interested in Rastafari with its motto 'bridging the gulf between time and eternity.' This is worth noting, since this open-minded approach to broad public and even global outreach permeates Muta's attitude towards Rastafari publicity, from his early days of lecturing in a hotel in Negril to his latter worldwide touring as an artiste and his thirty-odd years of constant appearance on air.

However, it would mean a vain attempt trying to categorize or even shelving Mutabaruka into any of the broadly circumscribed Rasta Houses or communities. Even more so than most other Rastafari, he refuses any closed descriptions from the outset. His radio audiences know about his often surprising and unorthodox views that sometimes clash with other Rasta conceptions, but in a constructive amicable way. When others would appear as strict opponents in heated debates, Muta will always start his argument with something like 'bredrin or sistren, hear me now,' expressing respect and equality. It is well known within the Rasta community and beyond that he privileges Afrocentric ideas over what he calls the Judeo-Christian tradition based on Bible revisions.

He is also keen on Asian or Eastern philosophies and a collector of Buddha statues, which should not be mistaken for some sort of 'cultural appropriation,' but rather as a symbolic sign for his sincere attraction to the spiritual-philosophical tradition attached.[5] Occasionally, some Rastafari question his free-spirit. For instance, for Priest Fego from the Bobo Shantis in Bull Bay, this presents a case of non-allegiance: 'Muta showed me that he is not a Twelve Tribes, not an Orthodox, not a Bobo, not a Nyahbinghi. … You cannot be neutral in this thing here, you know. You cannot be neutral in this war here. It is a war, you know. Either you are on God's side, or you are on Satan's side.'[6]

The honourable priest is certainly not the only one taking issue with Muta's distancing from the Bible as the single authoritative source for the faith. In fact, Muta even denies that Rastafari represents any such thing as a faith or a religion. All the different Rasta Houses 'differ' in their views and reasonings on what Rastafari is all about in terms of *livity*, spirituality, philosophical guidelines, and practical aims. There exist variations or divergent ideas on how the movement started or who may be identified as a Rasta.[7] All this supports Muta's aforementioned assertions that Rastafari has little uniformity, but sufficient unity. Its 'lack' of uniformity, to him, is a simple, logic consequence of the plurality of individual experiences in the absence of a fixed doctrine (written or not). This may appear 'confusing' to sociologists, theologists, or those anthropologists, who aim to categorize Rastafari as yet another religious denomination, as Muta discussed lucidly in his keynote speech at the Vienna conference of the Society for Caribbean Research in 2001:

> ... the nucleus of this experience is Haile Selassie. That mean you will hear the man in New York saying Haile Selassie and you will hear the man in the hill saying Haile Selassie and you will hear the man on the ground in Kingston saying Haile Selassie. But how he got to Haile Selassie is totally different, totally different. And this is what is confusing the sociologists. It is confusing the sociologists because they want a pattern to study. A lot of people they want a pattern. How do we study Rastafari when you have one Rasta saying one thing and a next Rasta saying the next thing? Yes, because it's an experience. So most Rastas will tell you that Rasta is not a religion, even though the form, having a theological nucleus, appears like a religion to some.[8]

Muta agrees with many Rastafari voices, uttered not least by countless Reggae tunes, calling for more unity, but warns against any misinterpretation of this as uniformity, as the latter would threaten the creative dynamism embedded in Rastafari communication or reasoning.[9] He, therefore, embraces diversity within Rastafari, sometimes in tension with Rastafari organizations claiming philosophical or spiritual leadership. The following quote from the same speech at the University of Vienna, elucidates his view, acknowledging the confusion it may create for outsiders (or 'tourists'):

> So we are saying here that the Rastaman in the hill, who is articulating Rastafari, who most of the time did not read any book, because he did not have the information

like the man on the ground in Kingston, he is articulating
Haile Selassie out of an experience. Very important.
An experience, not a written thing, an experience. So if
someone who speak to this Rasta in the hill, he will hear a
total different articulation than from the man in the streets
of Kingston, who is a Rasta. Now to the normal tourist
this is weird. How come the Rasta over there so saying a
different thing of the Rasta over there so? Because it is not
a conform and a uniform religious believe, as we know it.
Because when people studying religion, they are studying
it based on a belief system. There is no Rasta religion per
se! There is not a Rasta religion. People want to say 'Rasta
religion.' There is a Rastafari experience. The experience
is a way of life. And the man in New York City, who is
experiencing Rastafari, will not say the same thing like the
man who is living in Kingston, like the man who is living in
Westmoreland. It's a total different experience.[10]

Unity exists in the central focus on Haile Selassie I., the 'nucleus' of
Rastafari, proclaimed as Black people's redeemer by one important
founding father of Rastafari, namely Leonard Percival Howell.
Yet even the relationship with Haile Selassie I. is quite personal for
most followers of the philosophy, as Muta explains on the origins of
Rastafari in a broadcast:

Before Haile Selassie was on the throne of Ethiopia, his
name was Ras Tafari. You had people in Ethiopia and
Africa who used to follow Ras Tafari before his name was
Haile Selassie. That's why you hear people saying they are
Rastafari, meaning that they follow Ras Tafari. ... How
Rastas are behaving now? They turn the thing in just a
religion. They perceive and really validate Haile Selassie
through the Bible. When they quote the Bible, they say:
'Haile Selassie said his foundation is in the holy mountain.'
Haile Selassie never said anything like that! So the reasoning
is that you have some original Rastaman who couldn't read
nor write, but they listened to Leonard Howell who said
that Haile Selassie is ushering a new perspective for the
redemption of Black man and is going to redeem Africa
and Black people out of white supremacy and slavery!
... The people in Jamaica who started to follow Leonard
Howell were Christian-minded people, and they read the
Bible, you know. So, since reading the Bible, they started to
associate certain passages of the Bible with Haile Selassie,

> like Revelation 5 and Psalms 87. Thus, when they declared
> that now, they started to feel like they have to use the Bible
> to validate their perception of Haile Selassie. The Rastafari
> who I know, who don't read Bible, never used the Bible to
> validate Haile Selassie nor used what Haile Selassie said
> in the autobiography and in the selected speeches. They
> used Leonard Howell and then started to tread an *ital livity*,
> and in that experience it started to open up lots of nature
> arguments.[11]

According to this statement, the coronation of Ras Tafari Makonnen as Haile Selassie I. on November 2, 1930, in Ethiopia was perceived as the fulfilment of Old Testament prophecy in Jamaica and interpreted as a divine sign for liberation of downtrodden Africans in the diaspora. Its global coverage in media became the catalyst for the foundation of early Rastafari followers who started to revere Haile Selassie I. as Black people's redeemer and interpreted his coronation as remedy from white supremacy.[12] In the latter quote, Muta points to the Christian background of some of Jamaica's early Rastafari, which eventually has led to a Bible-based conception of Haile Selassie's personality in many Rasta Houses to this day. However, some 'original Rastaman,' as Muta refers to the founding fathers, further developed Leonard Howell's fundamental philosophical and theological arguments about Selassie as the Black God but eschewed over-dependency on the Bible. Their *livity* took the path of a recollection of traditional African values, or 'a natural way of life.' Of course, this must be seen as a creative and dynamic recovery, not a return to a particular ethnic culture. In the so-called Pinnacle community in the parish of St Catherine, which was the most important hub of the Rastafari movement in the late 1930s and throughout the 1940s, Howell and his followers designed the principles that are still relevant amongst various Rasta communities and organizations: self-sufficiency, the practice of *oneness* and a re-education with an Afrocentric mindset.[13]

Due to its rebellious anti-church and anti-government proclamations, the nascent community faced considerable pressure from colonial authorities and Jamaica's then Chief Minister Alexander Bustamante (later to become the country's first prime minister). Bustamante eventually ordered a devastating raid on Pinnacle in 1954, which dispersed thousands of communal farmers to Kingston and other regions of the island, eventually contributing to the dissemination of Rastafari philosophy and culture in Jamaica.[14] Pinnacle was not the only Rastafari community exposed to atrocities carried out by the British colonial government and the early post-independence government of Jamaica.[15] Muta, in this regard, recollects police shooting practices, providing evidence for the extreme persecution of Rastafari in those days:

> There was a time in Jamaica when Rastafari couldn't walk on the roads. And not only that, you know. Many people don't know that the police in Jamaica used to use the image of Rasta as target practice at their gun place to fire after.[16]

At times, the Rasta manhunt by the authorities came close to pogrom-like dimensions. On top, public opinion in Jamaica was shaped by an insulting and dooming stance towards the Selassie-praising, ganja-smoking, and dreadlocks-wearing early practitioners, as Muta reports in a programme:

> Rastafari have gotten certain persecution and humiliation since their time. Everything bad that is happening to a Jamaican, happens to Rasta, by the society! There was a time when Rasta couldn't walk on the road! And we didn't scam somebody, because the only two things they could lock up Rasta for was ganja and badword (swearword; authors' note), according to them. As a matter of fact, the times when I went to jail, it was for these two things. Ganja and badword![17]

Despite being a respected intellectual and radio presenter today, Mutabaruka was unjustly (albeit briefly) imprisoned due to allegedly possessing ganja and using swearwords, as the ready-made standard reasons for incarceration in prisons or mental asylums.[18] Muta often stresses that Rastafari are still humiliated nowadays, though the outward deprivation of the most basic civil rights has somewhat eased after Haile Selassie's visit to Jamaica in 1966.[19] This ground-breaking event of the first state visit by an African king – the King of Kings, in fact – facilitated the movement's legitimation in the public eye:

> Rastafari in its own soul became legitimized by the visit of Haile Selassie to Jamaica. Before that, in 1963 and in the

> 1950s, there was a brutal war against the Rastafari faith. …
> We were brutalized, but now we see that the struggle of a
> few has become the struggle of many![20]

The revolutionary poet, expanding his public appeal to mainstream radio, has been influenced by various Rastafari *brethren*, whom he occasionally credits in his radio shows. Two of Muta's erstwhile companions during his time in the Rastafari community of the Twelve Tribes of Israel are former PNP-opposition leader Peter Phillips and pan-Africanist Jerry Small, who used to host a talk show (on NewsTalk93 FM). Muta remembers that Phillips and Small were responsible for shaping a Rasta mentality for the youth (including himself) in the early 1970s:

> We used to go up and down between Peter Phillips and Jerry
> Small. And Jerry Small is the only one who is left out of
> the whole group. All of the others felt that they can join the
> government to change the thing and turn the system itself.[21]

Several Rasta-inspired individuals, such as Peter Phillips, became later involved in politics, which Muta doesn't regard as an appropriate space for social transformation loyal to Rastafari idea(l)s. He questions Phillip's progression as a political leader, for losing sight of his own Rastafari past.[22] One of his long-time *bredrin* or comrades is Prof I, a Rastafari in the Nyahbinghi tradition who, as Muta alleges, maintains 'a certain ancient kinda way' of how to live a Rastafari life.[23] As opposed to a mainstream conception, the notion of an 'ancient' Rastafari way implies a certain *livity* and way of keeping spiritual gatherings, the so-called *Binghis*. According to Muta, such perception is practised at *Redemption ground*, which is Prof I's *yard* and community spot for reasonings and gatherings.

Inspired by political reasonings, Muta uses his weekly time on air to follow a rights-based approach, wherever Rastas and common people fell victim to maltreatment, even in cases of atrocities from years back such as the Coral Gardens incident (equally remembered by a great number of Reggae tunes).

6.2. 'You Don't Have to Love Us, But You Better Respect Us': About the Coral Gardens Reparations

In his broadcasts, Mutabaruka vehemently and emphatically reminds his audience about the Coral Gardens massacre of 1963, which is also known as *Bad Friday*.[24] In the Coral Gardens Rasta community near to Montego Bay in the parish of St James, a government-sanctioned joint military and police raid resulted in multiple deaths and imprisonments of more than one hundred Rastafari.[25] Muta was one of the most vocal activists for a thorough investigation in the matter and relentlessly pleaded for an official apology from government. Eventually, the campaign led to a belated legal investigation more than half a century thereafter. It finally resulted in an official apology condemning the government's actions and the establishment of a J$10 million trust for reparations. The then equivalent of less than US$80,000 is not considered as adequate compensation by activist groups.

Since this subject exemplifies Muta's role and engagement as a public intellectual, the various episodes featured in his radio programmes will be presented along with his activism for reparations in the context of slavery. Let's start with the particular case, before we take a closer look on the much larger picture of reparations.

During the events of the Good Friday (respectively *Bad Friday*) weekend in April 1963, Rastafari clashed with state authorities and military forces following a fire at a gas station attributed to actions of the alleged culprit Rudolph Franklyn and members of a local Rastafari community. Alexander Bustamante, prime minister at the time, ordered a prosecution and allegedly demanded capture of all Rastafari 'dead or alive.' It triggered an island-wide campaign against Rastafari, who were forcefully trimmed off their dreadlocks.[26] For many decades, most mainstream media bought into the government's official version of an unlawful uprising of Rastas, calling for policing measures. But slowly accepting Rastafari views as ventilated through various Reggae tunes, legal representations, and not least radio programmes such as Muta's *Cutting Edge* and *Steppin Razor*, public opinion changed towards a critical review of the entire conflict, thereby shifting responsibility towards state-inflicted violence and systematic discrimination against the Rastafari community.

For years, in annual commemorations, Rastafari supported by some civil society actors, academics, and intellectuals scrutinized these brutal assaults, commemorated the victims, and fostered political dialogue.[27] To some sceptics of these commemorations, Muta countered in this way:

> We might be chanting and keeping these commemorations every year and people might ask which purpose it serves. When Irie FM took this march and the rally on the road for the recognition of the Coral Gardens massacre in 2013, when we started from Ward Theatre and moved up to Mandela Park, it was one of the biggest rallies anybody has ever seen. It is said that 'the race is not for the swift'! Or: 'The battle is not for the strong but is who can endure to the end.' Well, I know that something is happening. Because if I never knew that something is happening, I would have gone somewhere else. ... Rastafari have gone through all these tribulations and trials for years! For years! But we persuade and we stand tall! And I want to say to my Rastafari brethren and sistren to not let the thing get you giddy and twisted, you know! Because there is a light at the end of the tunnel! We know! We don't ask anybody that! African people must find their place in the scheme of things again!'[28]

The radio presenter reminds his listeners of the giant dimension of the 2013 protest march in Kingston that was organized by Irie FM, the Rastafari Millennium Council, the Coral Gardens Committee heads, and himself, in order to raise consciousness in the nation about apology and financial compensation of the Coral Gardens massacre.[29] He encourages his Rasta comrades to withstand in a long struggle, of which the final proclamation at Mandela Park appears highly symbolic, reminding of Mandela's long march to freedom. At once, Muta appeals for the support and participation of Jamaica's Rasta-affiliated Reggae artistes: 'The Rastafari cannot just jump up and down the place at stage shows every day and don't really take part in something that is relating to the history of Rastafari!'[30] Live on air, Muta appears as a Rasta activist who relentlessly claims compensation as well as recognition:

I am calling upon the government of Jamaica to recognize the importance and significance of compensating the ones who are still here and apologize to the Rastafari community. Because we have already seen where these atrocities against the Jamaican people by the state continue in different ways. … Rastafari is not a fringe group. Rastafari is one of the main characteristics of Jamaica! And it is not a likkle cult! People talk about Rastafari like it is a cult. I am not in a cult business! We have contributed to the development of the Jamaican society holistically! We came and showed the people healthy food and a healthy lifestyle, whilst people mocked us and sent us to prison. And now we see that healthiness is part of the whole thing. … The two most visible faces on a T-shirt right now amongst people who are progressive and radical are Che Guevara and Bob Marley! At most places you go. If you go in a T-shirt shop in California, New York, or Amsterdam, the two faces that are most prominent are Che Guevara and Bob Marley! And it was Rastafari which shaped Bob Marley! So Rastafari is not any fringe thing in Jamaica.[31]

Muta is aiming here towards a broad and deep rectification of the inadequate image many Jamaican people (especially politicians and some Christians) may still nurture about Rastafari, namely that it is a marginal movement in society at large. He wants people to realize that it was Rastafari that had shaped global superstar Bob Marley, who in turn made Jamaica a popular and internationally known island with all economic benefits deriving from this upliftment. Therefore, in a broadcast in March 2016, he demands the recognition of the cultural momentum that Rastafari has built up over the years:

The Rastafari community is the community that has placed Jamaica on the map! Because if it wasn't for Rastafari, there would be no Bob Marley! We have to go to the root and give thanks to Rastafari which was able to shape and sanctify Bob Marley so that he was able to go out there and put Jamaica on the map! Rastafari has given the world what they want to call a new cultural expression in relationship to what they would call a religion. The cultural expression of Rastafari has spread wide and far, near and top and bottom. We want to say that Rastafari, undoubtedly without any dispute, has made Jamaica into a cultural mecca! The culture of Rastafari has enabled Jamaica to be a cultural mecca! We don't beg no one for any respect! Rastafari respect is due! And respect must be given![32]

Whilst addressing politicians, he calls for more broad-based social respect and elucidates that the quintessence of Rastafari has generated a new concept of self as it comes on to how African people see themselves in the Western world.[33] This concept appears tantamount to the preservation of an Afrocentric self-confidence. As indicated earlier, at last Muta's assertiveness and activism paid off. Following the pivotal commitment of public defender Arlene Harrison Henry and her extensive report on the Coral Gardens incident, an official governmental declaration was eventually accomplished in April 2017.[34]

Therein the Jamaican government under Prime Minister Andrew Holness issued a formal apology to the Rastafari community. Holness stated that the government (which belonged to the same party as in 1963, namely the JLP) deeply bemoaned the incident from 1963, which, according to this release, should never have happened. In addition to establishing a trust for the benefit of the attack's survivors, the prime minister promised that parts of the Pinnacle property, long sued for by Rastafari activists such as Bob Marley's eldest granddaughter Donisha Prendergast, should eventually be turned into a protected heritage site under the Jamaican National Heritage Trust.[35] What appears like a great achievement for the Rastafari community and its struggle for official recognition and respect substantiates only the beginning of the whole process of retributive justice, as Muta comments:

> Apology is one, but the mending is the next. But I for one accept the apology. We are going to see the next move between that and the government, what is going to take place now in order to what we call compensating the remained victims of that atrocity! So the struggle continues![36]

Acknowledging injustice committed is not the same as retributive justice, honouring the damage at least in the possible ways of material compensation. In April 2021, the government announced that in addition to the funded establishment of the so-called *Rastafari Coral Gardens Elders Home* in Norwood, regular monetary disbursements have been delivered to the Coral Gardens victims still alive since the formal apology four years earlier.[37] The political adoption and thus recognition of the Rastafari claims has indeed helped Rastas to accumulate symbolic capital. It is, however, the economic capital that matters in terms of retributive justice. Thus, the monetary compensation as well as the funding of a social and medical facility in the form of the mentioned elderly home by the responsible decision-makers may have constituted a formidable success for the Rastafari movement.

Although it is no longer a foregone matter, further action needs to be taken until formal reparations are achieved through legal compensation. Muta's aim is to attain the last facet of a three-level process towards these reparations. In his opinion, at first an apology should be articulated, then a compensation paid, and finally the compensation has to be broadened to the much larger pending claim of overall reparations.[38] Horace Chang, Jamaica's current Minister of National Security, promised that commitments for further development will be realized, such as a permanent structure to the Elders Home in Norwood, an office for the *Rastafari Coral Gardens Benevolent Society*, and fifty acres of land to develop a farm and community.[39] But could this suffice in the much broader context of reparations?

In general, Muta considers the yearning for reparations as decisive for establishing a Caribbean reparation movement at academic and political platforms.[40] These reparations focus on the international agenda of collective compensation for damages enslaved Africans suffered during slavery and the entire colonial era.[41] Addressing UK and Spain, the two former colonial powers ruling Jamaica, the radio philosopher sketches his concept of reparations:

> Reparation is when you accept the wrong that you did to a people, and then you do something about it! That is reparation! Reparation is not 'you are going to lend me money through IMF, so that I can build better schools.' That is not reparation! That is a system designed by the capitalist state to deal with economics and social order. Reparation is: 'You did something to my foreparents, so you are really sorry for that, and you are going to mend it.' That is reparation! Steppin Razor![42]

On the agenda of many Rastafari since at least independence, the plea for such reparations has now entered manifold spheres, e.g., Caribbean sports circles such as the *CARICOM Reparations Youth Baton Relays and Rallies*. Muta reports favourably on an event taking the shape of a run for reparations:

> It is a run to sensitize Jamaica and the argument of reparation for the atrocity that had been done during slavery days. We believe that Europe, especially Britain, France, and Spain, owes the people who were traumatized and are still traumatized for the atrocity that had been done. The worst atrocity that had ever been done against a people. And this reparation run is part of the sensitization of Jamaican people. Because when you talk about reparation, many people don't know what you are talking about. Some people mix up reparation with repatriation. When they say reparation, they mean repatriation. When they say repatriation, they mean reparation. But both come hand in hand. However, one is different from the other. Reparation means you are going to repair what was done to the people.[43]

At this point, Muta mentions *repatriation* as yet another crucial aspect of Rastafari demands for retributive justice besides reparation, namely claiming a physical return to the motherland of Africa.[44] Rastas started to claim reparations and repatriation not least through their musical medium of choice, in order to rectify the historical evil of slavery and colonialism. Primarily through famous Rastafari Reggae artistes, the demand for reparations and repatriation for the descendants of Africans (who were oppressively displaced from their continent during the transatlantic slave trade) received an internationally heard voice.

In recent years, Reggae artiste Chronixx was one of the protagonists singing about it, as the striking lyrics of his song 'Capture Land' (2014) exemplify. The lyrics brand America as 'capture land' referring to thieves like Columbus and the Queen from England causing a genocide among indigenous people and holding Africans in captivity on said 'capture land.' Repatriation therefore is still a must, as Rastafari declared ever since their rally for social justice. Recently, similar demands have been raised by the Caribbean political alliance CARICOM and Caribbean academics.

In 2014, CARICOM declared a *Ten Point Plan for Reparatory Justice*, which calls for regional rehabilitation programmes, formal apologies, repatriation rights, and further actions taken.[45] These programmes and activities are supported by famous scholars such as Jamaican professor of social history, Verene Shepherd, whom Muta calls his 'favourite radical.' Ultimately, as the radio host points out, one can identify a regional political and academic adoption of the Rastafari plea for reparation and repatriation.

An official political agenda can help to realize these legitimate claims. In the course of a formal meeting with UK's then-prime minister David Cameron in 2015, Jamaica's former leader Portia Simpson-Miller attempted to raise the issue of reparations, which, however, was ignored by Cameron.[46] Muta was deeply upset by Cameron's ignorance and his preparedness to negate the matter of reparations for slavery.[47] In line with all Rastafari organizations, particularly the Bobo Shanti of King Emmanuel Charles Edwards, who wrote hundreds of letters to so-called world leaders demanding a revision of the original compensation of slave masters for the 'loss' of their slaves at the event of emancipation, he keeps the memory of this absurd indemnification of the perpetrators alive. Muta points to the incomprehensible fact that former slave owners in British colonies were paid compensation up to the amount of £20 million after the abolition of slavery:

> After taking us from Africa, when the colonial master decided that he is going to free the African people from slavery, he paid 20 million pounds compensation to the backra masters (slave masters; authors' note) for the loss of work force! He gave the slave owners 20 million pounds! When he gave them the 20 million pounds, they said: 'Alright, slaves! You are free!' … Now, when the men let us free in a country where we don't own any land, and we never got any 20 million pounds, they say: 'Let them be sent back at their land, you know, make them repatriate to Africa. Because they came not by free will, but by force! And if they came by force and we let them go on a land which is not their own, and we don't give them any land or anything to fend for themselves, what are they going to turn?' They are going to turn scammer! Larceny! All the things that you don't want and don't like; it is going to breed these people! Because you never sent me back to Africa!'[48]

The wheels of justice grind notoriously slow, but they grind, if somebody keeps them going. It may not fully qualify under Muta's notion of reparations, but it may be a first breakthrough, when the University of Glasgow (Scotland) signed the first formal act of reparation for the Caribbean in the form of a £20 million contribution to the new Glasgow-Caribbean Centre for Development and Research in July 2019. It will be operated by the University of the West Indies and the University of Glasgow, guided by the principle of reparatory justice for the victims of slavery and colonialism, and is geared to deal with research in the context of reparation claims. Preceding this decision, the University of Glasgow has acknowledged the millions of pounds it received from the proceeds of slavery.[49]

For such progress, fiercely fought for almost a century, Muta shows pride in the resilience of his Rastafari *brethren* and *sistren* who have led Jamaican people (or the African diaspora in general) to the reconstruction and adequate comprehension of their Africanness and the justified calls for (diasporan) African redemption: 'When everybody seems to want to forget their Africanness, it is the Rastafari brethren and sistren that are reminding the Jamaican people: 'Look here, man, don't cut off your umbilical cord'!'[50] Sketching the intimate connection between Jamaica and the African continent, Muta uses a biological allegory, the umbilical cord. This allegory has also been used by Nelson Mandela during his public speech in Harlem (1990) when he referred to the relationship of Black Americans and Black South Africans.[51] Similarly, famous Black American sociologist and intellectual W. E. B. Du Bois wrote on this transatlantic (or rather global) bond of Africans with the motherland (in his autobiographical text *Dusk of Dawn*):

> On this vast continent were born and lived a large portion of my direct ancestors going back a thousand years or more. The mark of their heritage is upon me in color and hair. These are obvious things, but of little meaning in themselves; only important as they stand for real and more subtle differences from other men. ... But one thing is sure and that is the fact that since the fifteenth century these ancestors of mine and their other descendants have had a common history; have suffered a common disaster and have one long memory. ... But the physical bond is least and the badge of color relatively unimportant save

as a badge; the real essence of this kinship is its social
heritage of slavery; the discrimination and insult; and this
heritage binds together not simply the children of Africa,
but extends through yellow Asia and into the South Seas. It
is this unity that draws me to Africa.[52]

Rastafari were among the pioneers raising this awareness of
pan-African *kinship* or a common social and mental heritage in the
Caribbean and beyond. Particularly in Jamaica, Rastas tirelessly
evoked a collective memory and consciousness highlighting and
celebrating diasporan history and identification with Africa. Muta
affirms the necessity of returning to an African identification: 'Rasta
has become a beacon of hope for the salvation of the Jamaican people,
who must recognize themselves eventually as African people!'[53] It
presents one of his major achievements as a poet, musician, radio
host, and social activist to spread decolonizing thoughts and practices
in order to dispose of (post)colonial heteronomy and its vestiges in
unbroken structures of mental slavery.

6.3.   'The Slave Mill Still Ah Gwaan': On the Decolonization of (Post)Colonial Realities

Mutabaruka's rhetoric may at times appear militant to some, but
never alludes to violence. Of course, the context of Jamaica and other
Caribbean islands fundamentally differs from current developments
in the US, where the threat of racially biased violence is a permanent
daily experience, demanding preparedness for self-defence. For
instance, US-American Black nationalist Malik Zulu Shabazz, during
a call-in interview with Muta in a *Steppin Razor* show (August 2017),
talked about military preparations of the US-based New Black Panther
Party 'for the big war that is to come.'[54] Although Shabazz, called a
racist and extremist in the *Extremist Files* of the Southern Poverty Law
Center, didn't elaborate his statement, one can suppose he referred to
politics of self-defence the Black Panthers proclaimed from the late
1960s onwards, following the murders of Malcolm X and Martin
Luther King Jr.[55]

American anthropologist and pan-Africanist James Small, during an intense interview with Muta on air in 2016, spoke of war between US-police forces and the Black community. He, however, promoted an economic rebellion in the form of internal sanctions along ethnic lines, namely the economic boycott of white American businesses by Black citizens.[56]

Mutabaruka's militancy by and large has the communicative rational base of advocacy for socio-political transformation and refrains from escalation. From the assessment of a fair number of radio broadcasts, it may be concluded that it is still 'the system which is the fraud,' as one of his most successful poems stated.[57] He abstains from denigrating white people in general and certainly does not support segregation or much less physical violation in retaliation. But he could not be more outspoken about his rebuke of white structural racism embodied by white supremacy. Most of this rejection goes beyond lamenting historical suppression (or *downpression* in Rasta reasoning) by positively calling for resurrection of Black consciousness and knowledge of (African) history, in short, the African integrity for (Jamaican) people of African origin. Therefore, most westernized (colonial) ideas are brought to biting social commentary and questioning, thereby contextualizing the overall theme of political, economic, sociocultural, religious, and legal *decolonization*.

Occasionally, these talks refer to symbolic decolonization as, for instance, the renaming of Jamaica's roads and parishes in line with African experiences, instead of remaining mnemonic signs for the colonial past.[58] Often, his contextualization mirrors his African and global perspectives, for example, the so-called *Rhodes Scholarship* for students from former British colonies, a prestigious grant for the University of Oxford that is named in honour of white supremacist and imperialist Cecil John Rhodes:

> Cecil Rhodes killed thousands of Africans. The place is now called Zimbabwe. It was once called Rhodesia after Cecil Rhodes who killed thousands of people, like King Leopold in the Congo. But Black people are very proud to get the Cecil Rhodes scholarship. We love when we are honoured by our slave masters. When our slave masters honour us, we feel good. When our Jamaican people honour us, we say: 'That is a little local honour.'[59]

Through such deconstructions, lucidly challenging vaguely hidden colonial legacies, Muta educates his audience. Particularly, legacies considered 'good' in mainstream thinking, such as awarding the Rhodes Scholarship, are among his favourite targets. These considerations, reminiscent of literary criticism in academia, form an integral part of his practical mental decolonization: 'The slave mill still ah gwaan, and the slavery still exists. Even if it is in our mind, it still exists.'[60]

In the realm of geopolitics, his verbal swordsmanship happily slices the colonial residues of the British crown. He likes to sarcastically refer to the land ownership of Queen Elizabeth II as the *Queen of the United Kingdom and the other Commonwealth realms* over Jamaica, at least until the Jamaican government seriously decides to become sovereign state in the form of a republic (as prime minister Andrew Holness declared on March 23, 2022, at the occasion of a 'royal visit' of Prince William and Princess Catherine of Wales), following the example of Barbados (in 2021).[61]

Unsurprisingly, at the occasion of Queen Elizabeth's II death on September 8, 2022, Mutabaruka reinvigorated his call for a British apology with reparations in several national and international broadcasts. He declared the responsibility of the Crown for the deeds of 'her family,' culminating in a strategy to 'rebrand slavery and call it colonialism.'[62] Technically speaking, the British monarchy reigns in the fifteen Commonwealth realms, all of which are non-republican forms of government. Muta therefore reminds his audience and the Jamaican government that the Queen (and her successors) could reclaim her crown land at any time.[63] As mentioned before, ownership of land is an important and emotional topic for Muta. One of the dicta he always presents in the context of decolonization and the struggle for sovereignty and self-governance is 'Land is power,' which he had already highlighted artistically in his poem *Big Mountain*:

> dont let di whiteman tongue fool yu
>
> dont let his paper cool yu
>
> dont let his fire water get u down
>
> stand up and fight for your piece of ground
>
> stand on big mountain its your ancestors earth

> land is power without it life has no worth
>
> stand on big mountain you'll have to be strong
>
> good must overcome the struggle is long
>
> in afrika and asia he went to civilize nations
>
> yet in the land of liberty and justice he has reservations
>
> on the big screen he played his silly game
>
> usin the image of john wayne
>
> robbin and rapin he stole the land
>
> refuse and resist the whiteman plan[64]

So-called 'Indian reservations' exemplify the white imperialist strategy of taking the land by occupation, not only in the US but globally. It is but one historic example for the exclusion from the rest of a country. South Africa's 'homelands' in the days of apartheid would be another, just as the land grabbing in colonial Rhodesia, which remained basically untouched after independence until President Robert Mugabe's large-scale confiscation of white-owned farms after 2000. In a broadcast from November 2017, shortly after Robert Mugabe's ousting from Zimbabwe's presidency, Muta re-reads his controversial leadership over a period of almost four decades as a struggle over land reform from colonial occupation:

> Mugabe is the only leader who decided that he wants to take back the land for the people. And they put an embargo and sanctions on his country, make it look like the people are not in a good economical situation because he is wicked. But we must remember that the Americans and the British do that with everybody. And I see they are doing it all over the world. … Most of the wars that have been fought on earth were fought over land. People's desire is to own land. And when white people go into your country, it is land they are searching for. Land, land, land! When Columbus came to Jamaica first, it was the land he wanted to dig up to find gold. When America went into Iraq, it was land they went after to control. So land is power. If you don't have any land, you don't have power.[65]

Although the quote refers to colonizing countries, imperialist invasions, and occupations through war, the analysis refers to any circumstances. Following Garvey's footsteps, Muta emphasizes the socio-political and economic importance of land ownership for postcolonial Africa and Black people in the African diaspora. For an adequate evaluation of his narratives on controversial figures such as Robert Mugabe, it seems utterly important not to read anything into his statements, which he did not say. In a joint online interview lasting two and a half hours, updating information for this book in March 2022, Muta complained that he is often overinterpreted or sometimes entirely misrepresented.[66]

We consider it therefore incorrect to read these rhetorical provocations as signs of broad approval for particular autocrats. He nowhere says that Mugabe was a wise leader, or even that his almost four decades in power were examples of 'good governance.' Well aware of his 'steppin razor' dance on thin ice, given the abundance of critical voices from Zimbabwean authors and artistes such as Tsitsi Dangaremba and many others, he merely refers to the issue of land confiscation and the succeeding Western condemnation of Mugabe as terrorist or maniac or something similar.[67] This does not mean that he is an ardent supporter of Robert Mugabe's leadership or even the actual land redistribution in favour of the Black elite, which some politicians insinuate even in Jamaica, according to his own impression:

> In Jamaica, it's not a popular line to defend Mugabe, especially amongst people who claim politics. But we don't care because we see what they do to the people and our people, when I talk about defending land! When Mugabe toed the line, they loved and hugged him and gave him 'Sir.' But when they realized that he is going to take away the land from the white people, he was no longer whatsoever he was. He was denounced as a terrorist. You understand? If you check the history of America and England, other leaders get denounced as tyrants when they don't support their regimes.[68]

Beyond doubt, the later Robert Mugabe has been portrayed in Western media as a corrupt despot, after he was originally courted following independence with the expectation to bind Zimbabwe close to the West, economically and politically.[69] As someone with first-hand knowledge who has visited Zimbabwe under Mugabe's rule, Muta simply puts his finger to the double standards employed in Western discourses, which thinly veil self-interests in African resources, market-oriented trade relations, or even tourism. Only if these and other vital interests appear threatened, friends turn into dangerous enemies overnight. Thus, calling Muta names such as 'demagogue, Black populist, or even racist,' as probably everyone has heard people talking about him, finds little support in his words. It rather correlates with prejudices and random associative reinterpretations towards 'the man they love to hate,' as he himself ironically refers to these and other descriptions of his personality. Some of his subject matters in radio programmes are less portraits of actual situations or thorough political analysis but rather self-reflexive examinations of the (post)colonial psyche.

This becomes evident when he groups historic leaders with highly different leadership qualities in one breath (e.g., in the following quote). His prepared food for thought is therefore hardly the reign of Robert Mugabe, as influential he may have been, but the complexities often overlooked when a political leader or an entire country becomes discarded from Western favouritism.[70] George Bush's Jr. in/famous dictum 'You are either with us or against us!,' apart from its biblical origins, qualifies as the signifier for Western self-interest, which Muta frames in the Black/white dichotomy behind enslavement and other atrocities.[71] His target is the combination of two faces of power: the power of representation and the power of material domination:

> I still hear people putting Mugabe in a certain light because of these white media that feeds them with news about African leaders. Just like how they tell you about Muammar Gaddafi, Idi Amin, Kwame Nkrumah, Patrice Lumumba, Jomo Kenyatta, all of them. The only one white people love is Nelson Mandela. And you see the ones who the white people love, Black people love them, too. The ones who the white people hate, Black people hate them, too. You don't see anything wrong with that? ... Why is it that every time African leaders look out for their country and the interest of their country, it turns out like they are evil, and they are painted evil. ... They listen to BBC, CNN, and Fox Channel; all these channels which support white people things. And then now they form their view about African

leaders. Show me one African leader in Africa right now
that the media doesn't vilify except Nelson Mandela?![72]

In many of these challenges to his (Black) audience, Muta instigates a
critical revision of mainstream Western (or 'white' in his words) media.
He questions people's dependency on mainstream Western media.[73]
When Nelson Mandela is singled out as the only positive example of
Black leadership, more radical and perhaps militant leaders such as the
great Steve Biko become forgotten or silenced by (media) historiography.
'They want everybody to be like Nelson Mandela,' Muta wonders
about the singular adoration of the former South African president.[74]
A comparison between South Africa and Zimbabwe draws attention
to the burning question of land transformation after the legal land
grabs. Among these laws, the Natives Land Act of 1913 in South
Africa and the Land Apportionment Act of 1930 in (then) Southern
Rhodesia (now Zimbabwe) are of exemplary importance. The first
limited African land ownership to mere 7 per cent of entire South
Africa, the latter made it illegal for Africans to purchase land outside of
established *Native Purchase Areas* in Southern Rhodesia.[75]

Juxtaposing the two countries' different status of land reform in the
new millennium, Muta highlights the almost unchanged continuation
of the status quo in South Africa against the sweeping expropriation of
white farmers in Zimbabwe under President Mugabe.[76] His revaluation
of their contrasting 'white media' representation, according to him,
has nothing to do with racism. In the following passage, illustrating his
view on the indelible connection of racism and power, he distinguishes
criticism – 'racism is not talking' – from disenfranchisement,
exploitation, and suppression, or *downpression*:

> Racism is a philosophy which says that you don't like
> another racial group because the group is destined to be
> inferior. And you use your influence and power to hold
> something over that group. Racism cannot be without
> power. It is power that drives racism. Economical, social,
> and political power. If you don't have the means by which
> to decide another race's standing socially, economically,
> and politically, it cannot be racism! ... White people created
> societies and structures to keep themselves as supreme.
> They call it white supremacy, and white supremacy

maintains itself through power! So there is no argument about Black people being racist! How the hell can Black people be racist, and they don't have any power to decide the economical and political welfare or well-being of other races? As a matter of fact, we are the only group of people that cannot decide the political, economical, and social condition of any other group of people! ... Whether in a society, as a nation, or as a group of people, superior means you are above a group. Black people are in no position to decide any other race's political or social order! If I talk on the radio and I talk about what white people did to us, people start to say: 'Muta is a racist when he talks about white people.' How can talking about white people make you a racist? Racism is not talking. Racism is when you act, when you decide that your race is superior to the next race and then you use power. ... Me talking about white people, or Black people talking about white people, or white people talking about Black people, it may have racial slurs, but it doesn't reach racism! ... I don't know of any Black people as a group of people who can decide that about any group of white people or any group of Chiney people. Yet for hundreds of years, racism has decided how we function in earth and has kept us down and oppressed us.'[77]

His paraphrasing of racism restricts the adequate use of the notion to oppressive practices, enforcing subordination, exclusion, and stagnancy through deprivation of basic rights. Muta understands 'race' as an impregnable historical distinction between Black and white.[78] This shows the profound influence of his favourite book *The Autobiography of Malcolm X* on his thinking.[79] As he emphasizes in chapter 1, no other book had a comparable impact on his thinking, his work as an artiste, and his radio presence as Jamaica's most poignant social critic. *The Autobiography of Malcolm X* became something like the guiding star for his project of decolonizing the mind.

Muta regularly interfaces his call for multi-level decolonization with a thorough deconstruction of globalization. He targets positive connotations of globalization as a necessary and unavoidable subscription or subordination of 'postcolonial' nations, for instance when he analyses the political economy of food chain dependencies and the colonization/globalization of food consumption. Of course, processed food, or so-called 'fast food' is his favourite target, from the early days of his artistic campaigns on Dub and/or Reggae riddims. The aptly titled 'Junk Food' (1983b) proves prophetic today:

> Junk food fullin' up de place
>
> Dis is a nada disgrace
>
> Junk food fullin' up de place
>
> A now good food a guh guh to waste

Given the take-over of junk food in Jamaica, he warns against the next waves of food consumption globalization, potentially creating havocs in many African countries. The more African countries are seen as the prime emerging markets, the more the devastations of predominantly US-American food chains for people on the ground will be felt, according to this quote from a radio programme:

> Globalization is the raping of your food and eating habits. That is what globalization does. It makes you become like a zombie to what they place in front of you to put in your mouth to eat. They call it fast food. It kills you quick! … Globalization doesn't allow sovereignty of people from different historical backgrounds or different cultural perspectives. It puts you under one order. That is what it is. It puts you under one order, economical, social, political, religious, sexual, and any other 'al' you can find come under that. A terrible thing, and we must watch it! Because now they are really pinpointing Africa. All roads lead to Africa. That is what is happening.[80]

Like Muta, Jamaican anthropologist Donald Robotham regards globalization as a hierarchy-reinforcing and hegemony-generating process, which is determined by political, economic, and cultural power games.[81] It is interesting to examine the obvious congruities with Muta's verbal slashes:

> This global racial-cultural hierarchy places Anglo-American culture at the apex and Sub-Saharan African culture at the base. Hegemony is exercised, first of all, within the complex racial and cultural hierarchies internal to the United States and Europe, and through this route, extends itself globally.[82]

This conforms in content with Muta's arguments about globalization and its evocative *one order*. Furthermore, Muta's notion of sovereignty resembles the philosophy of Marcus Garvey, who pursued a similar conception of a (Black) nation's sovereignty.[83] Garvey invoked his followers: 'Never be a race of servers, but a race of sovereigns.'[84] Talking about sovereignty, Muta does less refer to national sovereignty, but to independent thinking and democratic participation, often referred to as popular sovereignty.

As with all other subjects, there is no debate too controversial and no topic too hot for Muta getting involved. Pluralist gender perspectives and the decolonization of sexuality and gender equality is such a theme. Jamaica, and particularly its Reggae and Dancehall scene, has been targeted by LGBTQ+ rights activists, leading to the blacklisting of many artistes, internationally. The politics of blaming and shaming are questioned by Muta with his keen historicization, clearly exposing colonial morality steeped in Victorian ethic codes. He leaves no doubt that homophobia was no invention by the enslaved but an indoctrination by slave masters' mentality:

> Imagine, they (the former slave drivers; authors' note) gave us a book and told us: 'Look here, the thing (homosexual activity; authors' note) is not supposed to work that way.' And now they turn to these uneducated slaves and say: 'Look here, you better work it out!' So what must we think?! ... Because from the Bible, these what they would call uneducated, backward, and former slaves got their ideas from. And it were the Europeans who gave them that book! Why is it that when the former slaves start to read it and realize that this thing cannot work out, you hear: 'Bwoy, right now the former slaves are homophobic!' Homophobic, that is how them call us! Terrible, terrible, terrible.[85]

Muta addresses the international pressure on countries like Jamaica to immediately consent to a change in international morality, referred to recently in Western countries, 'as an important marker of civilizational status.'[86] Western countries' considerable economic and political pressure on African nations, according to him, reveals an element of hypocrisy.[87] Historically, Jamaica and all other former British colonies were indoctrinated and trained in religiously encoded homophobia, heteronormative sexuality, and binary gender constructions. There existed no second opinion in the moral code of acceptable sexuality since it was civil law enacted by the Parliament of England in 1533. This first so-called *sodomy law* transferred jurisdiction in such cases from ecclesiastical courts to civil courts. It was enacted more than one hundred years before the British occupation of Jamaica and determined sexual and gender socialization for the last centuries. It was finally repealed after Jamaican independence in England and Wales in 1967, relating only to consensual homosexual acts in private, and unsurprisingly retained in many former colonies, including the Anglophone Caribbean.[88]

Therefore, Muta correctly points out that the anti-homosexuality stance and the conventional gender constructions in many former colonial countries had primarily been shaped by British slave drivers, their mind control practices by harsh punishments, and the later forced devotion to the sexual rules of the Bible.[89] The legal codes in former British colonies known as *buggery law* still maintain punishment for homosexual acts, for instance in Jamaica imprisonment for up to ten years.[90] These statutory regulations based on a slave system legal heritage should be critically reviewed for a still common homophobic stance. Muta's history lessons on homophobia defer guiltiness from the banned Dancehall artistes to the colonial legacy.

However, as recent international reports show, the social climate and situation for the LGBTQ+ community in Jamaica has improved in recent years, and there is a visible trend for revisiting those colonial rules.[91] Yet the removal of the archaic law appears to be a lengthy process as some sectors of Jamaican society are not prepared to easily decline moral standards, deeply ingrained by religious upbringing. A first breakthrough attempt was launched by former prime minister Portia Simpson-Miller. The PNP-affiliated politician and first female prime minister of Jamaica had raised hopes for the LGBTQ+ community with her announcement to review the buggery law during her 2011 campaign.[92] In retrospect, however, Muta reads her statements as triggered by outside forces, and less her own initiative, namely, to sustain the foreign aid threatened to become sustained by foreign governments such as the UK, the former colonial motherland. Muta rebukes Simpson-Miller for empty promises made to please foreign donors:

> There was something going on three years ago when the prime minister of England said that they are going to rethink aid to countries that are homophobic, and where governments don't recognize the rights of the gay community. So Portia Simpson-Miller played into that by saying that! And now we haven't heard her saying anything more about it. ... Why she originally said that is not because of the Jamaican situation! She said that because at the time David Cameron and his friends declared: 'If you keep discriminating against gays, we are going to draw in and withhold aid from you!' So she had to say that![93]

A close reading of this and other Muta quotes on the issue indicates that he is framing the much-debated subject within a decolonizing, postcolonial perspective. Accusations of homophobia and heteronormative sexism severely harmed individual artistes and, indeed, the entire Jamaican share in the Reggae industry. By implication, Muta discloses international pressure for transformation, as related to old hegemonic orders, in the double sense of an entire moral order forced upon colonial subjects and orders directed to appropriate thought and action. This stance is strikingly different from apologetic statements of some Dancehall artistes defending the presumed morality of a 'natural binary sexual order.' He does not relate to the content, but rather the form, when criticizing the submissive stance taken by then Prime Minister Simpson-Miller to demands by UK Prime Minister David Cameron. In the absence of any attempts of rational conviction based on the force of argumentative reasons, the naked resort to power, comes to the fore: 'And if you don't accept that, they want to create problems for your economy because they have power. So they can decide about your moral or ethical perspectives.'[94]

Such a regress to hierarchical superiority clearly shows the continuation of age-old power structures to him. Far from admitting their own moral mistakes in puritanical colonial orders backed by Christian ethics, the threat of economic sanctions for insubordination under the new rules reveals ongoing conditions of dependency. Anthropologist Raymond Smith argues, '(that) small nations are pawns in a game that is played by others.'[95] However, these politics of unilateral control may often prove counterproductive, as they rather provoke resistance and a degree of stubbornness, when they clash with experiences of freedom struggles, decolonization, and self-determination.

Mutabaruka does not hide his own upbringing within a heteronormative ideology that suggests binary sexual relationships as 'more natural' than others. He thematizes his scepticism of transgender identities as a road to social progress and has some reservations about the promotion of sexual diversity on public television, but does not condemn homosexuality or show disregard for the LGBTQ+ community.[96] Debating anti-gay sentiments in society and (post) colonial law take another direction, particularly when he criticizes some intolerant mindsets of many Jamaicans and calls for a review of some ubiquitous crude attitudes.[97] Never afraid to touch hot potatoes, Muta puts the spotlight on emerging social conflicts between sex workers with different gender identities and sexual orientation. In recent years, gay sex workers, often forced into these relations of dependency by extreme poverty and homelessness in downtown Kingston, appear to take over the red-light district of New Kingston, catering for the middle and upper class.[98] In a broadcast from December 2014, for instance, he warns against the rise of violent conflicts, potentially harming female sex workers and their dependent single-parent households:

> I want to give a cry out to the female prostitutes! The female prostitutes told me: 'Muta, these boys (alluding to the gay prostitutes; authors' note) come on the road and take away our job. You know, we have to fight about men with them!' ... They are not easy when they sit down there and say: 'Mutabaruka, I listen to you on the radio all the while, you know. You have to tell them that they must stop taking over our corner, because they don't have any children to feed!' The women complained to me. ... I am just warning the people who are in authority! There is a bomb that is going to explode in that area of Kingston! You have the youths right now who are creating havoc in New Kingston with their gay lifestyle in the gully. And also, now they are coming up on top of the road to terrorize people with their situation! The authorities need to rectify this red-light district in New Kingston.[99]

Certainly, such statements can be easily misread, especially by listeners unfamiliar with Muta's world views and predominant concerns. Most of his rhetorical targets focus on precarious situations of the (Jamaican) majority, including even sex workers, who hardly ever find recognition or attention in public debates, at least not in their interest. We have therefore attempted to contextualize Muta's *Steppin Razor* and *Cutting Edge* strikes. Our focus was on the background of his Rastafari philosophy, his notions of decolonization and postcoloniality, in their relevance for Black social justice struggles, for instance claims for reparations, repatriation, and, in general, the liberation from habitualized structures of mental slavery.

His radio shows certainly play a huge role in decolonizing colonial impositions and thereby challenging the hegemonic Western system of knowledge and power, through both his own social commentaries and debates with selected guests and random callers. Determined by his ardent stance against white supremacy, he promotes Black Power as well as Rastafari world views and practices. His constant agency for justice towards African-Caribbean, African, and African-diasporan people employs an Afrocentric perspective that has contributed tremendously to the rise of Black (historical) consciousness in Jamaica and beyond, over a period of more than three decades. Whether establishment and authorities in Jamaica like it or not, most, if not all Jamaicans grow up or have been accompanied with Mutabaruka's philosophy and opinions for most of their life. This book may be seen as a first step to emphasize and acknowledge his tremendous influence on Jamaica's moral standards.

NOTES

1. That was one of his key messages in his keynote at the Eighth International Conference of the Society for Caribbean Research in Vienna (July 4–7, 2001). It is aptly captured by the title of his talk and article 'Rasta from Experience,' cf. Mutabaruka (2006a, 21–41). The oral transmission of the philosophy by knowledgeable elders was already one important subject of his inaugurating speech of the Nyahbinghi Center in Pitfour in early August 1984, witnessed by Werner Zips.
2. SR 13 (2015).
3. Mutabaruka (2006a, 37).

4. Interview 1 (2018).
5. Cf. Interview 1 (2018); Mutabaruka (2006a, 29); SR 13 (2015); Zips (2011a); Zips (2015, 116).
6. Interview 3 (2018).
7. Cf. Barnett (2005).
8. Mutabaruka (2006a, 29).
9. However, he is worried that the globalization or universalization of Rastafari through Reggae music, somehow 'proselytizing' people living at the four corners of earth, threatens the integrity of inherent conceptions of Black Power or Black Liberation, as he strongly emphasized in a statement on YouTube: 'Mutabaruka Speaks About White Rastas and The Rastafari Movement,' link: https://www.youtube.com/watch?v=LnwIN8VVeRQ.
10. Mutabaruka (2006a, 29).
11. SR 13 (2015).
12. Although slavery was officially abolished in 1834, almost one hundred years before, the miserable situation for Jamaica's Black majority hadn't changed a lot. Colonial power relations were maintained by the white minority succeeding the planter class whose repressive measures were pervasive. Cf. Andwele (2006, 11f).
13. Cf. Chevannes (1994, 121–24) and Lee (2003, 143–51).
14. Cf. Lee (2003, 209–220).
15. Cf. *Jamaica Observer* (2015).
16. SR 35 (2017).
17. SR 12 (2015).
18. Cf. SR 12 (2015) and SR 46 (2017).
19. Cf. CE 20 (2021) and SR 12 (2015).
20. SR 22 (2016).
21. SR 21 (2016). See also CE 7 (2015).
22. Cf. SR 21 (2016).
23. SR 12 (2015).
24. The documentary film *Bad Friday: Rastafari After Coral Gardens* provides an inclusive insight into the events of that time and interviews with some of the victims, cf. Thomas/Jackson/Wedderburn (2011). A personal memory of the incident features Rasta elder Prince Elijah Williams in *Book of Memory: A Rastafari Testimony* edited by Michael Kuelker (2004).
25. Cf. Campbell (2014).
26. Sadly, isolated cases still happen today like they did back then. In 2021, Jamaican police cut off the dreadlocks of a teenage Rasta lady while she was in custody. This incident was vigorously debated by Muta in a *Cutting Edge* episode, cf. CE 20 (2021). See also Fleary (2021) and McLean/Gordon (2021).
27. Cf. Frater (2018).
28. SR 21 (2016).
29. Cf. McGibbon (2013).

30. SR 21 (2016). Note: His use of the same wording of 'jumping up and down' for his fellow Jamaican artistes and his statement directed towards white Rastas (in the YouTube statement quoted in endnote 9) should be noticed, as providing evidence for his impartiality in this regard, calling for action speaking louder than words.

31. SR 30 (2016).

32. SR 21 (2016).

33. SR 35 (2017).

34. Cf. Barnett (2018: 149).

35. Cf. Atlanta Black Star (2017).

36. SR 37 (2017).

37. Cf. Newell (2021).

38. Cf. SR 21 (2016) and SR 30 (2016).

39. Cf. Newell (2021).

40. Cf. SR 21 (2016).

41. Beckles' *Britain's Black Debt* (2013) provides an in-depth discussion of Britain's slave markets and reparations in the Caribbean.

42. SR 14 (2015).

43. SR 47 (2017).

44. Cf. Zips (2006b).

45. Cf. Caricom (2015).

46. Cf. Mason (2015).

47. Cf. SR 14 (2015).

48. Ibid.

49. Cf. Jamaica Global (2019).

50. SR 21 (2016).

51. Cf. Talton (2018).

52. Du Bois (2007, 59).

53. SR 12 (2015).

54. SR 42 (2017).

55. For more information about the Extremist Files, visit: https://www.splcenter.org/fighting-hate/extremist-files/individual/malik-zulu-shabazz.

56. Cf. SR 27 (2016).

57. The poem is included in the form of the song *De System* on the album called *Check It!* (1983a).

58. Cf. SR 9 (2015). Note: Unaltered since the pre-independent era, Jamaica has been divided into fourteen parishes. For instance, the parish of St James was given its name in honour of King James II., who was the reigning monarch in the seventeenth century. See also Jemmott (2021, 11).

59. SR 9 (2015).

60. English translation: 'The slave mill is still going on'; SR 45 (2017).

61. Cf. Burke (2022) and *Jamaica Gleaner* (2022). Note: Regular proposals by Jamaican politicians for a constitutional amendment to make Jamaica

a republic and replace the Queen with a president as head of state have been made since the 1990s and came to nothing until the time of writing (2022).

62. In an interview for the US-American news channel MSNBC (on September 14, 2022; see https://www.youtube.com/watch?v=rF2JDph-9sA).

63. Cf. SR 23 (2016).

64. Mutabaruka (2005, 24).

65. SR 45 (2017).

66. In this online interview (2022) Mutabaruka stated the following:

> A lot of Jamaican people have never travelled yet. When they hear me talking, it sounds alien to them. ... So when you tell these people those things, it is kind of far-fetched for them. But a person who is outside of Jamaica, who has travelled like yourself, knows what has validity out there. ... Two white people have always come and written about Reggae. The problem is, are they writing from their guts or just because they feel a euphoria when they come to Jamaica? And they write it in some utopian way rather than really remember what the person said to them?

67. See Dangaremba's novel *The Mourning Body* (2020), which in many ways does not only refer to her female protagonist, but Zimbabwean civil society at large, for which she was nominated for the Booker Prize and received the Peace Price of German book sellers.

68. SR 45 (2017).

69. Cf. Escher (2019).

70. Mugabe's political philosophy is also known under the term *Mugabeism*, as described by Sabelo Ndlovu-Gatsheni (2009, 1,154):

> Mugabeism as form of populist reason is a multifaceted phenomenon requiring a multi-pronged approach to decipher its various meanings. At one level it represents Pan-African memory and patriotism and at another level it manifests itself as a form of radical left-nationalism dedicated to resolving intractable national and agrarian questions. Yet to others, it is nothing but a symbol of crisis, chaos and tyranny emanating from the exhaustion of nationalism.

71. Bush's dictum was uttered in a joint press conference with French president Jacques Chirac on November 6, 2001, preceding the US-led invasion of Afghanistan and later Iraq in 'coalition of the willing,' cf. CNN (2001).

72. SR 45 (2017).

73. Beyond reasonable doubt, key figures of the Black Liberation struggle, particularly African liberation heroes and Black nationalists in the US, such as Malcolm X, were presented as *hate preachers* by many, though not all Western media, even when they merely tackle blatant racialized unbalances, demanding social justice for all. See also Zips/Kämpfer (2001, 27f.).

74. SR 45 (2017).

75. An excellent example of the cynicism of British colonial administration regarding land expropriation is provided by the former Native Land Commissioner of colonial Southern Rhodesia, cf. Powys-Jones (1955).

76. Cf. SR 45 (2017).

77. SR 18 (2016).

78. Cf. Zips (2015, 118).

79. Cf. Haley (1999).

80. SR 22 (2016).

81. Cf. Robotham (2000, 2).

82. Robotham (2000, 3).

83. Cf. Martin (1986, 36, 105).

84. Garvey cited by Martin (1986, 105).

85. SR 11 (2015).

86. Hubbard (2017).

87. Cf. SR 22 (2016). Note: For many African countries, e.g., Uganda, a legal adoption of the decriminalization of same-sex practices not to mention marriages is unimaginable and the pressure from Western countries to do so (and, hence, the aid cuts by those) is oftentimes regarded as a hegemonic ambition and an approach of keeping African countries dependent, cf. Molloy (2014).

88. Cf. Bailey (1955) and Ramsay (2018) for homosexual law reform.

89. The reasons for the present-day anti-homosexual disposition are very complex. Helber (2015) provides a detailed review of the convergent socio-historic and (post)colonial aspects.

90. Cf. Offences Against the Person Act (2014, 26). Note: In fact, the law, which officially is called The Offences Against The Person Act, doesn't formally interdict homosexuality per se, nor does it prohibit a lesbian or gay lifestyle. However, anal intercourse is one of the main activities associated with same-sex intimacy, and that's why gays and lesbians are technically more likely to be charged with the offence of that law.

91. Cf. Faber (2018).

92. Cf. *Jamaica Gleaner* (2013).

93. SR 7 (2015).

94. SR 41 (2017).

95. Smith (1988, 178).

96. Cf. SR 41 (2017).

97. Cf. SR 18 (2016).

98. Cf. SR 4 (2014) and SR 20 (2016).

99. SR 4 (2014).

CHAPTER 7

CONCLUSION AND OUTLOOK
'Life and Lessons'[1]

By means of his weekly platforms, the *Cutting Edge* and *Steppin Razor* radio shows, Mutabaruka dissects existent societal values and idea(l)s, religious norms, domestic issues, and international affairs. Being an insurgent host or lifelong *rebel*, as he likes to refer to himself, he often assails Jamaica's political elite and its presumably corrupt and dysfunctional governance. He regards most politicians as upholding a colonial system that resembles the oppressive and hierarchical structures introduced by colonial rule. In a country with a colonial legacy of elitism based on the exploitation and indoctrination of the masses, Mutabaruka serves as a Black Power role model. He fearlessly and unapologetically takes responsibility for the promotion of an Afrocentric world view. His radio shows motivate the deprived and disadvantaged segments of Jamaica's society to overcome the (post-) colonial mindset, as it relates to 'race,' class, religion, politics, gender, or sexuality: 'It's all about trying to make the people understand themselves on a next level,' as he frames it.[2] He scrutinizes the often-hidden causes of unequal social conditions and inspires self-empowerment. Almost ten thousand hours of live broadcasts – an unimaginable number that could well fit into the *Guinness Book of Records* – articulate a policy of resistance and resilience of *Africanness*.

Mutabaruka is one of the loudest voices demanding a comprehensive decolonization, including the mind of formerly colonized people. His rallies for overall Black Liberation target not just the continuity of suppression and exploitation by former colonial powers and their allies, but internal structures, likewise, often circumscribed as 'mental slavery' by Rastafari. For thirty-odd years, the weekly radio broadcasts played havoc with colonial mindsets still prevalent in parts of powerful elites ruling postcolonial nations such as Jamaica.

This book had the intention to amplify some of his recurrent thoughts for a broader audience and thus contribute to current debates on postcolonial change by all-inclusive decolonization. Contributing to the global agenda of decolonization has been increasingly imperative to social scientists, including the co-authors of this book. Though perhaps not sharing Muta's views in every small detail, the two anthropologists believe like him in the imperative of equal rights and justice, overcoming the manifold historical wrongs based on racism in all its manifold manifestations.

His reasonings and narratives expose the geopolitical climate from a historical perspective on slavery and colonialism. Like a sociologist or anthropologist, for that matter, Muta keenly observes everyday life in Jamaica within the overall historical context of Black-white relationships. Despite his mostly constructive criticism geared for social transformation and meaningful change, Muta still occasionally infuriates powerful actors. But even his biggest foes may increasingly come to terms with a public Rastafari intellectual feeding the nation with his charm and charisma, spiced up by an adequate dose of irony and sarcasm. Many prominent scholars, artistes, activists, and the common people in the hills and so-called ghettos see Muta stepping in line with earlier Black leaders, such as Marcus Garvey, Malcolm X, Martin Luther King Jr, or Yaa Asantewaa, Nanny, and Angela Davis on the female side that he foregrounds wherever and whenever possible. In content, Muta regularly relies on Garvey's concepts of Black sovereignty, self-reliance, and pan-Africanism. On the rhetorical level his militancy reminds of Malcolm X, whereas his lesser acknowledged but obvious (at least to the two co-authors of this book) humanism brings Martin Luther King Jr to mind.

Muta's radio programmes full-heartedly endorse upliftment of an Africa-oriented consciousness. The different chapters illustrate that Mutabaruka is not only an opinion leader but also an opinion maker. Due to his broadcasts' call-in format, he is also an opinion pollster, catching public sentiments and needs. This book compiled in cooperation with Mutabaruka should be seen as a first step of appreciation concerning his role as educator, moral conscience, and cultural critic in Jamaica, and beyond. A much more comprehensive volume debating the 'Philosophy and Opinions of Mutabaruka,' initially envisioned by Carolyn Cooper, the first co-ordinator of the Reggae Studies Unit at The University of the West Indies, appears more than desirable.

NOTES

1. Mutabaruka's album *Life and Lessons* (2009) was released by Gallo Record Company in South Africa.
2. SR 42 (2017).

Muta, St Andrew, Jamaica 2007
Photo: Sabriya Simon

Amba and Muta at Rebel Salute, Port Kaiser, Jamaica 2008

Photo: Werner Zips

Muta as MC of Eastfest,
Jamaica 2008

Photo: Werner Zips

Muta live at Poetry Africa,
South Africa 2010

Photo: Mutabaruka private archive

Louis Farrakhan and Muta, Jamaica 2011

Photo: Mutabaruka private archive

Muta, St Andrew, Jamaica 2011

Photo: Sabriya Simon

Muta in the Atlas Mountains, Morocco mid-2010s

Photo: Mutabaruka private archive

Werner Zips and Mutabaruka, Vienna, Austria 2011

Photo: Manuela Zips-Mairitsch

Muta with Katana sword, Vienna, Austria 2011
Photo: Werner Zips

Muta live in Wiesen, Austria 2011

Photo: Manuela Zips-Mairitsch

Muta during his shows at Irie FM, Ocho Rios, Jamaica

Photos: Mutabaruka private archive

Sebastian Schwager and Carolyn Cooper, Kingston, Jamaica 2018

Photo: Sebastian Schwager private archive

APPENDIX

Jamaican Patois Vocabulary

Jamaican Patois word or phrase	English translation
a nada	another
ah	is/are; of
big up	to give respect
boasy	boastful
bun	to burn
buss	to burst
bwoy	boy
caw	because
Chiney	a person of Asian descent
cock it up	to dance coitus-like
cyaan	can't
dat	that
dawg	dog/friend
deh	there
dem	they/them
di/de	the
dis	this
dung	down
dutty	dirty
fi	for/to
full a	full of
guh	to go
gwaan	going/go on
gyal	girl
inna	in/in the
ketch	to catch
killy killy	murderer
likkle	little/small
load a	a load of

Jamaican Patois word or phrase	English translation
mek	to make
'memba	to remember
mi	I/me/mine
mikkle	middle
mout'	mouth
nah	not
neva	never
nuff	plenty/a lot
nuh	no, don't/doesn't
nuttin	nothing
ooman	woman
'pon	on/upon
rhaatid	damn
riddim	rhythm, instrumental
round a	around of
seh	that (conj.)
sistren	a group of women
skin teeth	to laugh/smile
soun'	sound
suh	so
tek	to take
watch yah	watch out
weh	where (conj.); who/what (pron.)
wha'	what
whappen	what's happened/happening
wi	we/us/our
yah	here
yu/yuh	you

BIBLIOGRAPHY

Discography:

Aidonia. 'Flying Dagger (Aka 100 Stab).' *Sky Daggering Riddim.* Equiknoxx Musiq, 2008.

Beat Pharmacy/Mutabaruka. 'Wata (Water).' Single. Deep Space Media, 2006.

Bob Marley & The Wailers. 'Babylon System.' *Survival.* Island Records, 1979.

———. 'Selassie Is The Chapel.' Single. N.P., 1968.

———. 'War.' *Rastaman Vibration.* Island Records,1976.

Bounty Killer. 'Spy Fi Die.' Single. Dynamic Sounds, 1993.

Buju Banton. 'Informer Fi Dead.' Single. Rude Boy Kelly Records, 1991.

Chronixx. 'Capture Land.' *Dread & Terrible.* Chronixx Music, 2014.

Eek-A-Mouse. 'Wa-Do-Dem.' Single. Greensleeves Records, 1981.

Higgs, Joe. 'Steppin' Razor.' Single. N.P., 1967.

I Jah Man. 'Jah Heavy Load.' Single. Island Records, 1978.

I-Octane. 'Informer A Work.' *Ragga Ragga Ragga.* VP Records, 2012.

Lucky Dube. 'Different Colours, One People.' *Victims.* Shanachie, 1993.

Major Mackerel. 'Pretty Looks Done.' Single. Jammy's Records, 1987.

Malcolm X. 'A Message to the Grass Roots.' *Message to the Grass Roots.* Afro Records, 1965.

Mr. Vegas. 'Daggering.' Single. Kirkledove Records, 2008.

Mutabaruka. *Black Attack.* Album. Ariwa Sounds, 2023.

———. *Check It!* Album. Alligator Records, 1983a.

———. 'Every Time A Ear De Soun.' Single. High Times, 1980a.

———. 'Junk Food.' Single. Alligator Records, 1983b.

———. 'Killin.' *Melanin Man*. Shanachie, 1994a.

———.'Life and Debt.' *Life Squared*. Heartbeat Records, 2002.

———. *Life and Lessons*. Album. Gallo Record Company, 2009.

———. 'Out Of Many One.' *Word Sound 'Ave Power: Dub Poets and Dub*. Heartbeat Records, 1994b.

———. *Outcry*. Album. Shanachie, 1984.

———. 'Skins.' *Any Which Way … Freedom*. Shanachie, 1989.

Popcaan. 'El Chapo.' Single. Notnice Records, 2017.

Rdx. 'Daggering (Feat. Bermuda Kidd).' Single. Apt. 19 Productions, 2008.

Scott-Heron, Gil. 'The Revolution Will Not Be Televised.' *The Revolution Will Not Be Televised*. Flying Dutchman, 1974.

Tarrus Riley/Konshens. 'Simple Blessings.' *All Night Riddim*. Chimney Records, 2017.

Tosh, Peter. 'African.' Single. Intel Diplo, 1977a.

———. 'Stepping Razor.' *Equal Rights*. Columbia Records, 1977b.

Vybz Kartel. 'Mr. Broadcast Commission (Anuh My Music).' *The Voice of the Jamaican Ghetto – Incarcerated But Not Silenced*. Whirlwind Records, 2013.

Vybz Kartel/Gaza Slim. 'Reparation.' Single. Adidjahiem Records, 2012.

Vybz Kartel/Tommy Lee. 'Informer.' Single. UIM Records, 2012.

Films:

Black, Stephanie. *Life and Debt*. DVD. USA, 80 Min. 2001.

Campbell, Nicholas. *Stepping Razor: Red X*. DVD. Canada, 105 Min. 1992.

Gerima, Haile. *Sankofa*. DVD. Burkina Faso/Ghana/USA, 125 Min. 1993.

Thomas, Deborah A., John L. Jackson, and Junior Wedderburn. 'Bad Friday: Rastafari after Coral Gardens.' YouTube. USA, 63 Min. 2011.

Zips, Werner. *Mutabaruka: The Return to the Motherland*. DVD with Booklet and Bonus Interview Film 'From the Cutting Edge – Mutabaruka on Mutabaruka.' Vienna, 90 Min. 2011a.

Interviews:

Interview 1: Mutabaruka. Personal Interview on November 28, 2018. Golden Spring, Jamaica. 160 Min. 2018.

Interview 2: Cooper, Carolyn. Personal Interview on November 29, 2018. Kingston, Jamaica. 50 Min. 2018.

Interview 3: Priest Fego. Personal Interview on December 2, 2018. Bull Bay, Jamaica. 42 Min. 2018.

Interview 4: Ishiwawa Hope and Husband. Interview By Christian Moll, December 2018. Papine, Jamaica. 40 Min. 2018.

Interview 5: Tony Rebel. Interview by Christian Moll, December 2018. Kingston, Jamaica. 31 Min. 2018.

Interview 6: Mutabaruka. Online Interview on March 14, 2022. Zoom. 150 Min. 2022.

Legislation:

Law Reform (Fraudulent Transactions) (Special Provisions). 2014. Federal Law: The Law Reform (Fraudulent Transactions) (Special Provisions) Act. Kingston.

National Honours And Awards Act. 2002. Federal Law: The National Honours And Awards Act. Kingston.

Offences Against The Person Act. 2014. Federal Law: The Offences Against The Person Act. Kingston.

Literature Cited:

Achiume, Tendayi. 'Contemporary Forms Of Racism, Racial Discrimination, Xenophobia and Related Intolerance.' United Nations General Assembly. Seventy-Third Session, August 6, 2018.

Africa W. 'How The World Bank And The IMF Destroy Africa.' 2015. Https://www.Africaw.com/how-the-world-bank-and-the-imf-destroy-africa. (accessed August 21, 2022).

Amnesty International. Waiting In Vain. Jamaica: Unlawful Police Killings And Relatives' Long Struggle For Justice. London, 2016.

Andwele, Adisa. 'The Contribution of Rastafarianism to the Decolonization of the Caribbean.' In *Rastafari: A Universal Philosophy in the Third Millennium*, edited by Werner Zips, 7–20. Kingston: Ian Randle Publishers, 2006.

Arias, Enrique Desmond. *Criminal Enterprises and Governance in Latin America and the Caribbean*. New York: Cambridge University Press, 2017.

Atlanta Black Star. 'Jamaican Government Issues Apology, Reparations for the 1963 Brutal Attack on Rastas.' https://atlantablackstar. com/2017/04/09/jamaican-government-issues-apology-reparations-1963-brutal-attack-rastas.   2017.   (accessed November 2, 2019).

Bailey, Derrick Sherwin. *Homosexuality and the Western Christian Tradition*. London and New York: Longmans Green, 1955.

Bakan, Abbie. 'How the IMF Wrecked Jamaica.' *Socialist Worker*, Issue 2059.   https://socialistworker.co.uk/features/how-the-imf-wrecked-jamaica. 2007. (accessed August 21, 2022).

Barnett, Michael. 'The Many Faces of Rasta: Doctrinal Diversity within the Rastafari Movement.' *Caribbean Quarterly*, 51, no. 2 (2005): 67–78. Proquest.

———. *Rastafari in the New Millennium: A Rastafari Reader*. Syracuse, New York: Syracuse University Press, 2012.

———. *The Rastafari Movement: A North American and Caribbean Perspective*. New York: Routledge, 2018.

Barsch, Volker. *Rastafari: Von Babylon Nach Afrika*. 4th ed. Mainz: Ventil, 2008.

BBC. Jamaica 'Murder Capital of the World.' 2006. https://www.bbc. co.uk/caribbean/news/story/2006/01/060103_murderlist. shtml (accessed August 21, 2022).

Beckles, Hilary. *Britain's Black Debt: Reparations for Caribbean Slavery and Native Genocide*. Kingston: University of the West Indies Press, 2013.

Beirich, Heidi, and Susy Buchanan. '2017: The Year in Hate and Extremism.' In Southern *Poverty Law Center (Splc): Intelligence Report*, 2018 Spring Issue. Montgomery.

Bengal, Rebecca. 'The Last Poets: The Hip-Hop Forefathers Who Gave Black America Its Voice.' *Guardian*. https://www. theguardian.com/music/2018/may/18/the-last-poets-the-hip-hop-forefathers-who-gave-black-america-its-voice. 2018. (accessed July 6, 2022).

Bennett, Louise. *Anancy and Miss Lou*. Kingston, Jamaica: Sangster's Book Stores, 1979.

Bernal, Richard. *Chinese Foreign Direct Investment in the Caribbean: Potential and Prospects*. Inter-American Development Bank, 2016.

Bourdieu, Pierre. *Distinction: A Social Critique of the Judgement of Taste*. London and New York: Routledge, 2010.

———. *The Logic of Practice*. Stanford, 1990.

———. *Outline of a Theory of Practice*. Cambridge: Cambridge University Press, 2013.

Brau, Eduard, and Ian Mcdonald. *Successes of the International Monetary Fund: Untold Stories of Cooperation at Work*. Hampshire and New York: Palgrave Macmillan, 2009.

Bureau for International Narcotics and Law Enforcement Affairs. *International Narcotics Control Strategy Report – Volume 1: Drug and Chemical Control*. Washington, DC: United States Department of State, 2019.

Burke, Kieran. 'Jamaica Looks To Cut Ties with British Monarchy.' https://www.dw.com/en/jamaica-looks-to-cut-ties-with-british-monarchy/a-61240993. 2022. (accessed March 24, 2022).

CARICOM. 'Reparations for Native Genocide and Slavery.' https://caricom.org/reparations-for-native-genocide-and-slavery. 2015. (accessed November 2, 2019).

Campbell, Horace. 'Coral Gardens 1963: The Rastafari and Jamaican Independence.' *Social and Economic Studies* 63, no. 1 (2014): 197–214.

———. 'Rastafari As Pan Africanism in the Caribbean and Africa.' *African Journal of Political Economy* 2, no. 1 (1988): 75–88.

Carmichael, Stokely, and Charles Vernon Hamilton. *Black Power: The Politics of Liberation*. New York: Random House, 1967.

Carson, Clayborne, Susan Carson, Adrienne Clay, Virginia Shadron, and Kieran Taylor. *The Papers of Martin Luther King, Jr.. Volume IV: Symbol of the Movement January 1957– December 1958*. Berkeley, Los Angeles; London: University of California Press, 2000.

Cassidy, Frederic. *Jamaica Talk: Three Hundred Years of the English Language in Jamaica*. Kingston: University of the West Indies Press, 2007.

Charles, Cristopher A.D. 'Political Identity and Criminal Violence in Jamaica: The Garrison Community in August Town and the 2002 Election.' *Social and Economic Studies* 53, no. 2 (2004): 31–73.

Charles, Cristopher A.D., and Orville Beckford. 'The Informal Justice System in Garrison Constituencies.' *Social and Economic Studies* 61, no. 2 (2012): 51–72.

Chevannes, Barry. 'Introducing the Native Religions of Jamaica.' In *Rastafari and Other African-Caribbean Worldviews*, edited by Barry Chevannes. New Jersey: Rutgers University Press, 1998.

———. *Rastafari: Roots and Ideology*. New York: Syracuse University Press, 1994.

Chung, Dennis. 'Understanding The Root Cause of Our Challenges.' 2017. http://dcjottings.blogspot.com/search? updated-max=2017-01-27t08:56:00-05:00&max-results=20&start=15&by-date=false. (accessed October 24, 2019).

Chung, Jordan. 'Choppa Rising: A History Of Trap Dancehall.' *Riddim No.* 99, Issue 1 (2020): 49–55. English Original. 2020. https://afropunk.com/2019/10/choppa-rising-a-history-of-jamaican-trap-dancehall. (accessed August 21, 2022).

Clarke, Paul. 'New China Era – More Investments to Flow into Jamaica after Ground-breaking Mou Signed.' 2019. https://jamaica-gleaner.com/article/lead-stories/20190412/new-china-era-more-investments-flow-jamaica-after-groundbreaking-mou (accessed August 21, 2022).

CNN. 'Bush Says It Is Time for Action.' 2001. https://edition. cnn.com/2001/us/11/06/ret.bush.coalition/index.html (accessed August 19, 2022).

———. Joaquín 'El Chapo' Guzmán Fast Facts. 2022. https://edition. cnn.com/2017/01/18/world/joaqun-el-chapo-guzmn-fast-facts/index.html (accessed August 21, 2022).

Cooke, Mel. 'Everytime A Ear Di Sound' Makes Mutabaruka Heard.' 2009. http://old.jamaica-gleaner.com/gleaner/20090712/ent/ent1.html (accessed July 11, 2022).

———. 'Mutabaruka Examined As an Icon, a Visionary.' 2010. http://jamaica-gleaner.com/gleaner/20100827/ent/ent4. html (accessed July 3, 2022).

Cooper, Carolyn. 'Di Ancestor Dem A Bawl.' 2015. https:// carolynjoycooper.wordpress.com/2015/10/21/di-ancestor-dem-a-bawl/ (accessed August 20, 2022).

———, ed. *Global Reggae*. Kingston: Canoe Press, 2012.

————. 'Mek Wi Talk Bout the Bottom A De Sea: Mutabaruka's Submarine Poetics.' *Caribbean Quarterly* 59, no. 2 (2013): 113–21. Routledge.

————. *Noises in the Blood: Orality, Gender and the "Vulgar" Body of Jamaican Popular Culture*. London and Basingstoke: Macmillan Education, 1993.

————. *Sound Clash: Jamaican Dancehall Culture At Large*. New York: Palgrave Macmillan, 2004.

Dalberg-Acton, John Emerich Edward. *Acton-Creighton Correspondence*. Indianapolis: Liberty Fund, 1887.

Davidson, Vernon. 'US, JA Move against Crime.' *Jamaica Observer.* 2015. https://www.jamaicaobserver.com/news/us-ja-move-against-crime/ (accessed August 21, 2022).

Davison, Phil. 'Mortimo Planno.' 2006. https://www.theguardian.com/news/2006/mar/23/guardianobituaries.religion (accessed July 11, 2022).

Dig Jamaica. 'Murder in Jamaica 2018.' 2019. http://digjamaica.com/m/blog/murder-jamaica-2018/ (accessed October 23, 2019).

Dixon, Leroy. 'Decry Popcaan's Murder Music.' *Gleaner*, 2019. https://jamaica-gleaner.com/article/commentary/20190812/leroy-dixon-decry-popcaans-murder-music (accessed October 29, 2019).

Doggett, Leroy. 'Calendars.' In *Explanatory Supplement to the Astronomical Almanac*, edited by Kenneth Seidelmann, 575–608. Sausalito, California: University Science Books, 2006.

Doumerc, Eric. *Caribbean Civilisation: The English-Speaking Caribbean Since Independence*. Toulouse: Presses Universitaires Du Mirail, 2003.

Dreisinger, Baz. 'Reggae's Civil War.' *The Village Voice.* 2010. https://www.villagevoice.com/2010/03/02/reggaes-civil-war/ (accessed October 29, 2019).

Du Bois, W. E. B. *Dusk of Dawn: An Essay toward an Autobiography of a Race Concept*. New York: Oxford University Press, 2007.

Edie, Carlene J. 'The 2007 Parliamentary Election: The Jamaica Labour Party's Return to Power.' *Social and Economic Studies* 60, no. 2 (2011): 1–39.

Edmonds, Ennis Barrington. *Rastafari: From Outcasts to Culture Bearers*. New York: Oxford University Press, 2003.

Edmonds, Kevin. 'Guns, Gangs and Garrison Communities in the Politics of Jamaica.' *Race & Class* 57, no. 4 (2016): 54–74. Los Angeles: Sage.

Eldemire, Summer. 'How Phone Scamming Has Fueled a State of Emergency in Jamaica's Tourist Capital.' *The Intercept*, 2018. https://theintercept.com/2018/10/16/jamaica-phone-scamming-state-of-emergency/ (accessed October 23, 2019).

Eriksen, Thomas Hylland. *Small Places, Large Issues: An Introduction to Social and Cultural Anthropology*. London: Pluto Press, 2015.

Escher, Manuel. 'Simbabwes Ex-Präsident Robert Mugabe Gestorben.' *Der Standard*, 2019. https://www.derstandard.at/story/2000108306862/zimbabwes-ex-praesident-mugabe-ist-tot (accessed August 21, 2022).

Euronews. 'Jamaica's Reggae Music Inscribed on UNESCO's World Heritage List.' 2018. https://www.euronews.com/2018/11/29/jamaica-s-reggae-music-inscribed-on-unesco-s-world-heritage-list (accessed July 3, 2022).

Faber, Tom. 'Welcome To Jamaica – No Longer 'The Most Homophobic Place On Earth.' *Guardian*, 2018. https://www.theguardian.com/global-development/2018/dec/06/jamaica-lgbt-rights-activists-pride-two-decades-of-progress-j-flag (accessed November 2, 2019).

Fanon, Frantz. *Black Skin, White Masks*. London: Pluto Press, 1966.

———. *The Wretched of the Earth*. New York: Grove Press, 1963.

Figueroa, Mark, and Amanda Sives. 'Garrison Politics and Criminality in Jamaica: Does the 1997 Election Represent a Turning Point?' In *Understanding Crime in Jamaica: New Challenges for Public Policy*, edited by Anthony Harriott, 63–88. Kingston: University of the West Indies Press, 2003.

Fleary, Sinai. 'Anger As Rasta Teen Says Jamaican Police Cut Off Her Dreadlocks.' 2021. https://www.voice-online.co.uk/news/2021/08/04/anger-as-rasta-teen-says-jamaican-police-cut-off-her-dreadlocks/ (accessed August 18, 2022).

FRA – European Union Agency for Fundamental Rights. Second European Union Minorities and Discrimination Survey: Being Black in the EU. Luxembourg, 2018.

Francis-Pitt, K'shema. 'Mutabaruka Elated over Lifetime Achievement Award.' 2019. https://www.iriefm.net/mutabaruka-elated-over-lifetime-achievement-award/ (accessed July 24, 2022).

Frater, Adrian. 'Rastas to Commemorate Coral Gardens Incident.' *Gleaner*, 2018. http://jamaica-gleaner.com/article/news/20180329/rastas-commemorate-coral-gardens-incident (accessed November 2, 2019).

Friederich, Jan, and Mahmoud Harb. 'IMF Bailouts in Africa Gain Only Marginal Success.' *Financial Times*, 2018. https://www.ft.com/content/a279ecd6-2908-11e8-b27e-cc62a39d57a0 (accessed August 21, 2022).

Gallup-Healthways. *State of Global Well-Being: 2014 Country Well-Being Rankings*. N.P., 2015.

Garvey, Amy Jacques. *The Philosophy and Opinions of Marcus Garvey*. Dover: The Majority Press, 1986.

Garvey, Marcus. 'Essay.' In *Marcus Garvey: Life and Lessons; A CEntennial Companion to The Marcus Garvey and Universal Negro Improvement Association Papers*, edited by Robert A. Hill and Barbara Bair, 29–32. Berkeley and Los Angeles: University of California Press, 1987.

Gilroy, Paul. *Small Acts: Thoughts on the Politics of Black Cultures*. London: Serpent's Tail, 1993.

Girvan, Norman. *Foreign Capital and Economic Underdevelopment in Jamaica*. Surrey: The Gresham Press, 1971.

Gordon, Shirley. *Our Cause for His Glory: Christianisation and Emancipation in Jamaica*. Kingston: The University of The West Indies Press, 1998.

Grizzle, Shereita. 'Lifetime Achievement Award for Mutabaruka – Set To Be Honoured at African Heritage Expo in NY.' 2018. http://jamaica-gleaner.com/article/entertainment/20180225/lifetime-achievement-award-mutabaruka-set-be-honoured-african (accessed July 24, 2022).

Habekost, Christian. *Verbal Riddim – The Politics & Aesthetics of African-Caribbean Dub Poetry*. Amsterdam: Rodopi, 1993.

Habermas, Jürgen. *Between Facts and Norms: Contributions to a Discourse Theory of Law and Democracy*. Cambridge and London: The MIT Press, 1996.

———. *The Theory of Communicative Action. Volume 2: Lifeworld and System: A Critique of Functionalist Reason*. Boston: Beacon Press, 1987.

Haley, Alex. *The Autobiography of Malcolm X*. New York: Ballantine Books, 1999.

Hamilton, Keegan. 'One FBI Agent's War on the Deadly Scam That Took Over Jamaica.' *Vice News*, 2017. https://news.vice.com/en_ca/article/595498/jamaica-lottery-deadly-scam-fbi (accessed October 23, 2019).

Harriott, Anthony. *Police and Crime Control in Jamaica: Problems of Reforming Ex-Colonial Constabularies*. Kingston: University of the West Indies Press, 2000.

Harrod, Jeffrey. *Trade Union Foreign Policy: A Study of British and American Trade Union Activities in Jamaica*. London and Basingstoke: Macmillan, 1972.

Haughton, Andre. 'The 13th IMF Test.' 2016. https://www.mona.uwi.edu/economics/news/2016/09/27/13th-imf-test (accessed August 21, 2022).

Hawthorne, Omar. 'Campaign Donation and Extradition of the Connected in Jamaica.' In *Corruption Scandals and Their Global Impacts*, edited by Omar Hawthorne and Stephen Magu, 97–119. London and New York: Routledge, 2018.

Helber, Patrick. *Dancehall und Homophobie: Postkoloniale Perspektiven auf die Geschichte und Kultur Jamaikas*. Bielefeld: Transcript Verlag, 2015.

Henke, Holger. *Between Self-Determination and Dependency: Jamaica's Foreign Relations 1972–1989*. Kingston: The University of the West Indies Press, 2000.

Henriques, Ainsley. 'Preface.' In *Out of Many, One People: The Historical Archaeology of Colonial Jamaica*, edited by James Delle, Mark Hauser, and Douglas Armstrong, ix–x. Tuscaloosa: The University of Alabama Press, 2011.

Henry, Okoye. 'It Is All About Survival – Mobay Prostitutes.' *Jamaica Gleaner*, 2016. https://jamaica-gleaner.com/article/western-focus/20160202/it-all-about-survival-mobay-prostitutes (accessed August 21, 2022).

Hollington, Andrea. *Traveling Conceptualizations: A Cognitive and Anthropological Linguistic Study of Jamaican*. Amsterdam and Philadelphia: John Benjamins Publishing, 2015.

Hope, Donna. 'From Browning to Cake Soap: Popular Debates on Skin Beaching in the Jamaican Dancehall.' *The Journal of Pan African Studies* 4, no. 4 (2011): 165–94.

————. *Inna Di Dancehall: Popular Culture and the Politics of Identity in Jamaica*. Kingston: University of the West Indies Press, 2006.

Hubbard, Edward Akintola. 'Britain Can't Just Reverse the Homophobia It Exported During the Empire.' *Guardian*, July 28, 2017. https://www.theguardian.com/commentisfree/2017/jul/28/britain-reverse-homophobia-empire-criminlisation-homosexuality-colonies (accessed November 2, 2019).

International Labour Organization. *Women in Business and Management: Gaining Momentum in the Caribbean*. Switzerland: International Labour Organization, 2018.

International Monetary Fund. 'Jamaica.' 2019. https://www.imf.org/en/countries/jam# (accessed October 18, 2019).

Irie FM. 'About Us.' 2022. https://www.iriefm.net/us/ (accessed August 20, 2022).

James, C.L.R. *The Black Jacobins: Toussaint L'Ouverture and the San Domingo Revolution*. United Kingdom, 1938.

Jamaica Gleaner. 'Buggery Law Debate for Parliament This Year.' 2013. https://jamaica-gleaner.com/gleaner/20130609/news/news2.html (accessed August 21, 2022).

———. 'We're Moving On: Holness Says Jamaica Intent on Removing Queen as Head of State.' 2022. https://jamaica-gleaner.com/article/news/20220323/royal-visit-were-moving-holness-says-jamaica-intent-removing-queen-head-state (accessed July 3, 2022).

Jamaica Global. 2019. 'Reparation for Slavery at Last! University of Glasgow and UWI Announce Multi-Million Pound Collaboration.' 2019. https://www.jamaicaglobalonline.com/reparation-for-slavery-at-last/ (accessed November 2, 2019).

Jamaica Information Service. 'Mutabaruka Honoured By Youth Groups.' 2010. https://jis.gov.jm/mutabaruka-honoured-by-youth-groups/ (accessed July 24, 2022).

———. 'Reggae Month.' 2015. https://jis.gov.jm/features/reggae-month/ (accessed November 2, 2019).

Jamaica Observer. 'Constant Spring Market: A Case For Public Education.' 2019. https://www.pressreader.com/jamaica/daily-observer-jamaica/20190312/281672551261872 (accessed August 21, 2022).

———. 'Dunn, Brown Burke, Golding Sworn in As MPs.' 2017b. https://www.jamaicaobserver.com/latest-news/dunn-brown-burke-golding-sworn-in-as-mps/ (accessed August 20, 2022).

————. 'Mount Salem in St James Declared First ZOSO.' 2017a. http://www.jamaicaobserver.com/latestnews/mount_ salem_in_st_james_declared_first_zoso?profile=0 (accesssed October 12, 2019).

————. 'Rastas Beaten, Forcibly Trimmed of Their Locks After Coral Gardens.' 2015. http://www.jamaicaobserver.com/news/ rastas-beaten--forcibly-trimmed-of-their-locks-after-coral- gardens_45946 (accessed November 2, 2019).

Jemmott, Jenny. 'The Parish History of St. James.' 2021. https://www.parishhistoriesofjamaica.org/wp-content/ uploads/2020/01/the-parish-history-of-st-james.pdf (accessed August 21, 2022).

Katz, David. 'No Rough Sex Please, We're Jamaican.' 2009. https:// web.archive.org/web/20090828190603/http://new.music. yahoo.com/blogs/mojo/10671/no-rough-sex-please-were- jamaican/ (accessed August 17, 2022).

Kuelker, Michael. *Book of Memory: A Rastafari Testimony*. Caribsound Ltd., 2004.

Kuwornu-Adjaottor, J.E.T., George Appiah, and Melvin Nartey. 'The Philosophy Behind Some Adinkra Symbols and Their Communicative Values in Akan.' *Academic Journals: Philosophical Papers and Review* 7, no. 3 (2016): 22–33.

Laville, Sandra. 'Beijing Highway: $600m Road Just the Start of China's Investments in Caribbean.' 2015. https://www. theguardian.com/world/2015/dec/24/beijing-highway- 600m-road-just-the-start-of-chinas-investments-in-caribbean (accessed August 21, 2022).

Lee, Helene. *Der Erste Rasta*. Höfen: Hannibal, 2003.

Lemard, Glendene. 'Jamaica.' In *Crime and Punishment Around the World: Volume 2 – The America*s, edited by Graeme Newman, 205–215. Santa Barbara, Denver, Oxford: ABC-CLIO, 2010.

Leslie, Glaister. *Confronting the Don: The Political Economy of Gang Violence in Jamaica*. Geneva: Small Arms Survey, 2010.

Lewis, Jovan Scott. 'Structural Readjustment: Crime, Development, and Repair in the Jamaican Lottery Scam.' *Anthropological Quarterly* 91, no. 3 (2018): 1,029–48. George Washington University, 2018.

Lewis, Rupert. 'Reconsidering the Role of the Middle Class in Caribbean Politics.' In *New Caribbean Thought: A Reader*, edited by Brian Meeks and Folke Lindahl, 127–43. Kingston: University of the West Indies Press, 2001.

Mandela, Nelson. 'We Should Forgive But Not Forget.' *Guardian*, 1999. https://www.theguardian.com/world/1999/jul/03/guardianreview.books7 (accessed August 31, 2022).

Manley, Michael. *Up the Down Escalator: Development and the International Economy – A Jamaican Case Study*. Washington, DC: Howard University Press, 1987.

Martin, Tony, ed. *Marcus Garvey: Message to the People. The Course of African Philosophy*. Dover, Massachusetts: The Majority Press, 1986.

Mason, Rowena. 'Slavery Reparations Call Overshadows Cameron's Visit to Jamaica.' *Guardian*, 2015. https://www.theguardian.com/world/2015/sep/30/slavery-reparations-call-overshadows-david-camerons-visit-to-jamiaica (accessed November 2, 2019).

Mbembe, Achille. *On the Postcolony*. Berkeley: University of California Press, 2001.

Mcgibbon, Anthea. '2013 Protest March of 1963 Coral Gardens Massacre in Jamaica Peaceful.' 2013. https://jamaicans.com/2013-protest-march-of-1963-coral-gardens-massacre/ (accessed November 2, 2019).

Mclean, Roxroy, and Temeka Gordon. 'Rasta Teen Trimmed in Lock-Up.' 2021. http://jamaica-star.com/article/news/20210803/rasta-teen-trimmed-lock (accessed August 18, 2022).

Mcleod, Sheri-Kae. 'Women Surge: Historic Number of Women Elected to Jamaica's Parliament.' 2020. https://www.caribbeannationalweekly.com/caribbean-breaking-news-featured/women-surge-historic-number-of-women-elected-to-jamaicas-parliament/ (accessed August 20, 2022).

Meeks, Brian. *Reinventing the Jamaican Political System*. New York: Palgrave Macmillan, 2008.

Ministry of Health and Wellness. *Jamaica Health and Lifestyle Survey III (2016–2017)*. N.P, 2018.

Mo Ibrahim Foundation. *2018 Ibrahim Index of African Governance: Index Report*. N.P, 2018.

Mockyen, Alma. *Rewind: My Recollections of Radio and Broadcasting in Jamaica*. Kingston: Arawak Publications, 2003.

Mohashin, K.M. Shazzad. 'IMF in Greece: In the Shadow of the Washington Consensus.' *Journal of Balkan and Near Eastern Studies* 19, no. 6 (2017): 666–83.

Molloy, Antonia. 'Ugandan President Yoweri Museveni Says Gay Rights Demands Attached to Western Aid Are "Sinful."' *Independent*, 2014. https://www.independent.co.uk/news/world/africa/ugandan-president-yoweri-museveni-says-gay-rights-demands-attached-to-western-aid-are-sinful-9584440.html (accessed November 2, 2019).

Monteiro-Ferreira, Ana. *The Demise of the Inhuman: Afrocentricity, Modernism, and Postmodernism*. New York: SUNY Press, 2014.

Moskowitz, David Vlado. *Caribbean Popular Music: An Encyclopedia of Reggae, Mento, Ska, Rock Steady, and Dancehall*. Westport: Greenwood Press, 2006.

Mphahlele, Ezekiel. *Writing Today in Africa*. Middlesex: Penguin Books, 1967.

MRSL – Market Research Services Limited. *All Media Survey 2016: Executive Report*. Kingston: MRSL, 2017.

———. *All Media Survey 2018: Executive Report*. Kingston: MRSL, 2019.

Mühleisen, Susanne. *Creole Discourse: Exploring Prestige Formation and Change across Caribbean English-Lexicon Creoles*. Amsterdam/Philadelphia: John Benjamins, 2002.

Mussa, Michael. *Argentina and the Fund: From Triumph to Tragedy*. Washington: Institute for International Economics, 2002.

Mutabaruka. 'Epilogue: The "Maroon" Struggle As Part of an African Freedom Struggle.' In: *Nanny's Asafo Warriors: The Jamaican Maroons' African Experience*, edited by Werner Zips, 219–27. Kingston: Ian Randle Publishers, 2011.

———. *The First Poems (1970–1979)*. Kingston: Paul Issa Publications, 1980b.

———. *The First Poems, The Next Poems (Double Volume)*. Kingston: Paul Issa Publications, 2005.

———. 'Ghana: Africa from Experience.' In *Rastafari: A Universal Philosophy in the Third Millennium*, edited by Werner Zips, 106–118. Kingston: Ian Randle Publishers, 2006b.

———. 'Outcry.' N.P., 1973.

————. 'Rasta From Experience.' In *Rastafari: A Universal Philosophy in the Third Millennium*, edited by Werner Zips, 21–41. Kingston: Ian Randle Publishers, 2006a.

————. 'Twenty-Four Poems.' N.P., 1972.

Mutabaruka, and Faybiene Miranda. *Sun and Moon*. N.P., 1976.

Mutabaruka, and Werner Zips. 'Fighting Injustice & Subordination: Mutabaruka's Return to the Motherland.' In *The Caribbean Writer As Warrior of the Imaginary*, edited by Kathleen Gyssels and Benedicte Ledent, 411–36. New York And Amsterdam: Rodopi, 2008.

Ndlovu-Gatsheni, Sabelo. 'Making Sense of Mugabeism in Local and Global Politics: 'So Blair, Keep Your England and Let Me Keep My Zimbabwe.' *Third World Quarterly* 30, no. 6 (2009): 1,139–158. Taylor & Francis.

Nelson, Jaevion. '"Informer Fi Dead": Is It Really the Key Obstacle to Fighting Crime?' 2015. https://petchary.wordpress.com/2015/06/05/informer-fi-dead-is-it-really-the-key-obstacle-to-fighting-crime/ (accessed October 24, 2019).

Nettleford, Rex. *Caribbean Cultural Identity: The Case of Jamaica*. Los Angeles: University of California Press, 1979.

Newell, Granville. 'Minister of Culture Pleased with Rastafari Coral Gardens Elders Home.' 2021. https://jis.gov.jm/minister-of-culture-pleased-with-rastafari-coral-gardens-elders-home/ (accessed August 19, 2022).

Ngwena, Charles. *What Is Africanness? Contesting Nativism in Culture, Race and Sexualities*. Pretoria: Pretoria University Law Press, 2018.

Paul, Annie. 'No Space For Race? The Bleaching of the Nation in Postcolonial Jamaica.' In *The African-Caribbean Worldview and the Making of Caribbean Society*, edited by Horace Levy, 94–113. Kingston: University of the West Indies Press, 2009.

Pearn, Julie. 'Poetry As a Performing Art in the English-Speaking Caribbean.' Doctoral Thesis, University Of Sheffield, 1985.

Phillips Fein, Charlotte. 'Marcus Garvey: His Opinions about Africa.' *The Journal of Negro Education* 33, no. 4 (1964): 446–49.

Powys-Jones, Lionel, C.E.B. 'The Native Purchase Areas Of Southern Rhodesia.' *Journal of Public Administration and Development* 7, Issue 1 (January 1955): 20–26. https://doi.org/10.1002/j.1099-162x.1955.tb00079.x (accessed October 28, 2022).

Planno, Mortimo. 'The Earth Most Strangest Man: The Rastafarian.' N.P., 1969.

Radio Jamaica News. 'Audley Shaw Racks Up $8 Million Phone Bill.' 2017.   http://radiojamaicanewsonline.com/local/audley-shaw-racks-up-8-million-phone-bill (accessed August 20, 2022).

Ramsay, Laura Monica. 'The Church of England, Homosexual Law Reform, and the Shaping of the Permissive Society, 1957–1979.' *Journal of British Studies* 57, no. 1 (2018): 108–137. https://doi.org/10.1017/jbr.2017.180 (accessed October 28, 2022).

Rapley, John. 'Jamaica: Negotiating Law and Order with the Dons.' NACLA Report on the Americas 37, no. 2 (2003): 25–29.

Rapport, Nigel, and Joanna Overing. *Social and Cultural Anthropology: The Key Concepts*. London and New York: Routledge, 2000.

Reynolds-Baker, Athaliah. 'Country Receives Funding From EU to Improve Justice System.' 2014. https://jis.gov.jm/country-receives-funding-eu-improve-justice-system/ (accessed August 21, 2022).

Roberts, Neil. 'Violence, Livity, Freedom.' *Small Axe* 18, no. 1 (2014): 181–92. Durham: Duke University Press.

Robinson-Walcott, Kim. 'Deconstructing Jamaican Whiteness: A Diasporic Voice.' *Small Axe*, 13, no. 2 (2009): 107–117. Durham: Duke University Press.

Robotham, Don. 'Blackening the Jamaican Nation: The Travails of Black Bourgeoisie in a Globalized World.' *Identities – Global Studies In Culture And Power*, Volume 7, no. 1 (2000): 1–37.

Rodney, Walter. *How Europe Underdeveloped Africa*. London: Bogle-L'ouverture, 1972.

Seattle Times, The. 'Key Player in Jamaican Lottery Scam Sentenced to 4 Years.' 2019. https://www.seattletimes.com/nation-world/nation/key-player-in-jamaican-lottery-scam-sentenced-to-4-years/ (accessed October 23, 2019).

Selassie, Haile. Speech on October 4, 1963, in General Assembly of the UN, 1963.

Shammas, Victor. 'A Prison without Walls: Alternative Incarceration in the Late Age of Social Democracy.' *Prison Service Journal*, Issue 217 (2015): 3–9.

Smith, Raymond. *Kinship and Class in the West Indies: A Genealogical Study of Jamaica and Guyana.* Cambridge: Cambridge University Press, 1988.

Stanley Niaah, Sonjah. *Dancehall: From Slave Ship To Ghetto.* Ottawa: University of Ottawa Press, 2010.

Stolzoff, Norman. *Wake the Town and Tell the People: Dancehall Culture in Jamaica.* Durham and London: Duke University Press, 2000.

Sulikowski, Ulrike, and Stefan Khittel. 'Postkoloniale Welt.' In *Lexikon Der Globalisierung,* edited by Fernand Kreff, Eva-Maria Knoll, and Andre Gingrich, 327–30. Bielefeld: Transcript, 2011.

Sunzi, and Lionel Giles. *Sun Tzu: The Art of War.* Tokyo: Rutland, 2008.

Sweet, James H., and Tejumola Olaniyan. *The African Diaspora and the Disciplines.* Indiana University Press, 2010.

Talton, Benjamin. 'The Mandelas at Harlem's Africa Square.' 2018. https://africasacountry.com/2018/12/the-mandelas-at-harlems-africa-square (accessed November 2, 2019).

Tate, Greg, ed. *Everything but the Burden: What White People Are Taking from Black Culture.* New York: Broadway Books, 2003.

Taylor, Lawrence J. 'Grenzen.' In *Lexikon Der Globalisierung,* edited by Fernand Kreff, Eva-Maria Knoll, and Andre Gingrich, 130–33. Bielefeld: Transcript, 2011.

Transparency International. *Corruption Perceptions Index 2018.* Berlin, 2019.

Trotsenburg, Axel Van. 'Jamaica Has Made An "Extraordinary" Economic Turnaround.' 2019. https://www.worldbank.org/en/news/opinion/2019/05/16/jamaica-has-made-an-extraordinary-economic-turnaround (accessed August 21, 2022).

University Office of Planning. 'Statistical Digest 2012/13 to 2016/17.' The University of the West Indies, 2018.

UNODC – United Nations Office on Drugs and Crime. *Global Study on Homicide: Homicide Trends, Patterns and Criminal Justice Response.* Vienna, 2019.

Urban Dictionary. 'Steppin' Razor.' 2007. https://www.urbandictionary.com/author.php?author=louisfromseattle (accessed August 20, 2022).

Waller, Lloyd, Paul Bourne, Indianna Minto, and John Rapley. *A Landscape Assessment of Political Corruption in Jamaica.* Kingston: Caribbean Policy Research Institute, 2007.

Wilson-Harris, Nadine. 'Crisis! – Scores of Jamaican Men Wanting a Gun to Prove Their Manliness.' *Gleaner*, 2017. https://jamaica-gleaner.com/article/news/20171119/crisis-scores-jamaican-men-wanting-gun-prove-their-manliness (accessed October 29, 2019).

World Bank. 'Jamaica Foundations For Competitiveness and Growth.' 2014. https://projects.worldbank.org/en/projects-operations/project-detail/p147665 (accessed August 21, 2022).

Wynands, René. *Do the Reggae. Reggae Von Pocomania Bis Ragga Und Der Mythos Bob Marley.* Oktober Kommunikationsdesign, 2000.

Zips, Werner. 'Bunny Wailer: Universal Teacher out of Trenchtown: The Living Legend For I-Ver More.' 2021. http://www.reggaestory.de/stories/bunny-wailer-zips-2021-12-en.html (accessed December 8, 2021).

———. *Gerechtigkeit Unter Dem Mangobaum. Rechtsanthropo-logische Forschung Zu Einer Insel Des Rechts (Anthropologie Der Gerechtigkeit, Band 2).* Wien: Facultas, Wiener Universitätsverlag, 2007.

———. '"The Good, The Bad, and the Ugly": Habitus, Feld, Kapital (Im Feld) Des Jamaikanischen Reggae.' In *Ethnohistorie: Rekonstruktion Und Kulturkritik. Eine Einführung*, edited by Karl Wernhart and Werner Zips, 221–38. Wien: Promedia, 2008.

———. 'Mutabaruka: Das Hattori Hanzo-Schwert Von Rasta.' In *Hail Di Riddim: Reportagen Aus Dem Reggaeversum*, edited by Werner Zips, 115–27. Wien: Promedia, 2015.

———. 'Mutabaruka: The Return to the Motherland. Notes on a Documentary Film of an African-Jamaican Artist's His-Story of Africa.' In *Rastafari: A Universal Philosophy in the Third Millennium*, edited by Werner Zips, 72–105. Kingston: Ian Randle Publishers, 2006c.

———. *Nanny's Asafo Warriors: The Jamaican Maroons' African Experience.* Kingston: Ian Randle Publishers, 2011b.

———. *Rastafari: A Universal Philosophy in the Third Millennium.* Kingston: Ian Randle Publishers, 2006a.

———. '"Repatriation Is a Must!": The Rastafari Struggle to Utterly Downstroy Slavery.' In *Rastafari: A Universal Philosophy in the Third Millennium*, edited by Werner Zips, 129–68. Kingston: Ian Randle Publishers, 2006b.

Zips, Werner, and Heinz Kämpfer. *Nation X: Schwarzer Nationalismus, Black Exodus & Hip-Hop*. Wien: Promedia, 2001.

Radio Shows:

Cutting Edge (CE) 1: Mutabaruka. Cutting Edge. Irie Fm. Ocho Rios, January 30, 2013, 10:00 p.m.–2:00 a.m.

Cutting Edge (CE) 2: Mutabaruka. Cutting Edge. Irie Fm. Ocho Rios, August 14, 2013, 10:00 p.m.– 2:00 a.m.

Cutting Edge (CE) 3: Mutabaruka. Cutting Edge. Irie Fm. Ocho Rios, April 16, 2014, 10:00 p.m.–2:00 a.m.

Cutting Edge (CE) 4: Mutabaruka. Cutting Edge. Irie Fm. Ocho Rios, October 18, 2014, 10:00 p.m.–2:00 a.m.

Cutting Edge (CE) 5: Mutabaruka. Cutting Edge. Irie Fm. Ocho Rios, November 19, 2014, 10:00 p.m.–2:00 a.m.

Cutting Edge (CE) 6: Mutabaruka. Cutting Edge. Irie Fm. Ocho Rios, January 14, 2015, 10:00 p.m.–2:00 a.m.

Cutting Edge (CE) 7: Mutabaruka. Cutting Edge. Irie Fm. Ocho Rios, August 5, 2015, 10:00 p.m.–2:00 a.m.

Cutting Edge (CE) 8: Mutabaruka. Cutting Edge. Irie Fm. Ocho Rios, August 24, 2016, 10:00 p.m.–2:00 a.m.

Cutting Edge (CE) 9: Mutabaruka. 2017. Cutting Edge. Irie Fm. Ocho Rios, March 15, 2017, 10:00 p.m.–2:00 a.m.

Cutting Edge (CE) 10: Mutabaruka. Cutting Edge. Irie Fm. Ocho Rios, May 3, 2017, 10:00 p.m.– 2:00 a.m.

Cutting Edge (CE) 11: Mutabaruka. Cutting Edge. Irie Fm. Ocho Rios, August 24, 2017, 10:00 p.m.–2:00 a.m.

Cutting Edge (CE) 12: Mutabaruka. Cutting Edge. Irie Fm. Ocho Rios, September 7, 2017, 10:00 p.m.–2:00 a.m.

Cutting Edge (CE) 13: Mutabaruka. Cutting Edge. Irie Fm. Ocho Rios, October 18, 2017, 10:00 p.m.–2:00 a.m.

Cutting Edge (CE) 14: Mutabaruka. Cutting Edge. Irie Fm. Ocho Rios, November 8, 2017, 10:00 p.m.–2:00 a.m.

Cutting Edge (CE) 15: Mutabaruka. Cutting Edge. Irie Fm. Ocho Rios, January 24, 2018, 10:00 p.m.–2:00 a.m.

Cutting Edge (CE) 16: Mutabaruka. Cutting Edge. Irie Fm. Ocho Rios, December 25, 2019, 10:00 p.m.–2:00 a.m.

Cutting Edge (CE) 17: Mutabaruka. 2020. Cutting Edge. Irie Fm.
Ocho Rios, January 29, 2020, 10:00 p.m. –2:00 a.m.
Cutting Edge (CE) 18: Mutabaruka. 2020. Cutting Edge. Irie Fm.
Ocho Rios, February 5, 2020, 10:00 p.m.–2:00 a.m.
Cutting Edge (CE) 19: Mutabaruka. 2020. Cutting Edge. Irie Fm.
Ocho Rios, December 9, 2020, 10:00 p.m.–2:00 a.m.
Cutting Edge (CE) 20: Mutabaruka. 2021. Cutting Edge. Irie Fm.
Ocho Rios, August 4, 2021, 10:00 p.m.–2:00 a.m.
Steppin Razor (SR) 1: Mutabaruka. 2014. Steppin Razor: The Art of
War. Irie Fm. Ocho Rios, November 27, 2014, 2:00–6:00 p.m.
Steppin Razor (SR) 2: Mutabaruka. 2014. Steppin Razor: The Art of
War. Irie Fm. Ocho Rios, December 4, 2014, 2:00–6:00 p.m.
Steppin Razor (SR) 3: Mutabaruka. 2014. Steppin Razor: The Art of
War. Irie Fm. Ocho Rios December 10, 2014, 2:00–6:00 p.m.
Steppin Razor (SR) 4: Mutabaruka. 2014. Steppin Razor: The Art of
War. Irie Fm. Ocho Rios, December 17, 2014, 2:00–6:00 p.m.
Steppin Razor (SR) 5: Mutabaruka. 2014. Steppin Razor: The Art of
War. Irie Fm. Ocho Rios, December 25, 2014, 2:00–6:00 p.m.
Steppin Razor (SR) 6: Mutabaruka. 2015. Steppin Razor: The Art of
War. Irie Fm. Ocho Rios, February 19, 2015, 2:00–6:00 p.m.
Steppin Razor (SR) 7: Mutabaruka. 2015. Steppin Razor: The Art of
War. Irie Fm. Ocho Rios, April 2, 2015, 2:00–6:00 p.m.
Steppin Razor (SR) 8: Mutabaruka. 2015. Steppin Razor: The Art of
War. Irie Fm. Ocho Rios, April 30, 2015, 2:00–6:00 p.m.
Steppin Razor (SR) 9: Mutabaruka. 2015. Steppin Razor: The Art of
War. Irie Fm. Ocho Rios, June 11, 2015, 2:00–6:00 p.m.
Steppin Razor (SR) 10: Mutabaruka. 2015. Steppin Razor: The Art
of War. Irie Fm. Ocho Rios, June 25, 2015, 2:00–6:00 p.m.
Steppin Razor (SR) 11: Mutabaruka. 2015. Steppin Razor: The Art
of War. Irie Fm. Ocho Rios, July 2, 2015, 2:00–6:00 p.m.
Steppin Razor (SR) 12: Mutabaruka. Steppin Razor: The Art of War.
Irie Fm. Ocho Rios, July 23, 2015, 2:00–6:00 p.m.
Steppin Razor (SR) 13: Mutabaruka. Steppin Razor: The Art of War.
Irie Fm. Ocho Rios, September 17, 2015, 2:00–6:00 p.m.
Steppin Razor (SR) 14: Mutabaruka. Steppin Razor: The Art of War.
Irie Fm. Ocho Rios, October 1, 2015, 2:00–6:00 p.m.
Steppin Razor (SR) 15: Mutabaruka. Steppin Razor: The Art of War.
Irie Fm. Ocho Rios, October 15, 2015, 2:00–6:00 p.m.

Steppin Razor (SR) 16: Mutabaruka. Steppin Razor: The Art of War. Irie Fm. Ocho Rios, November 19, 2015, 2:00–6:00 p.m.

Steppin Razor (SR) 17: Mutabaruka. Steppin Razor: The Art of War. Irie Fm. Ocho Rios, December 3, 2015, 2:00–6:00 p.m.

Steppin Razor (SR) 18: Mutabaruka. Steppin Razor: The Art of War. Irie Fm. Ocho Rios, January 7, 2016, 2:00–6:00 p.m.

Steppin Razor (SR) 19: Mutabaruka. Steppin Razor: The Art of War. Irie Fm. Ocho Rios, January 15, 2016, 2:00–6:00 p.m.

Steppin Razor (SR) 20: Mutabaruka. Steppin Razor: The Art of War. Irie Fm. Ocho Rios, January 20, 2016, 2:00–6:00 p.m.

Steppin Razor (SR) 21: Mutabaruka. Steppin Razor: The Art of War. Irie Fm. Ocho Rios, March 17, 2016, 2:00–6:00 p.m.

Steppin Razor (SR) 22: Mutabaruka. Steppin Razor: The Art of War. Irie Fm. Ocho Rios, April 7, 2016, 2:00–6:00 p.m.

Steppin Razor (SR) 23: Mutabaruka. Steppin Razor: The Art of War. Irie Fm. Ocho Rios, May 26, 2016, 2:00–6:00 p.m.

Steppin Razor (SR) 24: Mutabaruka. Steppin Razor: The Art of War. Irie Fm. Ocho Rios, June 9, 2016, 2:00–6:00 p.m.

Steppin Razor (SR) 25: Mutabaruka. Steppin Razor: The Art of War. Irie Fm. Ocho Rios, June 23, 2016, 2:00–6:00 p.m.

Steppin Razor (SR) 26: Mutabaruka. Steppin Razor: The Art of War. Irie Fm. Ocho Rios, July 28, 2016, 2:00–6:00 p.m.

Steppin Razor (SR) 27: Mutabaruka. 2016. Steppin Razor: The Art of War. Irie Fm. Ocho Rios, August 18, 2016, 2:00–6:00 p.m.

Steppin Razor (SR) 28: Mutabaruka. 2016. Steppin Razor: The Art of War. Irie Fm. Ocho Rios, August 26, 2016, 2:00–6:00 p.m.

Steppin Razor (SR) 29: Mutabaruka. 2016. Steppin Razor: The Art of War. Irie Fm. Ocho Rios, October 13, 2016, 2:00–6:00 p.m.

Steppin Razor (SR) 30: Mutabaruka. 2016. Steppin Razor: The Art of War. Irie Fm. Ocho Rios, October 20, 2016, 2:00–6:00 p.m.

Steppin Razor (SR) 31: Mutabaruka. 2016. Steppin Razor: The Art of War. Irie Fm. Ocho Rios, November 24, 2016, 2:00–6:00 p.m.

Steppin Razor (SR) 32: Mutabaruka. 2016. Steppin Razor: The Art of War. Irie Fm. Ocho Rios, December 22, 2016, 2:00–6:00 p.m.

Steppin Razor (SR) 33: Mutabaruka. 2017. Steppin Razor: The Art of War. Irie Fm. Ocho Rios, January 26, 2017, 2:00–6:00 p.m.

Steppin Razor (SR) 34: Mutabaruka. 2017. Steppin Razor: The Art of War. Irie Fm. Ocho Rios, March 2, 2017, 2:00–6:00 p.m.

Steppin Razor (SR) 35: Mutabaruka. 2017. Steppin Razor: The Art of War. Irie Fm. Ocho Rios, March 16, 2017, 2:00–6:00 p.m.

Steppin Razor (SR) 36: Mutabaruka. 2017. Steppin Razor: The Art of War. Irie Fm. Ocho Rios, March 30, 2017, 2:00–6:00 p.m.

Steppin Razor (SR) 37: Mutabaruka. 2017. Steppin Razor: The Art of War. Irie Fm. Ocho Rios, April 13, 2017, 2:00–6:00 p.m.

Steppin Razor (SR) 38: Mutabaruka. 2017. Steppin Razor: The Art of War. Irie Fm. Ocho Rios, May 11, 2017, 2:00–6:00 p.m.

Steppin Razor (SR) 39: Mutabaruka. 2017. Steppin Razor: The Art of War. Irie Fm. Ocho Rios, June 22, 2017, 2:00–6:00 p.m.

Steppin Razor (SR) 40: Mutabaruka. 2017. Steppin Razor: The Art of War. Irie Fm. Ocho Rios, July 13, 2017, 2:00–6:00 p.m.

Steppin Razor (SR) 41: Mutabaruka. 2017. Steppin Razor: The Art of War. Irie Fm. Ocho Rios, August 3, 2017, 2:00–6:00 p.m.

Steppin Razor (SR) 42: Mutabaruka. Steppin Razor: The Art of War. Irie Fm. Ocho Rios, August 10, 2017, 2:00–6:00 p.m.

Steppin Razor (SR) 43: Mutabaruka. Steppin Razor: The Art of War. Irie Fm. Ocho Rios, November 2, 2017, 2:00–6:00 p.m.

Steppin Razor (SR) 44: Mutabaruka. Steppin Razor: The Art of War. Irie Fm. Ocho Rios, November 9, 2017, 2:00–6:00 p.m.

Steppin Razor (SR) 45: Mutabaruka. Steppin Razor: The Art of War. Irie Fm. Ocho Rios, November 23, 2017, 2:00–6:00 p.m.

Steppin Razor (SR) 46: Mutabaruka. Steppin Razor: The Art of War. Irie Fm. Ocho Rios, November 30, 2017, 2:00–6:00 p.m.

Steppin Razor (SR) 47: Mutabaruka. Steppin Razor: The Art of War. Irie Fm. Ocho Rios, December 7, 2017, 2:00–6:00 p.m.

Steppin Razor (SR) 48: Mutabaruka. Steppin Razor: The Art of War. Irie Fm. Ocho Rios, December 14, 2017, 2:00–6:00 p.m.

Steppin Razor (SR) 49: Mutabaruka. Steppin Razor: The Art of War. Irie Fm. Ocho Rios, December 21, 2017, 2:00–6:00 p.m.

Steppin Razor (SR) 50: Mutabaruka. Steppin Razor: The Art of War. Irie Fm. Ocho Rios, December 28, 2017, 2:00–6:00 p.m.

ABOUT THE AUTHORS

Mutabaruka

Born in Jamaica, Mutabaruka has established himself as an artiste, performing poet and philosopher, who is also the host of the famous interactive talk shows *Cutting Edge* and *Steppin Razor* on Jamaica's most popular radio station, Irie FM. During his weekly broadcasts, the outspoken Rastafari debates socio-political, philosophical, and Rastafari-related topics. He has contributed to Black consciousness globally transcending his own Rastafari, Reggae, and poetry community. He advocates Black Power and opposes Eurocentric and neo-colonial thinking. He unapologetically voices his notions on multifaceted matters and particularly creates space for Black freedom struggle. His poem collection *Outcry* (1973) and his music album *Check It!* (1983) are among his great achievements. Above all, he played the rebellious slave Shango in Haile Gerima's drama movie *Sankofa* (1993) and was the protagonist in the documentary film *Mutabaruka: The Return to the Motherland* (2011). Some of his formal awards are Order Of Distinction (Commander Class) from the Jamaican government in 2016, the Lifetime Achievement Award awarded at the Black Royalty African Heritage Expo in Connecticut (USA) in 2018, or Best Dub Poet from the Jamaican Music Awards (repeatedly awarded).

Sebastian Schwager:

Sebastian Schwager works in the social sector (with people with disabilities) and is a freelance anthropologist, filmmaker, and musician.

His research mainly focuses on media and visual anthropology in the context of post-colonialism, ethnohistory and ongoing globalization. He holds a master's degree in social and cultural anthropology and involves in field research in Jamaica, Greece, Australia, Bali, and Austria. His documentary film *Rebels outta Vienna* (2022) deals with the Viennese Reggae scene being embedded in the Rastafari movement (for more information: www.rebelsouttavienna.com). A saxophonist and producer, he regularly releases music under the pseudonym *Sabolious* (www.linktr.ee/sabolious). Exploring a variety of sounds and genres within his tracks, he found himself immersed in the vibes of Reggae/Dub, Chillhop/Lofi, Electronic, and Trap. Also establishing his record label *Anaves Music* (www.anaves-music.com), he is eager to promote various artistes worldwide. Lately he has collaborated with singers like the legendary Fred Locks or the highly talented Italian-Senegalese singer Awa Fall aka Sista Awa.

Werner Zips:

Werner Zips is professor of Social and Cultural Anthropology at the University of Vienna, Austria. The trained lawyer and anthropologist is the author of numerous articles and books on Jamaican Maroons (*Nanny's Asafo Warriors. The Jamaican Maroons' African Experiences*, 2011; *Black Rebels. African-Caribbean Freedom Fighters in Jamaica*, 1999), Rastafari (*Rastafari. A Universal Philosophy in the Third Millennium*, 2006), and Black Nationalism. He has edited volumes on Legal Pluralism, the African Diaspora, and Black Economic Empowerment in South Africa. His recent research deals with issues of conservation in Africa, with a special focus on community-based natural resource management, indigenous rights, and climate crisis mitigation. In cooperation with Manuela Zips-Mairitsch he has edited the volume *Bewildering Borders: The Economy of Conservation in Africa* (2019). He has also directed and produced numerous ethnographic films and television documentaries on Southern Africa, West Africa, the Caribbean, and Asia, including the DVD *Mutabaruka: The Return to the Motherland* (2011).

INDEX